Literacy and Learning

An Expeditionary Discovery through Children's Literature

Suzanne W. Hawley
Carolyn V. Spillman

The Scarecrow Press, Inc.
Lanham, Maryland, and Oxford
2003

Dedication

For all of my best beloveds: Dave, Pete, and Mark, who have been characters in many of my reading stories—especially the funny ones! SWH

For Emma and Jack, whose passions for literature since their births have given me such joy and inspiration, and for the rest of the family who have supported this endeavor, with love! CVS

KH

SCARECROW PRESS, INC.

Published in the United States of America
by Scarecrow Press, Inc.
A Member of the Rowman & Littlefield Publishing Group
4501 Forbes Boulevard, Suite 200, Lanham, MD 20706
www.scarecrowpress.com

PO Box 317
Oxford
OX2 9RU, UK

British Library Cataloguing in Publication Information Available

Library of Congress Cataloging-in-Publication Data

Hawley, Suzanne W., 1943-
  Literacy and learning : an expeditionary discovery through children's
literature / Suzanne W. Hawley, Carolyn V. Spillman.
     p. cm.
  Includes bibliographical references (p.) and index.
  ISBN 0-8108-4731-0 (alk. paper) -- ISBN 0-8108-4732-9 (pbk. : alk.
paper)
  1. Children's literature, American--History and criticism. 2.
Children--Books and reading--United States. 3. Literacy--United
States. I. Spillman, Carolyn V. II. Title.
PS490.H39 2003
810.9'9282--dc21

                                            2002156064

10/25/04

Contents

Preface

He spooned the honey onto the cover of one of her books. "Taste,"
he said, almost in a whisper.
Mary Ellen savored the honey on her book.
"There is such sweetness inside of that book, too," he said
thoughtfully. "Such things . . . adventure, knowledge, and wisdom.
But these things do not come easily. You have to pursue them. Just
like we ran after the bees to find their tree, so you must also chase
these things through the pages of a book!"
Then he smiled and hugged her.

—Patricia Polacco, *The Bee Tree*, 1993

As you enter the world of children's literature you too will be chasing adventure, knowledge, and wisdom. You will embark on ventures that will change your life forever. You will meet characters that will impact your thoughts and actions for a lifetime. You will pursue them through places and times that will expand your mind and your sensitivities.

Perhaps to your surprise, you are opening a book on journeys—which we call Expeditionary Discoveries. As teachers of today and tomorrow, you will learn how each day in the classroom entices, welcomes, and encourages travelers on their journeys of learning. You will plan for your students' growing experiences, you will nurture them along the way, and celebrate when they have traveled a fine distance and you can see that they are far beyond where they started. These are the journeys that we hope to promote in this book.

These journeys have many facets. This book is a textbook of children's literature and will provide information for the classroom teacher to use in expanding students' interest and knowledge of literature and literacy. This book is a road map for teachers to plan expeditions for students to make profound discoveries—not only about children's literature but also about their lives. This book is a reference for guiding teachers in locating and using children's literature that is appropriate for various purposes that are both educational and that promote lifelong learning.

Expeditionary Learning

The idea of pushing one's boundaries to give depth and meaning to the learning of new skills and concepts has been associated with rugged, outdoor expeditions known as Outward Bound.[1] During such an expedition, participants solve problems, think for themselves, and trust the others on their team. The rigor is often extreme and the rewards at the end of the journey are worth the effort.

The extension of this notion is found in schools where authentic learning, field experiences, teamwork, and integration with the community are valued. In 1992, Expeditionary Learning officially became a part of Outward Bound and educators began looking at the parallels in learning between the physical accomplishments and those of the character and educational focus.

Expeditions of learning challenge students to ask difficult questions and to find the answers from a variety of sources. The curriculum is an immersion of genuine interest in topics, driven by skill building, project work, and final presentations to a responsive audience.

Since the inception of Expeditionary Learning, more than ninety-nine schools have affiliated with the program and are actively pursuing curriculum that reflects the ten design principles.

Ten Curriculum Design Principles of Expeditionary Learning/Outward Bound

These principles are desirable doctrines to guide life as well as education. If our schools can keep them in the forefront of curriculum, by using materials and planning activities that support the principles, students will be exposed to them and should recognize the value of them for their lives. They are presented below with a brief description of each. For additional information and insights on these principles, explore the website http://www.elob.org.

The Primacy of Self-Discovery

When one has a passion to learn something, there is little that anyone can do to interfere. That emotion of wanting to learn and of personal searching for understanding is to be desired in the elementary schools.

The Having of Wonderful Ideas

Curiosity and the time to generate new ideas are nurtured by a community of learners who respect each others' ideas.

The Responsibility for Learning

When students take responsibility for their own learning, the roles of teaching and learning are strengthened by the symbiosis. Personal inquiry is a lifelong skill that can be nourished to take root in childhood.

Empathy and Caring

Small learning groups with members taking care of each other lead to trust and deep understandings.

Success and Failure

We learn through mistakes as well as victories. The mountains seem higher if we have traveled through a valley.

Collaboration and Competition

Team trust leads to working together and individuals competing against themselves with increased rigor in the standards.

Diversity and Inclusivity

Richness and depth of experiences come through differences among group members. When shared perspectives are viewed as a whole, creative thinking is expanded.

The Natural World

Being stewards of the environment and looking to nature as a model for life girds students with productive human habits.

Solitude and Reflection

We replenish our souls and minds when giving thought to experiences. They are even more profitable when shared with others.

Service and Compassion

We are crew members on the planet Earth, and we owe service to others.

Guide to the Expeditions

In chapters 2 through 11, you will find suggestions for expeditions at the end of each chapter. The suggested expeditions will provide possible resources and ideas for leading your students through learning expeditions. Below is the explanation of the framework for these expeditions.

Components of an Expedition

Guiding Questions

Expeditions ask guiding questions that lead to learning experiences across disciplines within the curriculum. Each expedition will begin with a set of questions that students should answer as they continue through the journey.

Standards

Expeditions integrate with regular classroom curriculum and become a vehicle for meeting state and national standards. Objectives from various national organizations will be stated, giving direction to the teacher for connecting the study to state and local standards. Most national educational standards are found on the Internet, so addresses will be provided.

Initial Reading Options for Teacher Read-Aloud, Shared, Guided, and Independent Reading

Expeditions must capture the imagination and interest of the students to maintain momentum while discovering answers to the questions. We recommend beginning each expedition with literature. Through group reading and discussion, guiding questions may be asked and plans may be made for finding answers. For each expedition, we list initial reading options that may be used as the teacher reads aloud to the whole group or shared or guided reading when students have access to texts and follow while others are reading aloud.

Following an initial reading, a planning strategy is to list the guiding questions before the reading, have the students think of these questions and others as they are listening to the read-aloud, and then compile all questions for a master question board. A subsequent planning session may determine how the group will find the answers and what experiences they may have on the journey. Culminating activities are planned at the end of the expedition for celebrating the experiences and acquired knowledge. We could call this strategy as it progresses through the entire expedition, the CRASH.

C (compile questions);

R (read literature to find answers),

A (answer questions through reading and projects), and

SH (share what has been found).

Fieldwork

Expeditions benefit students through authentic projects outside the classroom. Some projects may include doing things with other classes at school, interviewing administrative and office personnel, activities with homes, and extended families, neighbors, and friends. Teachers may take children on field trips, or in some situations, could recommend weekend or evening trips for parents to provide. Such outside activities may not be possible in all schools or with all children in a classroom. Teachers are cautioned to avoid recommending experiences that some of the children would not have access to and that might make them feel embarrassed or cheated.

Fieldwork needs to have the feel of the "field," so that the projects are different from the typical classroom activities. Fieldwork involves people outside the classroom, but may be conducted through the Internet, mail, or phone interactions for the purpose of gathering data or information. Suggestions are listed with each expedition for possible fieldwork opportunities.

Individual and Class Projects

Expeditions operate within a structured framework that allows for individual projects as well as class ventures. Teachers must hold each student accountable for meeting the objectives and standards of the study, so individual projects and assignments are a part of the expedition. Each person carries responsibility for meeting the goals and contributing to the total project. Individual projects may be compiled into a class project. Sometimes there are ongoing class projects to which individuals contribute along with personal projects that may or may not be a part of the class undertaking. Individual project suggestions are listed, followed by class project recommendations. Teachers should be selective in the ideas that suit their students' needs.

Sharing Outlets

Expeditions require sharing of information and responsiveness from an audience. Celebration is a form of sharing and confirms the value of what children are learning and doing. Festivities that include guests outside the school are powerful for opening vistas of the students to the greater world. The sharing opportunities also relay to students the importance of accurate information that is molded for clear communication and interest to the audience. The responsibility for sharing valuable information is on the shoulders of the youngsters who are learning. Possible sharing outlets are listed for each expedition and teachers will think of additional channels as they progress with Expeditionary Learning.

Assessment

Assessment is ongoing throughout the expedition and holds each student accountable for the objectives and standards. Expeditions are not "add-ons" to the curriculum but are an integral part of the instruction and evaluation. Students are expected to participate in all activities and demonstrate their competency in the objectives.

Assessment strategies are listed in each expedition that may be used with various assignments. Examples that are suggested include checklists, portfolios, and rubrics. These assessment instruments will be developed by the teacher to reflect the criteria for each activity.

Guide to Using This Book

In this book, we will guide you through the genres of literature that will be the bedrock of your curriculum: traditional folk literature, fantasy, realistic fiction, nonfiction, and poetry. The book provides information on materials and strategies for fulfilling requirements for standards, integration of subject areas, and ways to maintain the expeditionary design principles. Through the experiences in this book, you will become familiar with classic and current literature for the child and the selection criteria for assessing the five major genres. You will note topical issues of concern to educators as they relate to literature and literacy, and you will gain expertise in planning for the implementation of a literature program in your curriculum that includes learning expeditions.

Throughout the book, you will find references to the ten design principles that support Expeditionary Learning.[2] You will experience these principles with the suggested activities throughout the book. Each design principle is highlighted in a chapter with the plans for an expedition that is conducive to the integration of curriculum and based on a balance of the genres.

Our book is designed to give both beginning and experienced teachers tools and strategies to help their students gain literacy and life skills using children's literature. We have provided information about many of the finest offerings of children's literature and have recommended many more titles. We have also offered resources for teachers to explore and find out more about using children's literature in their classrooms.

Finally, there is an appendix with definitions of awards and the titles and authors of books that have won the awards. Internet websites are provided for further information on the books and awards.

The format for each chapter includes an epigraph from children's literature that reflects a relevant design principle. The epigraph sets the stage for themes within the chapter.

Upon completion of reading and responding to the content and activities in this book, you, as a teacher, will have a store of knowledge about children's literature, literacy processes, and integration of the curriculum, and will have the tools for planning for optimal student learning with literature.

Notes

1. Meg Campbell, Martin Liebowitz, Amy Mednick, and Leah Rugen, *Guide for Planning a Learning Expedition* (Dubuque, Iowa: Kendall/Hunt Publishing Company, 1998).

2. Emily Cousins, *Reflections on Design Principles* (Dubuque, Iowa: Kendall/Hunt Publishing Company, 1998).

Chapter 1

The Primacy of Discovery: Foundations of Literacy

"Only five books tonight, Mommy," she says.
"No, Olivia, just one."
"How about four?"
"Two."
"Three."
"Oh, all right, three.
But that's it!"

—Ian Falconer, *Olivia*, 2000

All of us who write, speak, and teach about children's literature realize that the foundation for literacy begins early in a child's life, even before birth. We know that the home environment provides the means for the infants and toddlers to acquire the literacy skills—listening, speaking, reading, and writing.

In Ian Falconer's *Olivia*, the young child, who happens to be a pig, is bargaining with her mother for as much literacy as she can get in her nighttime routine readings. During the first few years of life, when given an opportunity, children recognize the pleasures to be found in bedtime stories. Mama Pig in this story falls a little short as a great model for the love of literacy, but her scowl may represent reality reflecting tired parents who try to limit the length of the bedtime routine. The important point here is that Olivia was able to have her favorite book read to her, allowing her wonderful dreams throughout the night.

As Glazer states in her book, *Literature for Young Children,* linguists agree, "children are born with a natural capacity for oral language."[1] However, in order to nurture this natural capacity they need to be surrounded by a language-rich environment, in which people are speaking to them constantly, providing models to encourage their efforts toward the use of language. Family, friends, and caregivers should be using mature language to talk with children. In this way, children become familiar with language patterns and expand their vocabularies. Language development is critical for successful reading, writing, listening, and thinking skills.

1

Children are born with a natural desire to learn about their world. They are active learners who observe, manipulate, and experience their environment with all of their senses. Their future lives reflect what happens to them during the prenatal period and early months of infancy. They are innately primed for self-discovery and for taking on the responsibility for their own learning.

The design principle from Expeditionary Learning that is targeted in this chapter of the book and in the developmental stage of initial language and literacy is the "Primacy of Self-Discovery."

> Learning happens best with emotion, challenge, and the requisite support. People discover their abilities, values, "grand passions," and responsibilities in situations that offer adventure and the unexpected. They must have tasks that require perseverance, fitness, craftsmanship, imagination, self-discipline, and significant achievement. A primary job of the educator is to help students overcome their fear and discover they have more in them than they think.[2]

Infants need much support in the early years to sustain and guide the motivations that are present from birth. As teachers of young children, it is vital that we recognize the impact of prenatal and infancy development on later growth. For children to develop and function with their innate capabilities, good maternal health, both physical and mental, before and during pregnancy is crucial. Following birth, children need nurturing interactions, safe care, and expectations for timely growth and development in all areas. As a teacher, you will hope and expect that the children in your care have had safe and secure experiences during prenatal and infancy periods and come to school with the maximum potential.

The fact is, however, many will not have had optimal growing conditions. Their experiences and their environmental influences during critical periods for brain growth in the prenatal and early infant months will shape the brain. During the prenatal months, the fetus is subject to environmental experiences also. Upon birth, infants can perceive different levels of light and can respond to the differences, they can respond to familiar voices, and recognize stories they have heard in utero.[3] Those experiences and influences may be positive and will produce structural changes that increase the networking of pathways in the brain. On the other hand, intense stress, as well as exposure to toxic substances, can alter the genes of the fetus.[4] The effects on the child are then accented under negative environmental conditions, such as family or substance abuse and/or neglect.[5] The resulting behaviors of children under these circumstances may include hyperactivity, attention, and learning deficits.

Synaptic Development through Senses

In *Ghosts from the Nursery*, Karr-Morse and Wiley report from several sources that one to two hundred billion brain cells are present in a four-and-a-half-month-old fetus, but it is the stimulation of the environment both before and after birth, and the continuous interaction after birth, of the infant and the environment that builds the synaptic system that allows cognitive processing. Although the neurons are present long before birth, the connections through which impulses travel are just beginning to form at birth. These structures, called dendrites and synapses, become the network for developing schemas as the baby interacts with and explores the world. It seems that the phrase, "use it or lose it" applies in infants' brain development in that following a period of proliferation in growth of connections, a period of "pruning" will occur, followed by reorganization. There are at least thirteen stages of brain development, each one building on the previous one. There are untold unprogrammed circuits in the infant's brain just waiting to be stimulated and when that stimulation does not occur on a timely basis, pruning and reorganization of resources will eliminate these unused circuits.

On the other hand, these circuits are open and viable, waiting for external stimulation to catapult the infant's cognition, language, and human interaction skills. In *Ghosts from the Nursery*, Kotulak says, "The brain gobbles up its external environment in bits and chunks through its sensory system: vision, hearing, smell, touch, and taste." [6]

As adults, we must provide materials for the stimulation of these senses. Table 1.1 provides books that satisfy each sensory area and leave the infant searching for more. (The sense of taste is not listed. Of course, it is expected that infants taste each and every book they touch!)

Establishing a Literacy-Oriented Environment

Knowing how vulnerable infants are during the prenatal period and the early months of life, we must feel and act upon the urgency to provide the safest, most positive physical, intellectual, and emotional environment for these children. Varied interactions with adults and other children and many opportunities to explore and begin to understand the environment are indicative of children who will be ready for literacy and life experiences as they are encountered.

Table 1.1. Books to Stimulate Senses

Sense	Type of Book	Example of Book	Suggested Activities
Seeing	Age-appropriate picture books	*Baby in a Car* *Baby in a Buggy* (Monica Wellington)	Ask baby, "Where is . . .?" Baby can point and later say the name. Point from left to right and give infant the orientation of the directionality of print
Hearing	Sound books	*Country Animals* *Farm Animals* *Garden Animals* *Pet Animals* (Lucy Cousins)	Make sounds of animal for baby. Later ask baby to point to animals as you make the sounds. Then you point to the animal and let baby make the sound.
Smelling	Scratch and Smell	*I Smell Christmas* (Mercer Mayer)	Show baby how to rub a finger over the objects and then smell the fragrance. Talk about how each object smells.

Prenatal months and the first two years of life are the most crucial period for brain development, for social development, and for the human personality to form. There are sensitive periods in an infant's development for the acquisition of language. During this time, the establishment of a literacy-oriented environment will set the stage for a lifestyle that will include literacy and literature. Parents will hold and cuddle their babies and speak to them in soft sing-songy voices that signal security, love, warmth, and food to the child. That feeling then extends to the experience of reading or listening to a story when the child hears that same voice. The association of security and warmth with reading experiences is the first step toward a literacy-oriented environment and lifestyle.

Storytelling often bonds families. Babies' eyes will focus on the face of one who speaks to them, and the more the babies hear, the more they coo, babble, and respond. Babies of three or four months have been found to respond to stories told to them, so it is never too early to begin. Lack of stimulation during such a critical period means that the function will never develop to the level that it could have developed during that period. It may mean that these children will grow into toddlers without knowing the intense satisfaction of literacy experiences, such as the sounds and images of language, the interplay with books and toys, and the personal interaction with another person who is telling or reading a story.

Key elements of the literacy-oriented environment are the immersion of the infant in a language-rich atmosphere. It is during this time that the oral language foundation develops and becomes the base for future literacy. In *A is for Ox*, Barry Sanders states that "every young child recapitulates" the history of human cultures by passing first through a stage of orality as a precursor to written language."[7] The experiences during this oral stage that ultimately lead to success in reading and writing include acquisition of mental imagery from spoken words, development of vocabulary, beginning of cultural heritage of narrative concepts, and listening to stories read aloud.

Acquisition of Mental Imagery from Spoken Words

Descriptions of objects in the child's environment give opportunities for the infant to begin forming pictures in the mind. ("Look at the doggie. See his little tail wag. Look at his spotted, furry coat of hair. He is not as big as you are.")

Repeating lived-through episodes will allow the child to bring back to mind something that has been experienced. ("Remember when we saw the doggie? Did you touch the doggie? Did you hear him bark?")

Storytelling about toys and people in the child's life will allow the child to put familiar objects with identifying words ("Once there was a little teddy bear. He was lonely when he was left alone. One day, he decided to get out of the baby's bed and go for a walk.")

Development of Vocabulary

Expand on what the child says even if the language is fundamental. (If the child utters a sound, pick up on that sound and expand it into rich language: "Yes, you see the crackers and you'd like one, wouldn't you? Wonder what they will taste like. Do you think they will be salty? Crisp? Tasty? Do you like the crackers?")

Exchange conversation, expecting the highest level of communication possible. (After reading Margaret Wise Brown's *The Runaway Bunny*, talk with the child about favorite parts of the story, why the bunny wants to run away, how the bunny's mother feels, and how the bunny feels at the end after getting a big hug from mother.)

Read books to children, allowing them to identify pictures of words and actions. (From P. D. Eastman *Are You My Mother?* infants can point to and/or label the bird, the tree, the nest, all of the creatures who were asked the question, and finally, the mother.)

Beginning of Cultural Heritage of Narrative Concepts

Preconceptions of what makes a story seem to vary in many cultures. The traditional oral narrative, found in most folktales, is the prevailing concept of a narrative. These stories usually begin with a ritualistic beginning, such as "Once upon a time." In the story, we find flat characters about whom we know very little, a well-defined problem, and several (usually three) attempts to solve the problem. The final resolution comes quickly followed by another formulaic phrase, "and they lived happily ever after."

In some cultures, the narrative is an exchange of language between two characters, jokes, riddles, or chains of events that are totally lacking the sequence usually associated with narratives.

The cultural traditions that are passed from generation to generation through the oral channel begin during these first two years of infancy. They allow formation of the "story" schema, a network of criteria, and expectations for both the oral tellings and written narratives to come. These experiences are vital to the child's subsequent grasp of the language and its functions.

Reading Aloud

Reading aloud to a child is also fundamental in promoting early literacy. One study examined the nature of early socialization mothers provide as they shape babies' understanding of the value of books. Even with babies as young as six months of age, it was found that the mothers participate in specific literacy type behaviors, such as:

- using a higher pitch in their voices,
- asking questions,
- exaggerating facial and body movements,
- using various sound effects with excitement,
- verbally coaxing the baby to respond by bouncing or jiggling the infant,
- providing much eye to eye and body to body contact,
- pointing or patting pictures,
- moving the book to keep it in the baby's line of sight,
- modeling book-reading activity,
- answering their own questions,

- labeling the pictures, and
- describing the actions.

The infants' actions are also representative of conventional as well as nonconventional book-reading. They sit next to their mothers and often turn pages. They lean forward, looking at pictures or print, sometimes bouncing, sometimes patting the book or kicking it with their feet. They often perform the action named in the book. They point, reach, grab, kiss, and eat the books. Their language activities are related to labeling and describing the pictures, labeling the actions and events, and they relate the text to their own lives.[8]

Bettelheim, the famous child psychologist, wrote that he realized his most important task was to restore meaning to the lives of his severely disturbed patients. He searched for the most important experiences in children's lives, the best way to give meaning to their lives. "Regarding this task nothing is more important than parents and others who take care of the child; second in importance is our cultural heritage, when transmitted to the child in the right manner. When children are young, it is literature that carries such information best."[9]

Reading aloud is also a way for children to hear oral language and as they hear it, they realize there is a relationship between the words on the page and the words they are hearing. They delight in the illustrations and begin using their own knowledge of the world to make connections with the words and pictures on the pages before them. As they are read to, their abilities to listen and think are growing, and it won't be long before these youngsters will be writing.

Socialization through Literacy Routines

During the first two years of life, in addition to physical development, infants are developing cognitively, linguistically, and socially. It is through these three interrelated areas of growth that the infant begins socialization, through which tools for language and cognition are learned.[10] Bruner[11] describes how the parent provides the framework for the child's language to develop by structuring continuity and security through consistency. In this plan, a routine is established for activities such as reading to the child or playing with language at bath or mealtime. (Remember Olivia?) Through these activities, the parent is not only encouraging synaptic networking in the child's brain, but is providing a context for the child to learn and adopt linguistic knowledge and cultural mores.

The routine experiences that the child learns to rely on not only give comfort to him or her but provide a point of reference for other activities. When the parent says, "We will play after bath time," the child will realize that playtime will eventually come. It will be expected, and although the child does not have a concept of time, he or she can anticipate the playtime. The child begins to trust the parent or caretaker who takes the time to explain routines and makes the effort to maintain a regular schedule. Books shared during these routine times will help the child realize expectations of the family. The child will gradually recognize that at bedtime, the books are quiet, softly read, and make one feel comfortable and safe. At playtime, on the other hand, the books may be raucous and full of fun. These books bring a lesson to the child about how the family perceives bedtime and other routines. The child will internalize the family routines and identify that with family and those activities. It is through such experiences that children learn who they are and to whom they belong. Table 1.2 gives ideas of books, suggested routines, and activities during the child's day.

Table 1.2. Routine Books

Routine	Type of Books	Examples of Books	Suggested Activities
Bath time	Plastic or cloth	*Farm Faces* (Willable L. Tong) *Flower in the Garden* (Lucy Cousins) *Fun* (Jan Pienkowski) *Kite in the Park* (Lucy Cousins)	Keep a basket of plastic or cloth books near the tub. Read them to the child during bath time. Allow the child to hold the books even if wet!
Bedtime	Soothing Stories	*Where Does the Brown Bear Go?* (Nicki Weiss) *Goodnight Moon* (Margaret Wise Brown) *Jack: It's Bedtime* (Rebecca Elgar)	Establish bedtime routines of telling family members goodnight, reading books, and telling stories, giving hugs and wishing sweet dreams.

Language and Literature for the Infant

Karr-Morse and Wiley report that the intellectual and language abilities of parents are strong predictors of the cognitive functioning of their preschoolers.[12] Those parents with strong intellectual and language abilities are likely to interact with their children using those skills and will model language and thinking to their youngsters.

The more adults talk to their babies, the easier it is for the infants to select the sounds of their language and begin internalizing the grammar rules. The sound of human speech creates the path in the infant brain for language—and language learned begets more language. An absolutely essential responsibility of parents and caretakers of young children is to talk to them and with them, speaking about things of interest in their world, and listening to their responses. Their early language will be in the form of cooing and babbling, followed by one-word utterances, and gradually adding words according to the grammatical understandings they have achieved. Whatever their stage of linguistic development, language learning is sealed with love. As adults and babies communicate with words and sounds, much of it will be done with baby on the adult's lap, with arms around the baby, providing a safe haven and a comfortable setting.

As this language increases, parents will want to find materials that allow their infants to hear sounds and to begin walking the road toward phonemic awareness. Phonemes are the smallest units of sound in the English language, so there is a phoneme for each letter of the alphabet and then additional ones for multiple letters that make a specific sound. Some examples of these additional phonemes are /ch/ as in child; /wh/ as in what; /ng/ as in ring; and two phonemes for the /th/: this and thin. It is critical for children to begin hearing the distinctions among these sounds as they are listening to and developing their language. Further down that road when they approach preschool years looms the task of hearing the sounds and attaching a letter to each one. When this task is accomplished, the child is said to have phonemic awareness. Saturation with the sounds in the forms of rhymes, language play, sound games, and stories told and read to infants and toddlers will smooth that path toward phonemic awareness. It has been clearly established that phonemic awareness is a predictor of reading achievement. In fact, it has been suggested, tongue-in-cheek, that prenatal phonemic awareness may be in order.[13]

As children are playing with the sounds of the language, they are also processing a conceptual framework regarding the world around them. Concepts, or schemas, are the ideas that children construct that give them a baseline for comparing all new incoming information. When a child first sees a cat and hears the meow, feels the soft fur, and watches the four-legged, fuzzy animal play with a ball of string, the child has constructed a concept of cat. When the child then sees a dog that looks, feels, and sounds similar to the cat, it is likely that the child will assume this animal is a cat. More experience with cats and dogs will give more contrastive data so the child can accommodate his or her thinking to include another schema—an additional one for dogs.

Children certainly acquire much of the real-world information through actual, lived-through experiences of seeing, hearing, touching, feeling, (and of course, tasting whenever they can), the objects in their lives. A major secondary source for this conceptual development, however, is the picture book. Through this medium, children can distinguish attributes of different things in their world. They can take as much time as they want to muse over the colors found among dogs, the different sizes of horses, and other identifying characteristics of the constructs they are building. They have an opportunity through picture books to hear the labeling of objects in their environment. A common phrase heard among two-year-olds is, "do it again." They are asking you to read the pictures again, ask the questions that you have just asked, and play the games with the pictures on the pages another time and another time. As this interchange occurs between parent or caretaker and the young child, sounds are becoming firmly established, (sounds that are not heard are pruned to no longer be easily accessed), the foundation is being laid for rhymes, and growth abounds in concepts and the vocabulary to accompany the constructed schemas. Table 1.3 presents books for language development.

Teaching Strategies

1. Allow children to sense the environment with touch, sight, hearing, feeling, and, yes, tasting. Active is the keyword!
2. Provide many opportunities for sitting on adults' laps and pointing to objects of interest.
3. Provide real objects alongside the pictures in books (blocks, toys, stuffed animals, fruit, and anything concrete that children may make the connection between the real object and the symbol in the book.) Symbolism is a first step toward the type of thinking that is needed for reading.

4. Use lots of drama and auditory stimulation when reading to children. Vary voices with characters and use body language to explain actions in the books and stories.
5. Keep the story line simple when reading or telling, so they can follow the problem and the character's attempts to solve the problem.
6. Substitute the children's names for characters if the names are not important in the actual story. With characters whose names will be important to the children later in life (such as Winnie-the-Pooh and friends), use the character names without substitutions.
7. Let children hold the book and point to the pictures or words. If they are sitting next to or in the lap of an adult, they can see exactly what the reader sees. If sitting across from you, they are looking at the pictures from a different perspective. They need to experience both perspectives, so vary the physical arrangements of the reading time.

Implications for Teachers of Young Children

When teachers understand the relevancy of experiences of children during prenatal and infancy periods, they are more likely to provide activities that are linguistically, socially, and cognitively appropriate for the children in their care. They will also feel the responsibility for interacting with parents, providing guidance when possible for home experiences. They will value the cultural heritage of the children and make efforts to preserve the oral tradition from each family. They will guide children in the selection of materials, both print and nonprint, to build upon the foundation of oral language that was begun by the family. They will show the children who are in their care the joys and wonders that are to be found in both the spoken and written word.

Some Suggested Authors for this Age

Following are the names of some authors who write for children in this age group: Martha Alexander, Donald Crews, Lois Ehlert, Gail Gibbons, Kevin Henkes, Lynn Reiser, Anne Rockwell, Nancy Tafuri, Jeanne Titherington, and Rosemary Wells.

Table 1.3. Books for Language Development

Language	Type of Books	Examples of Books	Suggested Activities
Sounds	Song and Chant Lullabies	*Bang, Bang, Toot, Toot* (Rich Cowley) *Polar Bear, Polar Bear, What Do You Hear?* (Bill Martin, Jr.) *To Market to Market* (Anne Miranda)	Say and sing the sounds. Encourage the baby to repeat the sounds. Articulate clearly and avoid "baby talk." Use a lyrical voice. Accent the rhythm when possible. Sing them to sleep with some lullabies.
Rhymes	Nursery Rhymes	*Appley Dapply's Nursery Rhymes* (Beatrix Potter) *Cecily Parsley's Nursery Rhymes* (Beatrix Potter) *The Classic Mother Goose* (Armand Eisen, ed.)	Read the rhymes to the infant. Change your voice with different characters. Put hand and body motions with the rhymes. When possible, turn them into finger plays. Use exaggerated facial expressions.
Concepts	Concept Books	*Spot Goes to the Beach* (Eric Hill) *Count and See* (Tana Hoban) *A Rainbow all Around Me* (Sandra L. Pinkney)	Show the baby how to lift the flap and do it until the baby can do it. Count or say the letters in a rhythmic voice. Add surprise to your voice. As you model, the child will eventually interact with the book.
Vocabulary	Picture Books	*Number One, Tickle Your Tum* (Baby Bear Books) (John Prater)	Engage infants in the pleasure of the words. Help make connections so the words will mean something to the baby.

Notes

1. Joan I. Glazer, *Literature for Young Children* (Upper Saddle River, N.J.: Prentice-Hall, 1999), 98.

2. http://www.elob.org/aboutel/principles.html

3. Michael Cole and Sheila R. Cole, *The Development of Children* (New York: Freeman, 1996).

4. Ronald Kotulak, *Chicago Tribune* series: "Unlocking the Mind," April 11–15, 1993 and special section: "The Roots of Violence: Tracking Down Monsters within Us." December 12–15.

5. Robin Karr-Morse and Meredith S. Wiley, *Ghosts from the Nursery: Tracing the Roots of Violence* (New York: The Atlantic Monthly Press, 1997).

6. Ibid., 25.

7. Barry Sanders, *A is for Ox: The Collapse of Literacy and the Rise of Violence in the Electronic Age* (Newbury, Calif: Vintage, 1994), 36.

8. Anne Van Kleek and Ronald B. Gillam, "The Relationship between Middle-Class Parents' Book-Sharing Discussion and Their Preschoolers' Abstract Language Development," *Journal of Speech, Language & Hearing Research* 40 (1997): 1261–1272.

9. Bruno Bettelheim, *Uses of Enchantment: The Meaning and Importance of Fairy Tales* (New York: Knopf, 1976), 4.

10. Lev Vygotsky, *Thought and Language* (Cambridge, Mass.: MIT Press, 1962), 51.

11. Jerome Bruner, "Early Social Interaction and Language Development" in *Studies in Mother-Child Interaction*, ed. H. R. Schaffer (London: Academic Press, 1977).

12. Karr and Wiley, *Ghosts from the Nursery*, 28.

13. Stephen Krashen, "Phonemic Awareness Training for Prelinguistic Children: Do We Need Prenatal Phonemic Awareness?" *Reading Improvement* 35, no. 4 (1998): 167–171.

Chapter 2

Self-Discovery of Literacy: Emerging Readers and Writers

And up and down every day, morning moon evening star, morning star evening moon, running left and turning right, counting one and counting two, learning A and learning B, a hum today, a song tomorrow, they gaze at the heavens, rise before the sun, sail with the moon and dream of stars to read and write and write and read each night and each morning and each noon and each day one more letter and one more sound, one more sound and one more word, one more word and one more line one more line and one more page of their little songs, their little songs in the great and beautiful books on the Road to A B C.

--Denise Lauture, *Running the Road to ABC*, 1996

"If only children could learn to read and write as easily as they learn to listen and speak . . . " lamented a young teacher. Others have said that if we tried to teach children to talk in the same way that we teach them to read, we would have a nonverbal society. Those of us who have been around young children realize that listening and speaking develop naturally with exposure to the language and speakers of that language. Virtually all humans have a language. Exceptions are among those with brain damage or extremely low functioning cognitive capacities. Oral language is in all societies of the world today; however, taking the step to literacy is far from being spread worldwide.[1] Literacy is not a given in each and every human. It is, however, within reach of every human who has developed symbolic thought processes and who has the exposure to and opportunities for interaction with print in some form. The discovery of literacy is a milestone in a child's development. Once a child realizes what worlds are opened with literacy, there is little that can stop the momentum. As in the previous chapter, the primacy of self-discovery is a motivating factor that can lead learners to the rewards of literacy. "When students discover an idea that moves or excites them, they are inspired to research, reflect, and learn more."[2]

How Children Discover Literacy

Children with the best chances for discovering literacy at a young age are those who have experienced the oral language in the nursery rhymes, lullabies, and concept books for the very young (as described in the previous chapter). A rich oral background allows children to appreciate the sounds of the language, the rhyming patterns, and the ritual of storytelling with long-ago language, such as "Once upon a time."

Alongside the immersion of these children into their language are extensive experiences with the language in print. Scribbles and notes on the refrigerator door, cards and letters from Grandma, magazines and books for both children and adults in the household are a few of the obvious ways that children begin to value print. Parents and siblings are great models to show the young literacy learner the pleasures of reading and writing. It is important for them to read to the children in the family and to encourage writing at all levels. It is just as important for the adults to read and write themselves and make sure that children see why they are engaging in these literacy activities and the importance of having such abilities.

We, as educators, need to take advantage of the years that the Swiss psychologist, Jean Piaget, has called the preoperational stage. The stage is approximately from ages two to seven. It is during this time that children learn to use symbols. Language is, of course, the use of symbols to represent real objects. These children are also making sense of and developing their own theories about the world. Through picture books for the young ones, adults can confirm their understanding of these stages, and children can see a mirror of their lives and interests. Knowing the characteristics of children at certain stages makes it easier for parents and teachers to choose appropriate books for every age.

Kevin Henkes has written several charming stories about mice children encountering the same situations as human children. Owen in the book of his name, *Owen,* goes to extreme lengths to keep his blanket. Henkes's illustrations and text are equally enjoyable and kids shout with laughter when they see Owen putting the blanket inside his pajama bottoms on the night the blanket fairy is supposed to visit. Lilly in *Lilly's Purple Plastic Purse* is just as typical as Owen and just as engaging. She has some new things (a purple plastic purse that plays a jaunty tune when opened, three jingly quarters, and a pair of rhinestone movie-star glasses) that she HAS to share. She can barely control herself the next day at circle time in school. She adores her teacher, Mr. Slinger, but during his lessons on three different kinds of cheese and words that rhyme with "mice," she finds it impossible to keep her riches to herself any longer. She opens her purse and gleefully shares her treasures—Uh oh! She finds herself in the back of the room for the rest of the day and Mr. Slinger has the purple plastic purse and its contents.

In *Wemberly Worried,* Kevin Henkes has again worked his magic. A little mouse, Wemberly, worries about everything—big things and little things. Her first day at nursery school is a challenge and she clutches her toy rabbit, Petal. At school she makes a friend, Jewel, who also has a toy doll. The two little ones and their dolls have a very successful day together and Wemberly still worries "but no more than usual. And sometimes even less."[3] Many children can identify with this feeling on the first day of school.

Nancy Tafuri, another author/illustrator for the little ones, illustrates Henkes's *The Biggest Boy.* The tale begins with

> He is a big boy.
> He can eat with a fork.
> He can get dressed all alone.
> And he can even reach some of
> The cupboards in the kitchen.[4]

The biggest boy tells his parents over and over again how big he is becoming, and they agree. Finally, when he looks at the moon from his bed at night and thinks it no bigger than a marble, he is certain that he is the biggest boy. Henkes talks about close and familiar things and the story fits nicely into a child's imaginative play.

Nancy Tafuri writes and illustrates wonderful stories for the young set. *Have You Seen My Duckling?* is an almost wordless picture book that follows a worried mother duck as she leads her brood around the pond searching for one of her wayward ducklings. It's a warm and reassuring story about independence and motherly love that will appeal to young children.

Another delightful story about a mother's determination to keep her little one close is Margaret Wise Brown's *The Runaway Bunny,* a well-loved classic. "If you run away," said his mother, "I will run after you. For you are my little bunny."[5] In the following pages, the author shows us that no matter what form baby bunny takes, his mother will always find him. *Goodnight Moon,* another of Ms. Brown's classics, takes the sleepy child on a tour of the bunny's bedroom as his mother tucks him in. He says goodnight to everything in the room and finally, to the moon. This is a bedtime tactic with which all parents are familiar.

Betsy Everitt in *Mean Soup* and Molly Bang in *When Sophie Gets Angry—Really, Really Angry* . . . understand the minds of children this age. The protagonists in each book have had bad days. In Everitt's book, Horace has a bad day at school, but his mother knows how to make the day better. She sets water on the stove, screams into the pot, and urges Horace to do the same. He screams, growls, and bangs on the side of the soup pot until he and his mother are smiling and enjoying the day. In the Bang book, Sophie's sister grabs the toy gorilla that Sophie is playing with. Mother says it is sister's turn.

> Oh, is Sophie ever angry now!
> She kicks. She screams.
> She wants to smash the world to smithereens.[6]

Lucky Sophie. She has a system that helps her get over her anger. She runs to the beech tree and climbs and the "wild world comforts her."[7]

Margaret Wise Brown, Kevin Henkes, and Nancy Tafuri's books are good choices as read-alouds to the very young. Some other authors who write simple stories about familiar things for this age are Rosemary Wells, Frank Asch, Sue Williams, Mercer Mayer, Marc Brown, Jan Ormerod, Jeanne Titherington, Eric Carle, James Marshall, and Bill Martin, Jr.

Phases in Literacy Learning

Language development is a precursor to literacy. There are distinct phases in literacy learning and each has a specific focus. Literacy's foundation is established from birth through the first two or three years as the home or the caregiver is the source of materials and stimulation for literacy. Much of the interaction at this phase is on a one-to-one basis. When the child moves into social settings, such as preschool, nursery school, or day care at ages three, four, and five, the focus shifts to group enjoyment of stories along with independent pursuits in reading and writing. Toward the end of the latter phase, children are moving through the stages of emergent literacy from early readers to transitional readers.

Phase One: Early Literacy Learners

Early literacy learners are curious about books and want to handle them. They can quickly learn how to turn pages, how to look at the pictures, and how to match the pictures to the words read by an adult. They need to know where to find paper and markers for their scribbling and drawing. They must use their sensory learning with reading and writing materials.

These young learners are very interested in their own worlds, so the materials they read and write about will have relevancy to their lives. Their own world, consisting of their family, toys, pets, and home environment, are areas of their interest and they will enjoy stories about these familiar people, things, and places. Alexandra Day's *Good Dog, Carl* is a wordless book about the relationship between a baby and his dog. It will be easy for children to make their own story to go with this familiar event. Pat Hutchins's *Happy Birthday, Sam* is another book that connects children to their families—grandfather in this case. Rosemary Wells's *Noisy Nora* is another "family" book with sibling issues easily understood by young children. In fact, young learners have a large menu for selection from the author/illustrator Rosemary Wells, whose Max books touch many phases of life.

These children are active learners who are constantly testing theories of their world. They are patient in examining illustrations and see much more in each picture than most adults do. If the illustration does not match their concept, they will usually ask questions to satisfy the mismatch between their theory and that found in the book. The bright colors and unique, sometimes geometric, designs found in the books of Lois Ehlert allow children to study the pictures and compare them to their real world. Eric Carle's menagerie of insects and spiders in his books allows children the same opportunity to ponder the illustrations of ladybugs, caterpillars, butterflies, and spiders, while enjoying the stories and sensory delights.

Phase Two: Social Influences on Literacy Learning

Young learners are social and seem to know how much they can learn from others. They observe, they imitate, and they have successes and failures. When they work with other children who are at a slightly higher level of achievement, they are very likely to rise to the higher level. Jane Yolen's *Street Rhymes from Around the World* are fun chants, rhymes, and games for sharing with other kids. Shel Silverstein's *Where the Sidewalk Ends* and *Falling Up* are two poetry books of which most children never tire. They find other children doing silly things they would love to do themselves, such as "Jimmy Jet and His TV Set."

As children are growing in their own literacy, it is vital for them to see literacy as valued by those around them. Frank Smith identified a belongingness found among readers and writers who share the desire to engage in literacy events and who want to use literacy skills to expand their worlds. The Literacy Club[8] concept asserts that children who are literate form a camaraderie that is recognized by other children. The desire for membership into this club with a group of children who have literacy skills becomes an incentive for acquiring the skills needed to belong. If children are surrounded by others who read and write and value those activities, they feel a part of the "club" and they make every effort toward greater involvement and proficiency. It is not surprising that emerging literates like to read about characters who are learning to read. Patricia Polacco's *The Bee Tree, Thank You, Mr. Falker,* and *Mr. Lincoln's Way* are all books about children who are learning to read and write. Young children cannot yet read these books but will enjoy hearing them.

Emerging Readers and Writers: Breaking the Code

Much has been written about how children learn the sounds and letters of the language, first producing them for oral communication, listening to them, and distinguishing among the sounds as they grow in the ability to converse and communicate. As they move into the preschool years, they will begin matching the sounds they hear and speak to letters of the alphabet. Unfortunately only about fourteen of our twenty-six letters actual adhere to the alphabetic principle, allowing children to directly match a letter and one sound. Table 2.1 tells which ones they are.

Other phonemes, the smallest sound units in the language, are used with varied spellings. The major thrust in children's literacy development must first be to recognize that these sounds have symbols and make up the words that we speak, read, and write. Phonemes with these varied spellings can be seen in Table 2.2.

Table 2.1. Letters that Match Sounds

Letter	Sound in a Word
/b/	/b/all
/d/	/d/og/
/f/	/f/ox
/g/	/g/as
/h/	/h/ot
/l/	/l/amb
/m/	/m/ama
/p/	/p/ie
/t/	/t/ime
/v/	/v/iolin
/w/	/w/alk
/x/	bo/x/
/y/	/y/es
/z/	/z/ebra

Phonemic Awareness

Phonemic awareness may be supported through rhyming chants, nursery rhymes, rhyming poems, and alliterative tongue twisters. Alliteration is when the same sound is used over and over in a chant or rhyme. It may be in the initial syllable, such as "Sing a Song of Sixpence," or in the middle of the word, such as "Hey, Diddle, Diddle, the cat and the fiddle." Mother Goose rhymes are a wonderful place to start in giving children opportunities to hear and say these sounds. Dr. Seuss books provide such opportunities also, and there are tongue twisters available in bookstores that appeal to children five years of age and above.

Making the sounds is fun also as shown by their love for John Archambault and Bill Martin, Jr.'s *Chicka Chicka Boom Boom* or Bruce Degen's *Jamberry*. In *Chicka Chicka Boom Boom* the letters of the alphabet are found hopping up and down a coconut tree. Children will have many opportunities to locate the letters on the pages and sing their names along with the descriptions, "skinned-knee D and stubbed toe E." [9] *Jamberry* leads children through a rhyming series of berries, also delighting their tongues with the sounds of the language.

Chapter 2

Table 2.2. Additional Phonemes and Their Spellings

More Consonants	Sounds in Words
/j/	/j/ump; ed/ge/; /g/erm
/kw/	/qu/ick
/n/	/n/ame; /kn/ow
/r/	/r/at; /wr/ite; h/er/; b/ir/d; f/ur/
/s/	/s/it; /ci/ty
/sh/	/sh/irt; na/ti/on; spe/ci/al
/hw/	/wh/at
/ch	/ch/ip; ba/tch/
/th/	/th/in
/th/	/th/at
/ng/	ri/ng/; tha/nk/
/zh/	mea/sure/

Vowel Sounds	
/a/	c/a/ble; r/a/ke; r/ai/n; d/a/y
/a/	r/a/t
/e/	m/e/; k/ee/p; m/ea/n; safet/y/
/e/	b/e/t; h/ea/d
/i/	I; k/i/te; s/i/ght; m/y/
/i/	p/i/n
/o/	/o/h; c/o/ne; b/oa/t; m/o/w
/u/	f/u/t/u/re; f/u/se; n/e/w
/u/	pl/u/mb; /a/round; not/e/d; wag/o/n
/oo/	r/oo/t; R/u/th; cr/u/de; n/ew/
/oo/	t/oo/k; p/u/t
/oi/	/oi/l; b/oy/
/ou/	/ou/t; pl/ow/
/aw/	r/aw/; t/augh/t; f/a/ll
/ar/	j/a/r

Principles of Print

As children are developing their interest in reading, they are also internalizing some of the conventions of print.[10] As they are immersed in the written symbols of our language and pore over the picture books, they begin to understand that print is read from top to bottom and left to right. Prior to this understanding, you will see their scribbles and the symbols they create to represent various sounds all over the page on which they are writing. For a child without the print principle of "left to right; top to bottom," it is not unusual to see print move up or down the side of the page.[11] Once the child understands that the convention is for print to start on the left and move right, then return to the left for the next line, you will see this pattern in the writing.

As children begin writing their symbols, they initially write the same symbols over and over; then they realize that book print has a variety of symbols. As the young child progresses with the written word, an understanding of standard form of letters is required. For many children, the lack of that understanding is shown in their reversal of letters. Letters of the alphabet are among a few things in the world of the child that are rigid in the way they appear. A chair is still a chair even when turned backwards or upside down. So why is a "b" a "d" when turned backwards? By first or second grade, most children have acquired the concept of the inflexibility of the letters: they must be formed in one direction or they do not represent that letter.

Spacing between words is another concept that children must acquire for written competency. To know when to place spaces between words, children must know the boundaries of a word—where it starts and stops. As they are internalizing this concept, it is helpful to point to words as they are read, giving children a chance to see the words and the spaces between. Children are usually taught to place a finger between words for spacing. Even so, they don't always know where the word begins and ends. That realization comes with experience with print.

Big books are excellent for children seeing the print and conceptualizing the principles they will need for efficient communication in writing.

Using Concept Books

Some good book choices for these emergent readers and writers are simple alphabet and concept books with illustrations of limited objects representing each letter or word and accurate sounds for the letters. When selecting these books, look carefully at the pictures and what they represent on the page. It's important to use objects for the letters that only have one name. For example, is the little furry animal on the page with the letter D a dog or a puppy? Is the picture for the C page a cat or a cherry? Cherry does start with a /c/ but the sound of the initial phoneme is that of /ch/. There are numerous appropriate alphabet and concept books for these early literacy learners.

Alphabet books are written for the child who is a bit older as well. Suse MacDonald's unusual *Alphabetics* provides hours of discussion. Luci Tapahonso and Eleanor Schick give us *Navajo ABC: A Diné Al-*

phabet Book. Twenty-two of the letters are associated with words easily understood as English; however, there is a glossary for translations of the words into the Dinè language. Four of the letters of the English alphabet are used to introduce Dinè words.

Gathering the Sun: An Alphabet in Spanish and English, by Alma Flor Ada is her "homage to the farmworkers"[12] even as it is an excellent alphabet book. Flor Ada celebrates with twenty-seven short and simple poems presented in both Spanish and English.

Stephen Johnson produced the breathtaking *Alphabet City.* The paintings of different structures within the city capture each letter of the alphabet. They are so realistic that they appear to be photographs. These last three alphabet books have gone beyond the letter-sound recognition idea and are better saved for the older child, a child who already recognizes beginning letters and has a large vocabulary of "symbols."

Any teacher or parent who is looking for a counting book to provide one-to-one correspondence will not be disappointed. Tana Hoban has provided us with *1 ,2, 3* and *Let's Count* for the very young. Hoban's realistic photographs, while an excellent tool for developing numerical concepts, also provide support for a step from concrete, manipulative objects to symbols of those objects. Here are more of Hoban's books along with some from other authors that children will enjoy:

1. *26 Letters and 99 Cents* by Tana Hoban
2. *Colors Everywhere* by Tana Hoban
3. *Count and See* by Tana Hoban
4. *Color Farm* by Lois Ehlert
5. *Red Leaf, Yellow Leaf* by Lois Ehlert
6. *Ten Monkey Jamboree* by Dianne Ochiltree
7. *Whose Shoes?* by Anna Grossnickle Hines
8. *Turtle Splash! Countdown at the Pond* by Cathryn Falwell

Beginning Readers

Beginning readers are more successful when the materials are designed for "reading" words instead of pictures. These early reader materials will be printed with large fonts, much white space on the page, and simple, often repetitive, language. With beginning reader material characteristics there are also various levels because the early reader progresses in the amount of text that can be processed easily, the spacing around the words, predictability of text, frequency of vocabulary, and various other indicators as will be discussed.

Emergent Level

Beginning readers at the emergent level need reading text to be about familiar topics. These books will contain high frequency, easily recognized short sight words, such as "dog" or "cat." These books typically have five- to ten-word sentences, pictures to accompany texts, repetition, and prediction. To facilitate these understandings and to help the reader notice word boundaries, text size for easy reading and writing should be about eighteen points with extra space between words and lines with much white space on each page. The number of lines per page in these easy readers should be no more than fifteen.[13]

Levels

Literacy organizations such as Reading Recovery[14] and the National Literacy Coalition[15] are two examples of organizations with specific guidelines for leveling materials. Reading Recovery, an intervention program for low-achieving first-graders has a book list of 2,000 titles that have been leveled into a continuum of twenty progressively complex levels of material from the earliest emergent reader to second-grade juncture.[16]

The National Literacy Coalition's leveling method includes sequential complexity in these attributes and others at various levels:

- number of lines of text,
- predictable pattern of text,
- high frequency vocabulary,
- familiar topics,
- complexity of syntax,
- repetitious language, and
- mechanical conventions such as contractions and types of punctuation.

Levels that reach into middle-grade levels, and on into secondary education and beyond to adulthood, also reflect content of story structure, literacy elements of plot, characters, and setting as well as cultural variations.

Publishers are very aware of the early reader and are publishing sets of reading materials that are leveled. A simple Internet search for leveled reading materials produces lists of publishers whose materials have been leveled, with an average of fifteen to twenty developmental levels designated. Teachers have many resources at their fingertips for locating the appropriate reading materials for their early readers.

From the library bookshelves, many of the books that also meet the criteria for early reading are easily located. Here are a few that are particularly recognizable:

1. *The Cat in the Hat* by Dr. Seuss
2. *The Foot Book* by Dr. Seuss
3. *Jessie Bear, What Will You Wear?* by Nancy Carlstrom White
4. *Sheep in a Jeep* by Nancy Shaw
5. *Time for Bed* by Mem Fox
6. *Little Bear* by Else Holmelund Minarik
7. *Bony-Legs* by Joanna Cole
8. *Danny and the Dinosaur* by Syd Hoff
9. "Frog and Toad" series by Arnold Lobel
10. "Henry and Mudge" series by Cynthia Rylant
11. *Three by the Sea* by Edward Marshall

Transitional Readers and Writers

Typically, children develop through the emergent stages and early reading levels and by the time they reach third grade, they are interested in reading "chapter" books and those that appear more like "grown-up reading materials." Even though the readers are feeling more sophisticated, there is still a need to carefully consider materials for their continuing progress in reading. As was true for the easy reader material, the text for the transitional reader has

a large typeface and the number of lines per page never exceeds fifteen. The number of words per line, however, has been increased to an average of eight to twelve. Sentences are no longer broken down into shorter lines, and right margins are justified. There is plenty of white space on every page, with generous margins at the top, bottom, and sides and there is still a full line of leading after every line of type. The book includes frequent full page black-and-white illustrations, but there may be two or three spreads in a row with no illustrations at all.[17]

These books are usually written in short chapters with a complete episode in each chapter. Books in a series are particularly appealing to children who are reading at the transitional level. They like the familiarity with the characters and their background knowledge of the setting of the book aids in their developing fluency.

Some titles along with series books that you will want to consider for these readers are:

1. *The Chalk Box Kid* by Clyde Robert Bulla
2. *The Stories Julian Tells* by Ann Cameron
3. *Molly's Pilgrim* by Barbara Cohen
4. *Freckle Juice* by Judy Blume
5. "Amelia Bedelia" series by Peggy Parish
6. "Wizard and Wart" series by Janice Lee Smith
7. "Rookie Readers" series published by Children's Press
8. "Pinky and Rex" series by James Howe
9. "Junie B. Jones" series by Barbara Park
10. "Magic Tree House" series by Mary Pope Osborne
11. "Polk Street School" series by Patricia Reilly Giff
12. "Amber Brown" series by Paula Danziger
13. "Horrible Harry" series by Suzy Kline
14. "Bailey School Kids" series by Debbie Dadey and Marcia Thornton Jones

Teaching Strategies

Shared and Guided Reading

Teachers use shared reading, often in a whole group setting, to model enjoyment, routines, and skills to students who follow along with the text either in their own books or with an enlarged version, such as a big book or projection on a screen. Through this strategy, emergent readers are exposed to a higher level of material and see models of good writing.

Guided reading, on the other hand, is usually with a small group of students who have similar needs for the direct instruction that is a part of the guided reading session. Teachers identify selections of text, often expository, nonfiction text, with specific skills targeted.

Shared and Guided Writing

Shared and guided writing are similar to shared and guided read-ing. Sometimes the teacher will share personal writing with the students to model certain genres, points of view, or other literary elements. Guided writing focuses on specific skills and may include group com-position as a practice before an individual writing assignment begins.

Teacher Messages to Students

Teachers frequently model writing for their students by writing to them on transparencies on an overhead projector. It is a fact that if the teacher begins writing and it is projected on a screen, the students stop what they are doing to read the teacher's message. Good modeling, as well as information, may be shared in this manner.

Real-Life Literacy Experiences

Thinking time followed by writing time after a special event lends authenticity to the writing experience. The Language Experience Ap-proach to reading and writing has long been used in the primary grades. Following field trips or guest speakers or any special event, students group-write responses to the event on a chart. Children contribute while the teacher usually takes dictation and captures their thoughts for all the students to read later. Through the whole process of emerging reading and writing, there are few better strategies than giving students a reason to write about something they have experienced and know. Writing thank-you notes, summaries of plays they have seen, and memory logs following special occasions are just a few of the ways to read and write about real life.

Jump Rope Rhymes and Other Word Games

Primary grade students are developing skills with their bodies as well as their minds. They love jumping rope, hula hooping, hopscotch-ing, and other activities that combine the physical and the mental. For this reason, they love chants and word games to go with these activi-ties. Look at Joanna Cole's *Anna Banana: 101 Jump Rope Rhymes.*

Implications for Teaching

Mem Fox, noted author of children's books and an authority on reading has written about the three magic secrets that hold the key to reading. Teachers have known these secrets for many years. First, readers must have access to and knowledge of the world of print; second, the oral language foundation must be a part of the young reader's history; and finally, to really become engaged with reading and writing the child must have some life experiences to drive the interest and to motivate continual involvement.[18] Fox's magic, though not new and not innovative, is tried and true. Then why do we have children who are not successfully reading and writing at an early age?

Literacy Variances

Literacy appears through a variety of experiences that are different among children. Some children have little experience with print before coming to preschool or kindergarten; others have strong phonemic awareness or are reading when they enter school. Whatever the variances among children's preschool years, there are factors that seem to affect the emergence of literacy.

Valuing literacy is a basic prerequisite for its emergence. When children observe parents, other adults, and other children reading and writing with pleasure and with accomplishment, they begin to know that they, too, must learn how to read and write.

Modeling is a key component for the acquisition of literacy. Children watch as others turn pages in a "right side up book" or magazine and they notice as the eyes of the reader or writer move from left to right and top to bottom. If the child happens to be sitting on the lap of the reader, the child can also hear the sounds as they are articulated and may start guessing which of the symbols are associated with those sounds. The child also connects the warm, safe environment of the reader's lap with a wonderful event—reading—and the child wants to learn how to do it too!

Direct effort also has to be exerted for the accomplishment of the skills of literacy. It does not come as easily or naturally as speaking, although we would like to think that it could. Someone in the child's environment—teacher, parent, or another literate person—spends some time showing the child the ways of the word. Literacy learnings that are directly taught include:

- phonological awareness,
- print protocols, such as holding the book upright and turning the pages,
- strategies for rhyming,
- decoding, and
- using context clues, such as pictures.

These accomplishments work for most children.

I Am a Reader, Writer, and Learner: An Expedition

Guiding Questions

1. Why am I learning to read and write?
2. Why do we listen and say rhyming words?
3. Why do we read together and alone?
4. What does it mean to be a learner?
5. How do I learn by seeing, hearing, touching, feeling, and tasting?
6. What can I do to learn more?
7. What games can I play that will help me learn to read better?
8. How have children from the past learned to read?
9. How have children in other countries learned to read?
10. What books will help me read and write better?

Standards

The standards for this expedition are from the National Council of Teachers of English/International Reading Association (NCTE/IRA) at http://www.ncte.org

The students:

1. read a wide range of print and nonprint texts to build an understanding of texts, of themselves, and of the cultures of the United States and the world; to acquire new information; to respond to the needs and demands of society and the workplace; and for personal fulfillment. Among these texts are fiction and nonfiction, classic, and contemporary works.

place; and for personal fulfillment. Among these texts are fiction and nonfiction, classic, and contemporary works.

2. use spoken, written, and visual language to accomplish their own purposes (e.g., for learning, enjoyment, persuasion, and the exchange of information).

3. employ a wide range of strategies as they write and use different writing process elements appropriately to communicate with different audiences for a variety of purposes.

Initial Reading Options for Teacher Read-Aloud, Shared, Guided, or Independent Reading

1. *Running the Road to ABC* by Denize Lauture (picture book—preK)
2. *Virgie Goes to School with Us Boys* by Elizabeth Fitzgerald Howard (picture book—primary)
3. *Anastasia Krupnik* by Lois Lowry (chapter book—middle elementary)
4. *More Than Anything Else* by Marie Bradby (picture book—middle elementary)
5. *The Bee Tree* by Patricia Polacco (picture book—primary)
6. *Olivia Saves the Circus* by Ian Falconer (picture book—primary)
7. *Chicka Chicka Boom Boom* by John Archambault and Bill Martin, Jr. (picture book—primary)
8. *The Cat in the Hat* by Dr. Seuss (easy reader)

Fieldwork Options

1. Find things in the environment that students have learned by seeing, hearing, touching, feeling, and smelling and make a booklet of pictures describing these objects and events. They may find pictures in magazines or they may draw their own pictures.
2. Ask grandparents and aunts and uncles for stories about how they learned to read.
3. Find out if parents or grandparents had to walk to school like the children in *Running the Road to ABC* and *Virgie Goes to School with Us Boys*. Tell parents or grandparents about these stories.

Individual Projects

1. Write about your summer vacation after reading *Olivia Saves the Circus*.
2. Keep a reading log of all books read.
3. Make a hanging book report, such as a mobile on a clothes hanger.

Class Projects

1. Plan a Read Across America Project, such as a Dr. Seuss Day (Theodore Seuss Geisel was born on March 2, 1904) when community members are invited to school to read Dr. Seuss books.
2. Collect pictures of objects and sort them for sounds. Organize sorted pictures into a "phoneme book."
3. Create a mural to show the "Road to ABC."
4. Find out what Haiti looks like.

Sharing Outlets

1. Read Across America celebration.
2. Mural of "Road to ABC" in school library.

Assessment Options

1. Assessment of project using teacher-made criteria.
2. Assessment of reading level.
3. Inventory of reading attitude before and after this expedition.

Notes

1. Barry Sanders, A is for Ox: The Collapse of Literacy and the Rise of Violence in the Electronic Age (Newbury, Calif: Vintage, 1994).

2. http://www.elob.org/aboutel/principles.html.

3. Kevin Henkes, *Wemberly Worried* (New York: Greenwillow, 2000).

4. Kevin Henkes, *The Biggest Boy* (New York: Greenwillow, 1995).

5. Margaret Wise Brown, *The Runaway Bunny* (New York: HarperTrophy, 1977).

6. Molly Bang, *When Sophie Gets Angry—Really, Really Angry* . . . (New York: Scholastic, 1999), 5-7.

7. Ibid., 24.

8. Frank Smith, *Joining the Literacy Club: Further Essays into Education* (Portsmouth, N.H.: Heinemann, 1992).

9. Bill Martin, Jr. and John Archambault, *Chicka Chicka Boom Boom* (New York: Scholastic, 1989).

10. Marie, Clay, *An Observation Survey: Of Early Literacy Achievement* (Portsmouth, N.H.: Heinemann, 1992).

11. Marie, Clay, *Change Over Time in Children's Literacy Development* (Portsmouth, N.H.: Heinemann, 2001).

12. "Alma Flor Ada," in *The Eighth Book of Junior Authors and Illustrators*, ed. Connie Rockman (New York: H.W.Wilson, 2000), 2.

13. Kathleen Horning, *From Cover to Cover: Evaluating and Reviewing Children's Books* (New York: HarperCollins, 1977).

14. Reading Recovery Council of North America, Columbus, Ohio.

15. National Literacy Coalition. Professional development seminar, "Assuring Growth and Accountability Supervision and Evaluation in Balanced Literacy Schools," 2000. Seminar held at Collier County Public Schools Staff Development.

16. http://www.readingrecovery.org/sections/reading/basic.asp

17. Horning, *From Cover to Cover*, 42.

18. Mem Fox, *Reading Magic: Why Reading Aloud to Our Children Will Change Their Lives Forever* (San Diego: Harcourt, 2001).

Chapter 3

Acquiring Literacy through Children's Literature: Continuation of Self-Discovery

We're going on a bear hunt.
We're going to catch a big one.
What a beautiful day!
We're not scared.

—Michael Rosen and Helen Oxenbury,
We're Going on a Bear Hunt, 1989

Discovering literacy for one's self is as exciting as going on a bear hunt. Sometimes there are just as many obstacles to literacy acquisition as there are to catching a bear. Examine the concepts of literacy and literature, storytelling, and reading aloud. See how they are all connected to self-discovery, and to the confidence and security that comes with "knowing" literacy and literature. The most important element that would allow one to "go on a bear hunt" would be the trust in the surrounding community. It is that same trust that allows children to experiment with sounds, words, thoughts, and ideas. From the safe experimentation, sincere feedback from the community, and the motivation to "find that bear," students are active in their self-discovery of literacy and literature.

What is Literature?

Definitions of literature change over time and from culture to culture. Certainly all would agree with Charlotte Huck that "Literature is the imaginative shaping of life and thought into the forms and structure of language."[1] Notice that the definition refers to "language"—written, oral, and visual language. Contrary to what some think, the world of literature is much more than just the written words of text. The literature that was handed down orally includes a great body of early forms

of language, such as fables, myths, and folktales. Oral language of today is also a part of the definition of literature in the form of childhood
rhymes, games, nursery songs, and modern rap. Today's forms are usually passed on orally, but unlike the earlier versions of oral literature,
these are also found in written form. The vast media used in illustrations and the sophisticated art styles with which children can communicate represent the visual language of literature. The visual images in
picture books sometimes relay an entire message without a need for any
text. Usually, the text and the illustrations interact to give depth to the
implied meanings. Language and literature exist for the purpose of
communication.

Literacy

Regie Routman claims "Genuine literacy implies using reading, writing, thinking, and speaking daily in the real world, with options, appreciation, and meaningful purposes in various settings and with other
people."[2]

Literacy, then, is the process that encompasses all of the
communication methods that we use with literature.

How Do Children Acquire Literacy through Literature?

Literacy, literature, and life are intricately woven through the
threads of history and are conspicuously part of today's society. We
need only to spend some time with some of the world's oldest literature—folk literature—to realize how the oral form of communication
influenced our ancestors and continues to affect our lives today. Statements such as "sour grapes" or "steady but sure wins the race" are in-
grained in our lives with meanings associated with our own activities.
We seldom think about the origin of these moralizing quotes. In fact,
they are lessons from fables, a kind of folk literature told hundreds of
years ago and passed down in oral form. Many fables have been attrib-
uted to a Greek slave, Aesop, who is thought to have lived around 600
B.C. Since that time, parents have often used the messages in fables as
a means of teaching their children the morals and mores of the society.
Adults first told fables and many other forms of traditional literature to
other adults as entertainment.

Storytelling as a Foundation of Literacy

The importance of literature to early humankind is evident in reports of early storytelling. Storytelling was the principal means of communication. It served to spread news, to elicit pride among groups of people, and to promote heroes among the common folk. We know that traveling storytellers passed from village to village, collecting stories and telling their own, adapting their tales to the new twists they heard, and passing those on too. This process assured the preservation of much of our folk literature and provides a glimpse into the customs of our ancestors.

Storytelling and the preservation of the heritage of a group of people were closely related, so it is not surprising that this form of communication can be found in the earliest history of man and is still very much alive today. Teachers can uncover some of the storytelling traditions that are a part of the cultures and histories of our children. Children's stories are often reflections of their "story listening heritage." Their tales frequently have roots in stories passed down in their families for generations. When children tell their own stories, they begin with what they know. Usually they tell the story from the first person narrative (I or me). Often their stories will include bits and pieces of things they have heard others tell. Their tales may not be actual stories but strings of events. It is good to encourage children with their beginning storytelling because it provides them with a connection to the past.

The Historical Value of Literacy

While tales from children's own lives and those passed down by family members are great ways for children to recognize that stories are not just for the moment but are to be remembered and told over and over again, there is also value in reading about historical characters who have also lived tales worth telling.

Tales of former slaves in our country are full of examples of their belief that literacy provided an avenue to freedom. Pinkus Aylee, a young black soldier and former slave in Patricia Polacco's powerful *Pink and Say*, fashioned a pair of eyeglasses so he could read. They were a prized possession even though he knew they could lead to a severe beating if enemy troops discovered them in his pocket. The enemy troops would realize that he, Pink, could read. In the picture book, *More Than Anything Else*, Marie Bradby tells of Booker T. Washington's intense desire to read. Teachers can share with children the depth of his desire and the strength of his belief that literacy would lead to a better life.

Sarny, the former slave heroine of *Sarny* by Gary Paulsen, begins her story in 1930 when she is ninety-four years old and has outlived two husbands, a child, and most of those she remembers. Sarny's poignant memories are infused with her zeal for literacy, with her belief that literacy enriched and possibly saved her life. Reading was so important to her that she risked everything, including her family's safety, to help others read. When children read stories about people like Sarny, Booker T. Washington, and Pinkus Aylee, they understand that being literate, being able to read, write, speak, and listen, is important for living life well.

In Karen Hesse's *Letters from Rifka*, we read about a family's migration from Russia to the United States in 1919. We agonize over the trials that young Rifka endures as we read her diary entries to her cousin, Torvah. Torvah gave Rifka "the book of Pushkin," and during the journey, Rifka writes in the book's white spaces. At last, she arrives in America. "I will write you tonight a real letter, a letter I can send," she tells Torvah. "I will wrap up our precious book and send it to you too, so you will know of my journey. I hope you can read all the tiny words squeezed onto the worn pages. I hope they bring to you the comfort they have brought me."[3]

In the third tale of the *Sarah Plain and Tall* series by Patricia MacLachlan, Anna moves to town to work for a doctor and expects Caleb to continue the journals that she began in the first book. Caleb protests and Anna tells him, "Everyone's not a writer. But everyone can write,"[4] Caleb finds that this is not always the truth later in the story. One day, he discovers a ragged looking older man in the barn who turns out to be his grandfather. Grandfather had left Jacob when he was a boy without a word of explanation. Caleb learns that his grandfather is illiterate, so he teaches him to read using Anna's journals. Eventually Grandfather and Jacob reconcile.

Literacy and Literature Connections

In many cases, it is the high level of literacy that allows children to value their own competence. Stanley Yelnats, the main character in Louis Sachar's Newbery award-winning *Holes*, and Jeffrey Lionel Magee, the protagonist of Jerry Spinelli's *Maniac Magee*, are literate and their literacy helps them survive.

Stanley was not a bad kid and was innocent of the crime for which he was convicted. He'd just been in the wrong place at the wrong time—not unusual for the friendless, overweight middle schooler. Now Stanley has to serve time at Camp Green Lake, really a reform school, with a bunch of wackos. He's an outsider there, too, and spends the few moments of free time at the end of each day reading letters from his mom and writing back to her. Zero, one of the other inmates, notices Stanley laughing as he reads one of the letters. Zero asks what the joke is. Stanley responds that his mother wrote about feeling sorry for the old woman who lived in a shoe because it must have smelled bad in there.

> Zero stared blankly at him. "You know, the nursery rhyme?"
> Zero said nothing.
> "You've heard the nursery rhyme about the little old lady who lived in a shoe?"
> "No."
> Stanley was amazed.
> "How does it go?" Asked Zero.[5]

The two boys forge a friendship that is central to the story and includes Stanley teaching Zero how to read and write. Zero's newfound skill provides the final stroke when he reads the name "Stanley Yelnats" on a valuable suitcase. Stanley's literacy is crucial to his life and to the outcome of his story.

Early in Spinelli's book, *Maniac Magee* meets Amanda Beal and her suitcase full of books. Amanda lets Maniac borrow a book on Children of the Crusades after he begs. Later in the day, there is a huge commotion at 803 Oriole Street, an infamous address with the only "un-sat-on front steps" in town because all the kids were afraid of the owner, Mr. Finsterwald. If you valued your life, you never chased a ball into Mr. Finsterwald's yard or went in there for any other reason. As a cruel gag three or four high school boys dropped an eleven-year-old over the fence and into the dreaded yard. Then they backed away just watching, watching, watching. . . . Accounts of what happen next vary, but

> Real or not, they all saw the same kid: not much bigger than Arnold Jones, raggedy, flap-soled sneakers, book in one hand. They saw him walk right up to Arnold . . .
> The phantom Samaritan stuck the book between his teeth, crouched down, hoisted Arnold Jones's limp carcass over his shoulder, and hauled him out of there like a sack of flour . . .

As the stupefied high schoolers were leaving the scene, they looked back. They saw the kid, cool times ten, stretch out on the forbidden steps and open his book to read.[6]

And, as Stanley Yelnats did in *Holes*, Maniac teaches a friend, Old Mr. Grayson, how to read and write. Maniac does many things well, but he seems to get the most pleasure from reading. He becomes a legend in Two Mills.

Reading Aloud to Children for Literacy Development

Crucial to the entire literacy process is reading aloud to children. In 1983 the National Commission on Reading was formed to evaluate all the research of the last quarter century on how children develop, how they learn language, and how they learn to read. It took them two years to determine what works, what might work and what doesn't work.

In 1985 *Becoming a Nation of Readers*, the National Reading Commission's report on reading in the schools today, stated that "the most important activity for building the knowledge required for eventual success in reading is reading aloud to children."[7] The Commission found conclusive evidence to support the use of reading aloud, not only in the home but also in the classroom. It is a practice that should continue throughout the grades. They discovered the very disturbing news that the average classroom teacher spent one minute a day reading aloud to students.

There have been several studies that have focused on reading aloud at home.[8] The studies all conclude that children who are read aloud to at home perform much better in school and later in life.

Reading aloud conditions the child to associate reading with pleasure. Few things sell in our culture unless they are promoted. Shouldn't we promote reading by reading to the students and our children? Reading aloud helps improve the students' vocabulary and writing. The more you read, the better you write. Children hear words that they may not know within a context that will help them with the meaning. Once they hear and understand the word, it becomes a part of their vocabulary. By hearing the word used correctly, they will know how to use it.

Reading aloud helps build background knowledge. Students construct their own meanings and their own worlds in their minds while they listen to stories. By using their previous knowledge and backgrounds to create meaning, they "transact" with literature.

Transaction with literature, according to Louise Rosenblatt[9] occurs when readers (or listeners) combine the language of the text they are reading with their own experiences to make personal meaning. Transaction is the highest form of comprehension. We guide children action is the highest form of comprehension. We guide children of all ages toward that transactional process when we provide high quality literature with many opportunities for discussion and exchange of viewpoints.

Reading aloud provides a reading role model. Not only are the children connecting with an adult, but they are also seeing an adult take pleasure in the reading experience. Here it's important to emphasize that adults should always be thoroughly familiar with the materials they are reading aloud before they read them aloud. It's disturbing and embarrassing for students and adults to read and hear something that is inappropriate. For example, a fourth-grade teacher decided to read *The Giver* to his classroom because it was that year's Newbery award winner. Fortunately a colleague, who had read the book, heard him mention this and also heard him say that he had never read the book. She suggested that he become thoroughly familiar with the book first to see if it was appropriate for his particular class. He needed to be aware that the book includes references to sexual "stirrings," and the most powerful scene in the book involves the murder of a baby. The teacher read the book and decided that his class was not mature enough to appreciate *The Giver*.

Reading aloud helps develop a student's writing skills and style. It is imperative that children learn Standard English as a future survival tool. About one-tenth of the world's population uses English as its mother tongue. English has become the language of technology. In fact, 80 percent of the information stored on the world's computers is in English.

Reading aloud strengthens the bond between the reader and the listener. In classrooms and homes, adults and children share warm stories, exciting ideas, and helpful information. The sharing adds a different dimension to the experience. A special language develops between the reader and the listener. They've shared the same experience and can refer to it in different situations with a smile or a few words. Once a mother was driving down a wooded road and her son said, "Mom, stop," in a concerned voice. Impatiently, she stopped and the child got out of the car to run out and hold up his hand. The mama duck and her little babies waddled across the road, confident in the protection they received from Officer Pete. This was a scene right out of *Make Way for Ducklings* by Robert McClosky that the boy's mother had read aloud over and over again.

Reading aloud provides opportunities for the listener to ask questions about related subjects in a natural way. Examples of this can be found anywhere where reading aloud is taking place. Parents or preschool teachers could be chanting nursery rhymes with children and, suddenly a child asks, "How can a cow jump over a moon? Where is the moon? What is the moon? Do cows live on the moon?" Or how about a father and daughter reading Barbara Park's *The Graduation of Jake Moon* about the relationship between a boy and his grandfather. In the book Jake recounts his grandfather's painful journey from vital, productive middle age to an elder man in the grip of Alzheimer's. The daughter asks, "Why does this happen, Dad? Will it happen to you? What kind of medical research is being done to stop it? Is that what Grandma had?"

Expeditionary Learning with Literature

Learning to be literate, learning about literature, and learning about life interrelate as students navigate their journeys through the world of education and into the real-life environment.

When students embark on learning expeditions, comprehensive, guiding questions drive the direction of the journey. Students may search for meanings of multicultural literature and examine examples to discover the value of reading these books. When on such an expedition, students select from options in their learning experiences, which will lead to answers to some questions and will generate others. Each answered question leads to the next question along the journey. Expeditionary learning provides the connections among literacy, literature, and life.

Guiding the Children of Today toward Literature and Literacy

Teachers have daily opportunities to guide children in their literacy development and to chart courses for them that will lead to lifelong transactions with literature. Teachers can make a difference.

It is often said that kids of today are different from those of the past. It is true that many have different circumstances and different environments. We live in an instant world where we can often see news as it is happening. Nothing is hidden. Children see adults living their lives in all their glitzy brilliance as well as grim sleaziness. Some sports figures are human beings who evince all of the qualities that parents would like their children to have. There are others, just as visible, who are not the role models parents are seeking, but youngsters are drawn to their outrageous antics. Athletes and entertainers dominate the news. Even many of our politicians and public servants are shown as living exotic lives, often just over the line of legality. The disparity in the models for youngsters is not a new phenomenon, but communication technology has taken us right into the courtrooms to see the seamy sides of life. Children quickly lose their innocence in our society. In a few cases, there may even be contagion when children deliberately emulate attitudes, if not actions. Adults are often shocked at the graphic explicitness of the news showing sexual escapades and tragic violence. We can no longer protect our children from seeing real-world events. The children need to talk about what they see and hear and ask questions. Literature provides a perfect forum for such discussions, especially since most issues facing today's children are reflected in the literature.

Teaching Strategies

Regardless of age, when children make connections with literature and realize that there are characters in the stories who have goals or problems with learning to read and write similar to theirs, they find great interest in how those characters attained literacy. Strategies to support and encourage self-discovery of strengths and interests are productive.

Character Sets

Students locate a collection of characters who have similar interests or problems. The characters may be illustrated or created in a shoe box diorama and placed together. Dialogues among the characters may be written to share their perspectives on how they learned to read or write or why they thought these skills were important. What would a conversation sound like between Stanley Yelnats (*Holes*) and Pinkus Aylee (*Pink and Say*)? What would Anastasia Krupnik (*Anastasia Krupnick*) and Phoebe (*Mick Harte Was Here*) say about their brothers?

Character Webs

Children sort out the feelings, obstacles, or steps taken by readers as they make progress in their attempts with literacy and literature. Web each character in the four stories of *The Library Card*. How did each character use the library card? A web could also show the obstacles Caleb met while teaching his grandfather to read (*Caleb's Story*).

Plot Maps

Once students understand the basic plot scheme in narrative stories, they are able to draw the rising action on stair steps with each step leading to the climax of the story. Young readers can fill in the steps with stories, such as Eve Bunting's *Wednesday's Surprise*. The pages of this story lead to a wonderful surprise and children will enjoy recording the events. More mature students may use this strategy as they develop an awareness of how a story may unfold through the pages of a journal as happened in Margaret Peterson Haddix's, *Don't You Dare Read This, Mrs. Dunphrey*. The dark plot is revealed in this journal with continual reminders that the teacher, Mrs. Dunphrey, has assured her students that she will not read sections that students want to keep private. In actuality, the notes to Mrs. Dunphrey asking her not to read the entries are really pleas for help.

Literacy/Literature Treasure Hunts

Students can search databases, room collections, school and public libraries, and catalog systems for "themed" books. These books may be read and used for book talks when students try to "sell" their books to other students as Ramona does in *Ramona Quimby, Age 8*, or they may be read and discussed in literature circles. Any content in the curriculum could be a theme.

Implications for Teachers of Literacy Learners

Teachers realize that children will overcome almost any obstacle to find out "the rest of the story" if we match children with appropriate and appealing literature. Discovering their interests through personal interaction, inventories, reading logs, and opportunities for them to select their own reading will establish the baseline for meeting individual needs. Although we want students to read a balance of all genres and types of literature, it may be necessary to allow an "unbalanced diet" of a favorite genre while getting the student involved in the whole literacy process. Self-discovery is our goal for matching literacy and literature and the students will definitely discover both literacy and literature if given a wide range of materials and many opportunities for exploration.

I Need to Find Out: An Expedition

Guiding Questions

1. How can I find out about people, places and things through literature?
2. Where can I look for answers to my questions?
3. Who can help me if I get stuck? How can I help others?
4. Who are people who have gone on expeditions to find answers? What have they found? How have they shared their findings?

Standards

In this expedition, we look to selected standards of the National Council of Teachers of English and the International Reading Association at www.ncte.org/standards/standards.shtml.

The students:

1. read a wide range of print and nonprint texts to build an understanding of texts, of themselves, and of the cultures of the United States and the world; to acquire new information; to respond to the needs and demands of society and the workplace; and for personal fulfillment. Among these texts are fiction and nonfiction, classic, and contemporary works.
2. read a wide range of literature from many periods in many genres to build an understanding of the many dimensions (e.g., philosophical, ethical, aesthetic) of human experience.
3. apply a wide range of strategies to comprehend, interpret, evaluate, and appreciate texts. They draw on their prior experience, their interactions with other readers and writers, their knowledge of word meaning and of other texts, their word identification strategies, and their understanding of textual features (e.g., sound-letter correspondence, sentence structure, context, graphics).
4. employ a wide range of strategies as they write and use different writing process elements appropriately to communicate with different audiences for a variety of purposes.
5. apply knowledge of language structure, language conventions (e.g., spelling and punctuation), media techniques, figurative

language, and genre to create, critique, and discuss print and nonprint texts.

6. conduct research on issues and interests by generating ideas and questions, and by posing problems. They gather, evaluate, and synthesize data from a variety of sources (e.g., print and nonprint texts, artifacts, people) to communicate their discoveries in ways that suit their purpose and audience.

7. use a variety of technological and information resources (e.g., libraries, databases, computer networks, video).

Initial Reading Options for Teacher Read-Aloud, Shared, Guided, or Independent Reading

1. *A Year Down Yonder* by Richard Peck (chapter book—upper elementary)
2. *Dragon's Gate* by Laurence Yep (chapter book—middle elementary)
3. *Somewhere in the Darkness* by Walter Dean Myers (chapter book—middle school)
4. *The Watsons go to Birmingham—1963* by Christopher Paul Curtis (chapter book—upper elementary)
5. *The Wanderer* by Sharon Creech (chapter book—upper elementary)
6. *Crazy Weekend* by Gary Soto (chapter book—upper elementary)
7. *Hatchet* by Gary Paulsen (chapter book—upper elementary)
8. *Children of the Dustbowl: The True Story of the School at Weedpatch Camp* by Jerry Stanley (nonfiction chapter book—upper elementary)
9. *Wringer* by Jerry Spinelli (chapter book—upper elementary)

Fieldwork Options

1. Interview an editor or reporter from a newspaper and find out how they "find out" information.
2. Work in a library.
3. Spend time in a bookstore looking at the shelves and the way the books are organized. What are children reading?
4. Organize a reading survey.
5. Read to residents of health care facilities or assisted living residents.

Individual Projects

1. Read to brothers and sisters, others at after-school day care, parents, and grandparents.
2. Fill out applications for jobs in the classroom and in school.
3. Help parents with grocery shopping by reading the labels on the boxed and canned products.
4. Ask a variety of people the following: How has your life changed through literature? What have you learned?
5. Research a question and locate references for finding the answers.
6. Write your research project in a formal paper.

Class Projects

1. Tutor emerging literacy learners (young ones who are just entering literacy process). (Fifth graders read with first graders.)
2. Visit shelters or nursing homes to read to adults.
3. Assemble a class visual display (bulletin board or display board) with information on what works and what does not work as inspirations for reading—written from the viewpoint of children in the class.
4. Collect stories about people the students met during this expedition.
5. Assemble a booklet of stories about how each of the class members learned to read and write.
6. Sponsor a storytelling festival.

Sharing Outlets

1. Storytelling Festival.
2. Visual Display: Collections of materials written, drawn, and compiled during this expedition are prepared for others to see.

Assessment Options

1. Log of reading activities.
2. Responses to storytelling.
3. Participation in class projects.
4. Checklist of proficiency in reading and writing standards.
5. Rubric for research paper.

Notes

1. Charlotte S. Huck, et al., *Children's Literature in the Elementary School*, 7th ed., rev. Barbara Z. Kiefer (New York: McGraw-Hill, 1997), 5.

2. Regie Routman, *Transitions* (Portsmouth, N.H.: Heinemann, 1988), 19.

3. Karen Hesse, *Letters from Rifka* (New York: Holt, 1992), 145.

4. Patricia MacLachlan, *Caleb's Story* (New York: HarperCollins, 2001), 8.

5. Louis Sachar, *Holes* (New York: Scholastic, 1998), 75–76.

6. Jerry Spinelli, *Maniac Magee* (Boston: Little, Brown, 1990), 18–19.

7. Richard C. Anderson, et al, *Becoming a Nation of Readers: The Report of the Commission on Reading* (Washington, D.C: National Institute of Education [ED], 1985.

8. W. H. Teale, "Parents Reading to their Children: What They Need to Know," *Language Arts* 58 (1981): 902–912.

9. Louise Rosenblatt, *Literature as Exploration* (New York: Appleton, Century, Crofts, 1987).

Chapter 4

Steering Actions Guided by Character and Heart: Service and Compassion

From this moment I swear I will hunt nothing but the King's deer, and I will feed every hungry soul that lives in this forest. That is my vow. Let them catch me if they can.

—Michael Morpurgo, *Robin of Sherwood*, 1996

Most elementary schoolchildren know the legend of Robin Hood of Sherwood Forest. They listen to and read stories about how he was a champion of the underprivileged, taking from the wealthy to provide food and life needs for the unfortunate. They know that he was a hero; that he had compassion, and that he served others. Could there be ethical struggles in their minds over Robin Hood breaking the law? Probably not in elementary school. Typically students are college-age before they reach the postconventional morality level, recognizing that there may be morally justifiable reasons for breaking the law.[1] Children enjoy Robin Hood for his adventures and they know that he "helped others." Helping others is a sign of compassion and service. As we go through this chapter, we will examine characters who have exemplified these traits—or who have not!

The design principle of compassion and service is a worthy directive for the schools of today. To consider others and to be compassionate in all aspects of life are the goals for this principle. In this chapter, books will be discussed that may serve as guides toward this principle.

> We are crew, not passengers, and are strengthened by acts of consequential service to others. One of a school's primary functions is to prepare its students with the attitudes and skills to learn from and be of service to others.[2]

Character Traits in Traditional Folk Literature

Almost since the beginning of time, people have taught their children how to live and behave socially, ethically, and spiritually through stories. These stories, first told by word of mouth, were passed from one generation to another, and carried with them the heritage of their forefathers as well as a code of conduct for their lives. It is appropriate that when we consider a design principle based on character traits that we examine traditional folk literature.

Traditional means that this literature has been passed down traditionally through oral storytelling. This genre of literature is also called "traditional folk literature." It is literature from common humankind and is composed of the hopes, dreams, daily events, and principles by which they have lived over the centuries.

To children, traditional folk literature means fairy tales and nursery rhymes. The beginning words of "once upon a time" immediately make them think of times long ago and far away, of princes and princesses, castles and wicked stepmothers. It should also bring thoughts of love, of times listening to magical tales told in the midst of warmth and comfort. Unfortunately, many of our children's first encounters with traditional folk literature are in the classroom or on a big or little screen. We as educators need to make certain that they do, indeed, become familiar with this rich body of literature.

Traditional folk literature is a window through which children in today's world may view cultures of long ago. Within this genre of literature, there are several forms, or subgenres. However, often tales blend together easily, and it is common for one story to resemble a fairy tale while another version, a variant of the same tale, may have characteristics of myths or animal tales. A strict division of the various selections is almost impossible.

Subgenres of traditional folk literature may be clustered in poetry or prose classifications representing the literary form in which they were originally produced. We classify five prose narrative subgenres under the broad term of traditional folk literature:

- Myths
- Legends
- Tall tales
- Fables
- Folktales

Folktales include beast tales, tales of wonder (called fairy tales by many), pourquoi tales, trickster tales, and silly tales.

We also classify two poetry subgenres under traditional folk literature:

1. Nursery and childhood rhymes (Mother Goose rhymes discussed in chapter 11).
2. Epics.

Mythology

"Myths are stories that originate in the beliefs of nations and races and present episodes in which supernatural forces operate."[3] Most cultures used myths to explain natural phenomena, origins, customs, or human relationships. They are possibly the oldest type of traditional tale. They are set in the remote past and at least some of their characters are deities and supernatural powers, often with human characteristics. They are full of excitement and adventure, but not always appropriate for use with children.

Myths often explain natural phenomena as in the tale of Demeter, the goddess of the harvest, and her daughter, Persephone. Demeter could not bear to be apart from her daughter. When she descended to earth from her throne on Mount Olympus, she would take Persephone with her. Persephone's radiance and happy nature captivated everyone around her. Hades, the gloomy god of the dead, fell in love with her and wanted her to become his queen in the underworld. Knowing that Demeter would never consent, he kidnapped the pretty child. Grief-stricken, Demeter searched relentlessly for her beloved daughter. She refused to let anything grow on earth until she found her. Suspicious of Hades from the beginning, she appealed to Zeus for help. Zeus, anxious to return the earth to its former lushness, commanded Hades to return his new queen to her mother. However, Zeus had stipulated that if she ate the food of the dead, she would have to remain in the world of the dead. Unfortunately, Demeter had eaten a few pomegranate seeds while in the underworld. A compromise determined that Demeter would only spend six months in the underworld, one month for each seed she ate. The earth became cold and gray because Demeter grieved so during the months that her daughter was in the underworld. However, "as soon as her daughter's light footsteps were heard, the whole earth burst into bloom. Spring had come. As long as mother and daughter were together, the earth was warm and bore fruit."[4]

Conflicts between the gods and between gods and humans play significant roles in Greek mythology. Such conflicts show that the immortals had the same failings as humans. The pride of the goddesses, Hera, Aphrodite, and Athena ultimately led to the Trojan War. A golden apple was found with the inscription "For the Fairest." Each of the goddesses assumed the apple was intended for her. A mortal judge had to be chosen and he had to be the handsomest man on earth. Paris "was the Prince of Troy—an alarmingly good-looking boy who had not yet fallen in love." Paris became the judge and chose Aphrodite as the fairest because she promised him "The love of the loveliest woman on Earth." The promise was fulfilled. He won Helen of Troy. The only problem was that she was married and her angry husband appealed to the King of Greece for help. Thus began the Trojan War. With her retellings, British author, Geraldine McCaughrean instills the myths with humor and a sense of immediacy in her marvelous retellings of myths and legends from around the world in *The Golden Hoard, The Silver Treasure,* and *The Bronze Cauldron.*

Most of us were raised on myths and legends of the ancient Romans and Greeks. However, in today's multicultural society, we have the opportunity to explore stories from a variety of peoples and countries. John Bierhorst has been indefatigable in providing us with examples of Native American mythology. Paul Goble and Gerald McDermott have each written and illustrated several picture books that are examples of Native American myths. Virginia Hamilton collected a number of creation stories from different cultures and put them in the extraordinary book, *In the Beginning: Creation Stories from Around the World.* Students today are surrounded with opportunities to explore the culture and values of the world population of the past and present.

Legends

Legends are similar to myths, and often the boundaries between the two are blurred. However, humans are the main characters of legends, whereas deities are the main characters of myths. Legends are long narratives of well-known cultural heroes. There is usually a core of truth in the stories and they are set in the identifiable past. Often legends are nationalistic, glorifying the characteristics that a country holds dear. Stories of King Arthur and the Knights of the Round Table, along with Robin Hood, Odysseus, and Beowulf are familiar legendary heroes. There is some evidence that King Arthur lived, but the stories that surround him about pulling his sword from the stone, about the Round Table and his loss of Guinevere, are fictitious. King Arthur is the embodiment of chivalry and all the upstanding moral values of the British Isles. The stories about Robin Hood were told as early as 1360 and were based on the life of Robert Fitzooth, the Earl of Huntingdon in Nottinghamshire, England. Again, the man was real but the stories are not. Robin Hood was the perfect example of the hardworking Englishman, passionately seeking justice for all.

In *The Adventures of Hershel of Ostropol*, Eric Kimmel tells ten Yiddish tales that feature Hershel and his dealings with the community of a small village in nineteenth-century Ukraine. Kimmel maintains that Hershel was a real character, a wandering beggar, who made the pompous and arrogant look foolish. The common folk deemed him their hero.

Epics

Often legends are told as long, narrative poems known as epics. The first great pieces of literature in the Western tradition were epics written by the Greek poet Homer around 750 B.C. The *Illiad* and the *Odyssey* are large-scale narratives, based on stories that occurred during the Greek Bronze Age. They are tales that deal with great and noble subjects: heroes and gods, battles, legendary people, and events. Gods and goddesses still have a hand in the lives of the main characters, but the emphasis has shifted to the humans themselves. Odysseus wandered the earth for many years, suffering a series of trials that kept him from returning to his wife and son. He exemplified the qualities that the Greeks held dear: intelligence, resourcefulness, and perseverance.[5]

Another great epic is *The Adventures of Beowulf*, written in Old English around 1100 A.D. The story, the oldest surviving epic in British literature, describes the adventures of a great Scandinavian warrior of the sixth century. The original epics mentioned here were written for adults. The language and concepts are often too difficult for a child audience. However, there are a number of retellings that appeal to upper elementary and middle school students.

Tall Tales

Exaggerated tales of the daring-do of local heroes became known as tall tales. Most tall tales revolved around powerful men of grit and determination who excelled in their occupations. John Henry and Davy Crockett are among the best known. As with other kinds of legends, there is a kernel of truth in each story, but exaggeration is a characteristic of tall tales. Johnny Appleseed was the gentlest of the tall tale heroes. His real name was John Chapman and he supposedly crossed the United States planting apple trees. Lately, authors have been adding tall tales about women to even the gender balance. Sluefoot Sue was the wild and unruly wife of Pecos Bill, and Sally Ann Thunder Ann Whirlwind Crockett was the tough frontier woman married to Davy.

Fables

Fables are short stories that have a very plain lesson. Most often, the main characters are animals that act like people. The animal character shows traits that are usually connected with that animal. For instance, the lion acts bold, the bull is strong, and the turtle is slow.

In Western culture, one immediately thinks of Aesop in connection with fables. Aesop was reputedly a wise and witty Greek slave who lived between 620 and 560 B.C. Some say that his fables were a political commentary on society; others say Aesop, himself, is a fabrication. Either way, fables play an important role in our culture, often providing a quick way to remind us of appropriate behavior and attitudes. To accuse someone of behavior resembling "sour grapes" is to say that the person simply despises something because he/she cannot have it. The moral is stated in the fable, "The Fox and the Grapes" in which a fox sees grapes hanging from a bush and knows that they will be just the thing to quench his thirst. He jumps for them several times, missing each time. Finally, he gives up and walks off stating that the grapes were probably sour anyway.

LaFontaine was a French poet who wrote fables in poetic form in the seventeenth century. He primarily drew on Aesop's fables for his own. The fables of the Eastern world are known as the Jataka Tales. The Jatakas consist of over five hundred stories about the previous incarnations of the Buddha in both human and animal form. The stories, longer than Aesop fables, have moralistic verses interspersed throughout.

When Arnold Lobel was asked to illustrate some traditional fables, he claimed that he started reading them voraciously. It didn't take him long to realize that he didn't care for them at all. So he wrote his own book of original fables, appropriately entitled *Fables*. He won a Caldecott Medal for his original, humorous fables.

Folktales

Flat, one-sided characters distinguish folktales. The characters are all good or all bad. For example, Cinderella is pure of heart, hard-working and loving, whereas her stepmother is wicked and cruel. The plot is the heart of any folktale. It progresses steadily to the climax that occurs at the end of the story. The setting is sketchy, providing a feeling of universality that all readers can identify with. Action moves swiftly.

As children discover the fantasy world of folktales, they feel safe exploring in their minds unknown and faraway places. They delight in the antics of imaginary creatures and their ability to move in and around fanciful worlds. Students also relate to the illusory heroes who seem to accomplish the impossible without difficulty. They better understand their own behavior and that of their peers and adults after encountering similar actions portrayed in folktales.[6]

We divide folktales into cumulative tales, beast tales, trickster tales, pourquoi tales, tales of wonder (often called fairy tales), and silly tales.

Cumulative Tales

These are tales in which the lines are repeated and to which elements are added. They are wonderful for oral telling because they're easy to memorize, and they are fun for children because they are simple, humorous, and easy to learn. "The House that Jack Built" is probably the best known of all cumulative stories.

"The Gingerbread Boy" is a cumulative tale that enthralls children. They are at first amazed that the cookie comes to life, then delighted with his daring, and finally feel justification when the fox eats him! He wasn't really so smart when he kept saying, "You can't catch me, I'm the Gingerbread Man!"

"Soap, Soap, Soap," an Appalachian folktale found in Richard Chase's *Grandfather Tales* is one that leaves kids laughing out loud when the boy who is sent to the store by his mother to get soap encounters several incidents that lead him deeper and deeper into trouble. It's not his fault that he forgot what he was supposed to be buying at the store!

Beast Tales

Beast tales are probably the favorites of all children, and these they know well. Talking beasts are the important characters, although humans may appear in the story. Right away several such tales come to mind: "The Three Little Pigs," "Goldilocks and the Three Bears," "The Three Billy Goats Gruff."

Talking animal tales are found in every culture. The Latin American story, "Martina, the Little Cockroach," charms its listeners. Beautiful *la cucarachita* conducts an hilarious search for the perfect husband and finds that the mouse, *ratoncito*, is the one for her. Too bad he disobeyed her and fell in the soup!

Trickster Tales

Trickster tales "contain one central character, usually a wise trickster in animal shape. In some cultures, the animal character will assume a human shape at times. Anansi, the spider of African origin, is an old man in some stories or a young man in tales from the Antilles. Trickster tales are usually brief and direct and humorous. The story relies on one action, a trick or joke, as the solution to the problem."[7] Nearly every culture has trickster tales in which a character uses wit to triumph over a more powerful creature. Joel Chandler Harris, a Georgia journalist, collected the Brer Rabbit tales from Southern African Americans in the late 1800s.

> Harris' Uncle Remus told animal tales in fractured English to the little white boy of the plantation house. But author Harris was not concerned with reproducing exactly the tales or their language. Harris and his contemporaries used phonetic dialect as a literary device. They felt that an exaggerated colloquial language best symbolized what they regarded as the quaint appeal of lowly, rural people.[8]

The dialect made the tales difficult to read and understand. Now retellers are trying to tell the tales in a more understandable and readable way.

American children know how wily Brother Rabbit begged Brer Bear and Brer Fox to punish him any way they saw fit, except by throwing him in the briar patch.

> "Oh mercy, don't do that!" cried Doc Rabbit. "Whatever you do with me, don't dare throw me in those thorny briars!"
> "That's what I'll do, then," Bruh Fox said.
> And that's what Brother Fox did. He sure did. Took Doc Rabbit by the short hair and threw him—*Whippet! Whippet*—right in the briar patch.
> "Hot lettuce pie! This is where I want to be," Doc Rabbit hollered for happiness. He was square in the middle of the briar patch. "Here is where my mama and papa had me born and raised. Safe at last!"[9]

Tricksters from other cultures include Reynard the Fox from France, the Native American Coyote, and the Raven from Indian tribes in the Pacific Northwest.

Not all tricksters are animals. We've already mentioned Hershel of Ostropol, the central character is many Jewish legends. In the Appalachian tales, preserved by Richard Chase in *The Jack Tales*, Jack is the prototype of a trickster. In "Jack in the Giants' Newground" he tricks several many-headed giants and earns himself a whole pot of money from the "king."

Explanatory or Pourquoi Tales

Pourquoi tales are short prose narratives explaining the origin of certain characteristics of animals. Trickery is often involved in these tales that were never meant to be believed. Verna Aardema's East African pourquoi tale *How the Ostrich Got its Long Neck,* explains that long ago Ostrich had a short neck. Crocodile gets a terrible toothache and Ostrich sticks his head right into Crocodile's mouth and attempts to find the offending tooth so he can pull it out. Then Crocodile closes his mouth, and there's a huge tug-of-war until Ostrich tricks the crocodile into opening his mouth and letting go. Ostrich's neck is stretched out forever as a consequence of the tug-of-war.

Native American folklore is replete with pourquoi stories. The Navajos claim that chipmunks have small feet because an early chipmunk was the watchman for the Gila Monster. His job was to make sure that no one stole anything out of the garden. One day Gila Monster noticed that his cornstalks were looking pretty thin so he began an investigation and discovered that his watchman, Chipmunk, was the thief. To compound the problem, Chipmunk was arrogant and ignored his master's summons. Gila Monster went in search of Chipmunk and reduced him to the size of an ant. A penitent chipmunk asked for forgiveness and was returned to his normal size. The feet remained tiny so that he would be reminded never to steal from anyone again.

And, finally, who could overlook Ashley Bryan's retelling of "Frog and His Two Wives"? Do you know why frog sits in the marsh croaking day after day? Because he is saying over and over, "I am in trouble!" His two wives, whom he had placed in the east and west sides of his land, have called him to come at the same time. He is in BIG trouble!

Tales of Wonder

Commonly called fairy tales, these are unbelievable stories that contain an enchantment or elements of the supernatural, of magic. They have certain characteristics in common, but not all fairy tales have all of the characteristics. It is common to find fairies, witches, giants, and ogres in these stories. Often there is a hero who rescues a helpless maiden. The hero and heroine are always completely good; the villain is completely evil. The stories frequently begin with "Once upon a time . . . " and end with " . . . and they lived happily ever after." The numbers three and seven often figure prominently in the story. It is not unusual to find a magic object, such as a ring, a glass slipper, or a talking harp in a tale of wonder. "Cinderella," "Beauty and the Beast," and "Snowwhite and the Seven Dwarfs" are all examples of fairy tales at their finest.

Bruno Bettelheim, the well-known child psychologist, said "nothing can be as enriching and satisfying to child and adult alike as the folk fairy tale . . . more can be learned from them about the inner problems of human beings, and of their right solution to their predicaments in any society, than from any other type of story within a child's comprehension."[10]

The term "fairy tales" immediately brings to mind the names of Charles Perrault, Jacob and Wilhelm Grimm, and Hans Christian Anderson. Perrault, a French man of letters, was the first to publish tales that we call fairy tales today. His book *Histoires ou Contes du Temps Passe* (*Stories of Past Times*) was published in 1697 and contained versions of "Little Red Riding Hood," "Cinderella," and "Sleeping Beauty." His tales were actually written to entertain the French court and they contain irony that we wouldn't expect the children of today's society to understand. The matter-of-factness with which he treats the demise of Little Red Riding Hood startles us as well. The wolf simply eats her up at the end. She isn't saved by anyone. She is dead!

The Grimm brothers collected tales from literate middle-class acquaintances who had collected them from peasants. The brothers were actually scholars and linguists who wanted to record the old folktales to preserve their rich language and document old customs and superstitions. What is called Germany today was simply a loose grouping of duchies and princedoms. The Grimms intended that their stories would support unification by "finding basic linguistic and cultural oneness of the German people."[11] They did not really write their stories for a child audience. However, when they saw that children were reading their work, they adapted it to fit the audience. In fact, the authenticity of various Grimm stories would not meet the stringent demands of folktale scholars today. Perry Nodelman states that the brothers Grimm thought they could make a tale most authentic by selecting the best parts from its various versions. They also made their tales fit their middle-class Christian beliefs. Nodelman goes on to say that "the stepmothers in stories like 'Hansel and Gretel' and 'Snow White' as the Grimms originally recorded them were birth-mothers, an idea that seems to have disturbed the Grimms enough to disguise it."[12] William and Jacob Grimm's names did not immediately become household words, but by the 1860s they were widely revered.

Inspired by the Grimm brothers, folklorists around the world began compiling tales from their countries' rich stockpiles. In Norway, Peter Christian Asbjornsen and Jorgen Moe collected tales such as "The Three Billy Goats Gruff," "Henny Penny," and "East o' the Sun and West o' the Moon," in their book, The Norwegian Folktales. Joseph Jacobs in England adapted tales for a child audience and published them in his *English Fairy Tales* (1894), and Andrew Lang, a Scot, published his four-volume collection of folktales from around the world (*The Blue, Red, Green and Yellow Fairy Books,* 1889–1894.)

In Denmark, Hans Christian Andersen was also interested in fairy tales. He put together a collection of old Danish tales and new tales that he wrote to resemble traditional tales. This first collection, published in 1835, contained his retellings of "The Princess and the Pea" and "The Tinder Box" as well as some original tales, which we no longer hear. However, by 1863, H. C. Andersen was a name well known in literate households because of his unique style of retelling traditional tales and inventing new ones. His true legacy is in giving us what is known as the modern or literary fairy tale, which is a wonderful bridge between traditional folk literature and modern fantasy.

Connections from the Past to the Present

Postmodern Folktale Parodies

A recent trend found among single folktale picture books is that of a parody based on characters or some literary element of folk literature. The tales, with known authors, have been described as postmodern. They are compared to modernist writings with this distinction: while "modernists are concerned with how they can represent life as closely as possible to reality, postmodernists are trying to define reality in an increasingly confusing world—or to redefine reality."[13] Two of the most well-known postmodernist parodies are Jon Scieszka's *The True Story of the Three Little Pigs* and *The Stinky Cheese Man and Other Fairly Stupid Tales.* Folktales are not the only genre represented with postmodern literature, but there seems to be a growing number of old traditional tales that are retold for the new millennium. Cinderella tales from various cultures around the world have been noted, and it seems that postmodern retellings of the Cinderella characters are also abundant. Here are a few:

1. *Cinderhazel, the Cinderella of Halloween* by Deborah Nourse Lattimore (picture book—primary)
2. *Dinorella, Prehistoric Fairytale* by Pamela Duncan Edwards (picture book—primary)
3. *Cinder Edna* by Ellen Jackson (picture book—primary)
4. *Cinder Elly* by Frances Minters (picture book—primary)
5. *Smoky Mountain Rose* by Alan Schroeder (picture book—primary)
6. *Cinderella's Rat* by Susan Meddaugh (picture book—middle elementary)

Mythological Connections to Today's World

As children move beyond the early elementary grades in school, their interest declines in the traditional fairy and folk tales, especially the well-known ones that they first heard as young children. These parodies and books that have sprung from the original tales still hold interest for the child who is eight to twelve years old. These children are also fascinated with connections from the ancient world literature, particularly the myths, to today's world as shown in brand names of commercial products (Venus pencils), world events (Olympics), and names of the days of the week, months of the year, and planets in our universe:

Days of the Week
Monday, named for the Moon in Germanic literature
Tuesday, named for Tiw, a Norse god of war
Wednesday, named for Woden, a god from Norse mythology
Thursday, named for Thor, Norse god of Thunder and Lightening
Friday, named for Frigg who was married to Odin, a Norse god
Saturday, named for Saturn, a Roman god of farmlands
Sunday, named for the Sun[14]

Months of the Year
January   Roman god, Janus
February   Roman festival, Februa

March	Roman god, Mars
April	Roman goddess, Aphrodite
May	Roman goddess, Maia
June	Roman goddess, Juno
July	Julius Caesar
August	Emperor Augustus

September–December were numbered as the seventh through the tenth months of an old calendar.[15]

Middle elementary students are always interested in how the planets were named. Again, the ancient world mythology is evident:

Planets

Jupiter	King of the Roman gods
Mars	God of War
Venus	Goddess of Love
Mercury	God of commerce and thievery
Pluto	God of the Underworld
Neptune	God of the Sea
Saturn	Titan, father of Jupiter[16]

Often students wonder if Earth is also named for a Roman god. The goddess of the earth in Roman mythology was "tellis" or fertile land. In Greek mythology, mother earth was named Gaia. These stories and connections from the past to the present are intriguing to students and may be a way to hook them on traditional literature—even past midchildhood.

Connections to the Past: An Expedition

Guiding Questions

1. What evidence from traditional folk literature do we see in our lives today?
2. How did this literature originate?
3. How long ago was it told and who told it?
4. Why are there so many Cinderella stories and other stories that seem similar among fairy and folktales?
5. Why are some characters so cruel? Why are there so many tricksters in folktales?

6. Why are the characters in traditional folk literature so good or so bad?
7. How are fables, myths, legends, and tall tales part of the traditional folk literature?

Standards

The standards in this expedition are from the areas of history and language arts.

The students:

1. illustrate or retell the main ideas in folktales, legends, myths, and stories of heroism that disclose the history and traditions of various cultures around the world.[17]
2. develop an understanding of and respect for diversity in language use, patterns, and dialects across cultures, ethnic groups, geographic regions, and social roles.
3. employ a wide range of strategies as they write and use different writing process elements appropriately to communicate with different audiences for a variety of purposes.[18]

Initial Reading Options for Teacher Read-Aloud, Shared, Guided, or Independent Reading

Teacher will read aloud a postmodern parody of a folktale for comparison with similar traditional tales, such as these examples:

1. *The Three Little Wolves and the Big Bad Pig* by Eugene Trivizas. (picture book —middle elementary)
2. *The Tortoise and the Jackrabbit* by Susan Lowell (picture book—primary)
3. *Cinderella's Rat* by Susan Meddaugh (picture book—middle elementary)

Fieldwork Options

1. Complete library research to locate traditional folk literature from a specific country.
2. Notice brand names in the commercial world and identify all that have names related to traditional literature, such as

mythology, legends, epics, or fables. Make a word wall of such names.

3.   Listen to adults talk and note phrases that may have come from morals in fables, such as:

> "Sour grapes" from *The Fox and the Grapes*;
> "Slow but steady" from *The Hare and the Tortoise*;
> "A deed done is a deed returned" from *Androcles and the Lion.*

Individual Projects

1.   Research a country or culture and identify its folk literature.
2.   Draft, edit, revise, and publish postmodern parodies of folktales after reading many of them.
3.   Retell or adapt a source story from folk literature.
4.   Listen to recorded storytellers and determine what makes a good storyteller.
5.   Practice storytelling.

Class Projects

1.   Find out who the compilers of folk literature were and where they lived and worked:

> Grimm Brothers
> Charles Perrault
> Joseph Jacobs
> Peter Asbjornsen

2.   Make a collection of their tales by country and display in the library.
3.   Make comparison charts of variants of the same tale, such as:

> a.   *Mufaro's Beautiful Daughters: An African Cinderella Tale* by John Steptoe
> b.   *The Egyptian Cinderella* by Shirley Climo

4.   Identify the criteria for classifying folktales as postmodern parodies and collect them for a display.
5.   Invite local storytellers to visit the classroom and demonstrate storytelling.

6. Identify names from our contemporary society that are related to ancient folk literature and create a word wall of those names and their literature connections.

Sharing Outlets

1. Reading Celebration. Read postmodern parodies of folktales to children in other classes at school.
2. Cultural Folktale Display. Display collections of folktales from various cultures for the whole school to enjoy.
3. Traditional Storytelling. Schedule a day for student storytelling after much reading and practice.

Assessment Options

1. Self-evaluation for storytelling.
2. Rubric for evaluating the written parody.
3. Checklist for participation in all events.
4. Artifacts from the expedition may be organized for the portfolio along with a reflection of the importance of each artifact.

Notes

1. Lawrence Kohlberg, "The Cognitive-Developmental Approach to Moral Education," *Phi Delta Kappan*, 57 (1975): 670–677.

2. http://www.elob.org/aboutel/principles.html

3. Rebecca J. Lukens, *A Critical Handbook of Children's Literature*, 5th ed. (New York: HarperCollins, 1995), 24.

4. Ingri D'Aulaire and Edgar Parin D'Aulaire, *Book of Greek Myths* (Garden City, N.Y.: Doubleday, 1962), 62.

5. http://dir.yahoo.com/Arts/Humanities/Literature/Poetry/Poets/Homer/

6. Frances Goforth and Carolyn Spillman, *Using Folk Literature in the Classroom: Encouraging Children to Read and Write* (Phoenix, Ariz: Oryx, 1994).

7. Betty Bosma, *Fairy Tales, Fables, Legends, and Myths: Using Folk Literature in Your Classroom* (New York: Teachers College, Columbia University, 1987).

8. Virginia Hamilton, *The People Could Fly: American Black Folktales* (New York: Knopf, 1985), 18.

9. Ibid., 19.

10. Bruno Bettelheim, *Uses of Enchantment: The Meaning and Importance of Fairy Tales* (New York: Vintage Books, 1977), 5.

11. Perry Nodelman, *The Pleasures of Children's Literature,* 2nd ed. (New York, Longmans, 1996), 249.

12. Ibid., 11.

13. Nina Mikkelsen, *Words and Pictures: Lessons in Children's Literature and Literacies* (Boston: McGraw-Hill Higher Education, 2000), 35.

14. http://www.eliki.com/ancient/myth/daily/monday/

15. http://webexhibits.org/calendars/year-history.html

16. http://www.geocities.com/Athens/Troy/1203/

17. http://www.sscnet.ucla.edu/nchs/standards/standardsk-4-4.html

18. www.ncte.org

Chapter 5

Lighting the Imagination: Having and Celebrating Wonderful Ideas in Children's Literature

Harry had never even imagined such a strange and splendid place. It was lit by thousands and thousands of candles that were floating in midair over four long tables, where the rest of the students were sitting. . . . Harry looked upward and saw a velvety black ceiling dotted with stars.

. . . It was hard to believe there was a ceiling there at all, and that the Great Hall didn't simply open on to the heavens.

—J. K. Rowling, *Harry Potter and the Sorcerer's Stone*, 1997

What a wonderful idea J. K. Rowling had when she created her characters in the Harry Potter series! Only time will tell the lasting value of these books, but today they exemplify the wonders of having ideas. These books have been accepted so heartily by children (and many adults) across the world, they are ambassadors of cleverness and are celebrated for freeing children to soar with their own ideas. Of course, the genre is fantasy. However, with the wide array of genres—specific types of texts—in children's literature, the possibilities for matching interests and lighting the imaginations of children are endless. The hearing, reading, discussing, and writing of forms of literature are natural avenues for inspiring students in their pursuit of education and understanding of life.

The design principle from Expeditionary Learning that is targeted in this chapter is "The Having of Wonderful Ideas."

Teach so as to build on children's curiosity about the world by creating learning situations that provide matter to think about, time to experiment, and time to make sense of what is observed. Foster a community where students' and adults' ideas are respected.[1]

Great Ideas in Fantasy

Modern fantasy is a widely popular form of fiction. It has its origins in traditional literature, emulating many of the ideas and motifs of myths, legends, and fairy and folktales. Fantasy encompasses many exciting, impossible, scary, and fanciful things that young people enjoy. It carries the reader into worlds that are far different from the one we know.

However, the clever writer of fantasy makes the reader believe that the world in the story is real and possible, no matter how impossible the settings, characters, and events. "Fantasy literature is filled with visions of antiquity: lost kingdoms, ancient peoples and a stock of images and language rhythms drawn from folklore, fairy tales and religion." [2]

We identify four subgenres of modern fantasy: the modern fairy tale, low fantasy, high fantasy, and science fiction.

The Modern Fairy Tale

The modern fairy tale depends on the same form and many of the same devices as the traditional tales. They are filled with supernatural beings and magic. They have exciting plots, but stock characters. They are stories, not full-blown novels, even though they are often published in book form. The genuine differences are that they are first written down, not told, and their author is known.

Many think of Hans Christian Andersen as a reteller of traditional stories, but his original tales are just as well known. By 1863 his collection of traditional and original tales numbered one hundred and sixty-eight and the public had embraced him as a genuine presence in the literary world. The original tales or modern fairy tales include such enchanting ones as *The Little Mermaid*, *The Ugly Duckling*, *The Snow Queen*, *The Little Match Girl*, and *The Steadfast Tin Soldier*. Other appealing literary tales are Oscar Wilde's *The Selfish Giant*, and *The Happy Prince*, Antoine de Saint-Exupery's *The Little Prince,* Natalie Babbitt's *Ouch!*, and Margery Williams's *The Velveteen Rabbit.*

Low Fantasy

Low fantasy involves stories that are set primarily in the real world, but often move into an extraordinary world. They include characters or happenings that are impossible, but seem possible. The term "low fantasy" does not indicate the importance of the story—as opposed to high fantasy, for example. It is not evaluative in any way.

"Authors achieve fantasy in this subgenre by manipulating a few elements, while the rest of the elements are realistic."[3] The success of these stories depends on the reader's willing suspension of disbelief. In some low fantasies, dolls and toys talk. This is, indeed, a fantasy often engaged in by youngsters. Many children have stuffed animals that take on an identity, and the owners carry on imaginary conversations with their little friends. The beloved Winnie-the-Pooh is just such a stuffed animal. His conversations with his sidekicks, Tigger, Eeyore, Piglet, Owl, Kanga, and Roo are completely credible. Lynne Reid Banks startled readers with her use of miniature plastic cowboys and Indians as characters in *The Indian in the Cupboard* and its sequels. Readers are captivated by the idea that using a magic cupboard and magic key can bring toys to life. But now that the cowboys and Indians are alive, they experience all the pain of their history. How can Omri and Patrick stop this? The story deals with sensitive and difficult questions.

Animals also talk in fantasy stories. One of the earliest fantastic delights is the *Wind in the Willows* by Kenneth Grahame. The book is a series of tales about a group of engaging animals that experience all the day-to-day trials and tribulations of life. Rat, Mole, and Badger put forth valiant efforts to save Mr. Toad from himself and from his obsession with the automobile. The image of Toad sitting in the middle of the road whispering "poop, poop" as he remembers the passing car stays with readers forever and, inevitably, brings a chuckle.

Robert Lawson also wrote about an engaging family of rabbits in his well-known *Rabbit Hill*. Georgie was typically curious in his explorations of the terrain just as Beatrix Potter's Peter was. Thank goodness the "new folks" arrived on Rabbit Hill and encouraged the animals to share their land and help Georgie. And, thank goodness, Peter shed his jacket and escaped the wrath of Mr. MacGregor in *The Tale of Peter Rabbit*.

Another fantasy that has been the source of controversy and concern is Helen Bannerman's *Little Black Sambo*, a tale that was a staple in the early lives of many of us. However, in recent years there has been a swell of controversy over the appropriateness of this story. Names in the story and the illustrations have offended many and fueled a heated discussion on the Child Lit listserv. At about the same time, Julius Lester, an eminent philosopher, professor, and storyteller decided to write the story with a new twist. By partnering with well-known children's book illustrator Jerry Pinkney, he created a jaunty tale based on Bannerman's original story and told in the Southern folktale tradition. *Sam and the Tigers* was a needed addition to children's literature.

However, Little Black Sambo's purple slippers with the crimson lining will never be forgotten.

Talking animal fantasies are probably the most common kind of fantasy book. Ian Falconer's *Olivia* is another talking animal that no child or adult will soon forget. Olivia is "good at a lot of things," including wearing people out. A sequel, *Olivia Saves the Circus* stars our little piggy in the center ring of the big top. She recounts her adventurous summer vacation by telling her classmates that the day she went to the circus all of the performers were sick with ear infections. Luckily, Olivia knew how to do everything and she took over all of the entertainment. At the end of the story, she quietly tacks on that her father took her sailing one day. Anyone who has read the first two Olivia stories is eager for another, in fact many more!

Poppy by Avi is another fine animal fantasy. Poppy and her large family of deer mice are starving. Mr. Ocax, the great horned owl, rules the community through fear. He demands that they stay where they are and promises to provide them with protection from the fearsome porcupines if they do. Poppy displays remarkable courage and helps the community outwit Mr. Ocax. The ending is a satisfying one, and the story is so enthralling that one believes completely that a deer mouse could carry on a conversation with a porcupine.

Books that have eccentric characters and preposterous situations are also considered low fantasy. *Mr. Popper's Penguins* by Richard and Florence Atwater is a wonderful read-aloud even after all these years. Mr. Popper, a housepainter, is fascinated with the Antarctic. An explorer gives him a penguin, which Mr. Popper immediately names Captain Cook. A wife is found for Captain Cook and the Cook family quickly expands to twelve with the birth of ten baby penguins. In the meantime, Mr. Popper builds a freezer in his basement for the penguins and starts taking them on the road to perform.

Extraordinary worlds are often carefully detailed in low fantasy. Frequently the story will begin in the real world and the characters will enter an extraordinary world. Lewis Carroll wrote about Alice falling into a rabbit hole and entering a fantastic world in *Alice's Adventures in Wonderland*. *The Wonderful Wizard of Oz*, *The Borrowers*, and *Charlie and the Chocolate Factory* are other well-known titles that involve extraordinary worlds. Mary Norton makes believers out of her readers by painting the tiny world of her characters with amazing detail. The diminutive Clock family adapts discarded objects from the real world to their needs. Norton's descriptions delight readers. And what child doesn't dream of living in a world filled with chocolate as a chosen few do in Roald Dahl's *Charlie and the Chocolate Factory*? Now we have

Harry Potter who enters the world of wizards in the first of J. K. Rowling's wildly successful series. In the first book, *Harry Potter and the Sorcerer's Stone,* Harry leaves his common, nonmagical world of Muggles and enters an extraordinary world where small, timid Harry is famous.

As in the Harry Potter books, magical powers play a significant role in fantasy stories. Natalie Babbitt's *Tuck Everlasting* has become a modern classic. In it, a magical spring provides eternal life. The Tuck family kidnaps Winnie when she prepares to drink from it. After she spends time with them and learns to care for them, she is given the choice: to drink from the spring and become immortal, or not to and remain human. Magical powers are frequently found in William Steig's books also. Sylvester discovers a magical pebble and makes a wish that turns him into a rock in *Sylvester and the Magic Pebble*; a talking bone helps outwit a band of robbers and a fox in *The Amazing Bone.*

Finally, we need to look at the low fantasy that involves supernatural events and the "scary stuff" that kids beg for and read. Mary Downing Hahn wrote *Wait Till Helen Comes* in 1986 and treated readers to a fine piece of supernatural fantasy. Helen waits by the pond to drag children to their deaths, hoping to find a playmate. Molly needs to move quickly to save her stepsister, Heather, from certain death. Readers plead for "more stories just like this!" Although not as frightening as Hahn's book, Bruce Coville wrote *The Skull of Truth*, a story that involves the supernatural. Charlie Eggleston, an inveterate liar, stumbles into Mr. Elive's magic shop one night and steals the skull. The skull compels him to tell the truth as long as it is in his possession, but no one believes him. Coville has written an excellent story of a boy working through problems that many encounter in today's world, and the book has a supernatural twist.

Once again, we can turn to any of the Harry Potter books and find them to be a hotbed of the supernatural, the impossible, and the scary. When the elegant-sounding gentleman, sitting in a wing-backed chair and plotting with his butler, is revealed as not only the frightening Voldemort, but also a snake, readers shriek in terrified surprise! However, after they stop shivering, they demand more.

High Fantasy

High fantasy is far more serious in tone and demanding of the reader than low fantasy. It takes place in a carefully created world, a secondary world, and concerns itself with universal questions. The protagonist is frequently on a quest and is usually written about as though he were a legendary hero. Allusions to the myths and legends of traditional literature are often found in these works.

Susan Cooper writes that because the United States is such a young nation, we do not have a "mythological foundation." Instead, we have a gap. "I think perhaps that the task of fantasy, in our contemporary world, is to help fill that gap."[4]

Lloyd Alexander actually based his *Prydain Chronicles* on Welsh legend. The characters' names are difficult and one would think that the concepts would be foreign to a middle schooler. Taran searches for his identity and maturity throughout the series. He meets all sorts of extraordinary characters along the way.

Popular opinion among adults would be that this series would never appeal to struggling sixth-grade readers. However, we had the good fortune of witnessing an entire inner-city sixth-grade class eagerly soak up every detail in *The Book of Three*, the first of the five-volume series. The students were disgusted at Taran's initial bungling of his duties, Eilonwy enchanted them, and they laughed at Fflewddur Fflam posturing and took up Gurgi's chants. Most important was the fact that they could see parts of themselves in the hero and they grew taller and more confident as a result. Other books that we place in the category of high fantasy are C. S. Lewis's *Chronicles of Narnia,* Lloyd Alexander's *Prydain Chronicles,* Susan Cooper's *The Dark is Rising*, series and the *Redwall* series by Brian Jacques.

Science Fiction

Science fiction is the fourth subgenre of fantasy and often overlaps high fantasy. It creates a fantastic world that, with scientific advances, could be a real world. It not only stimulates the imagination, but also encourages readers to think about the future and what could be possible. "The most ambitious kind of fantasy is science fiction—it draws on the work and the language of science to imagine alternate, futuristic ways of thinking and living. Struggles between good and evil dominate both. So does social criticism, whether realistic or theological."[5]

A Wrinkle in Time by Madeleine L'Engle and *The Giver* by Lois Lowry are remarkable books that straddle the boundaries of science fiction and high fantasy. In L'Engle's book, Meg is the daughter in an intellectual family. Her brother Charles Wallace, is a child prodigy. Their friend Calvin joins the two to help them search for their lost father. They discover a world of sameness and the seductiveness of "It." Meg saves her father, but she and Calvin have to leave Charles Wallace behind—for a while. The story is unusual and exciting. Lowry's *The*

Giver is haunting, a story that everyone should read, and no one will forget. As in *A Wrinkle in Time*, an important theme in *The Giver* is that love and individuality are crucial.

Other wonderfully exciting and provocative science fiction stories for the middle readers are the books in the *Tripod Trilogy* by John Christopher. *The White Mountains* is the first in the trilogy and has kept readers on the edge of their seats for years. Will, a twelve-year-old, lives in a city of the future but when the reader begins the story, the city seems like one during the Middle Ages. The Tripods have taken control of the city by "capping" all thirteen-year-olds with a metal cap that controls their behavior. Will and Henry, joined by Beanpole, race to freedom in the White Mountains, pursued by the metal monsters.

William Sleator writes science fiction that gives a fierce look at today's society. In *The Duplicate,* sixteen-year-old David solves the problem of being in two places at once by duplicating himself. The fun stops when it becomes frightening. The book will spark some interesting conversations among more mature readers about the future of genetics, cloning, and medical ethics.

Pamela Service and Daniel Pinkwater have written some engaging science fiction for the younger reader, mostly dealing with alien creatures that come to earth. Service has written about a skunk named Stinker. When alien Tsyng Yr crashed his spaceship in midwestern America, he entered the body of a skunk. Two children discover him and try to help him return home, beginning a very funny chain of events.

Daniel Pinkwater has also written some hilarious books for both the younger and older readers of science fiction. In *Fat Men from Space* William comes home from the dentist with a filling that picks up radio signals from a spaceship occupied with fat men who wear plaid sports coats and discuss their impending attack on earth. It ends up okay because they only want to eat up all the junk food on earth. In *Mush, A Dog from Space,* Pinkwater writes with his usual energy and enthusiasm about a talking mushamute dog from the planet Growl-Woof Woof who turns out to be a terrific cook and manager.

The field of science fiction is drawing more and more attention and has expanded enormously in the last twenty years. It encourages mind expansion and the exploration of other worlds. It does, in fact, promote the origination of wonderful ideas.

Censorship and Selection

These are issues that each person runs into in daily life—and, in most cases we don't realize it. When you open your dresser drawer in the morning to choose a pair of socks, which one will you select? If you're going to wear them to work, you probably wouldn't choose the musical ones with flashing bunny eyes or the chartreuse and pink ones, if you have on a navy blue suit. You will select the pair that matches your outfit and the occasion.

Librarians and teachers can't buy every book, either. They have budgets that guide them in what they can choose (just like the drawerful of socks.) In order to make effective choices, teachers and librarians need to know the needs of their patrons and the community. Then they need to find the best materials to match those needs. The only way to do that is to know the materials.

Selection Tools

Can every librarian or teacher read every single book published every single year? Of course not. There are approximately 5,000 children's books published every year. However, they can find information about the books from numerous reputable sources. These include *Children's Catalog* published by H. W. Wilson, a resource that has been in existence and well used for many years. The catalog is published every five years and is a comprehensive annotated list of children's fiction and nonfiction books and magazines from preschool through grade six. It also discusses professional aides for teachers and librarians. Children's literature specialists from across the country have chosen the materials for inclusion. Another important resource, although recently retired, is the *Elementary School Library Collection* published by Brodart. Although the tool will no longer be published, it is still an extraordinarily useful tool for the "development, evaluation and maintenance of existing collections as well as the establishment of new library centers."[6]

Public and school libraries should be subscribing to several periodicals that review current materials. And librarians, media specialists, and teachers should read them assiduously. Among the periodicals that are important for keeping current with children's literature are:

- *Appraisal: Science Books for Young People,* Northeastern University, Children's Science Book Review Committee;

Dept. of Science and Mathematics Education, 1967, v. quarterly.

- *Arts and Activities: Creative Activities for the Classroom,* Arts and Activities, c/o Publishers Development Corp., 1932, v. 10 nos. per year.
- *Book Links: Connecting Books, Libraries, and Classrooms,* American Library Association, v. bimonthly.
- *Booklist,* American Library Association, 1905, v. semimonthly.
- *Bulletin of the Center for Children's Books,* University of Illinois Press, 1947, v. monthly.
- *CBC Features,* Children's Book Council, 1945, v. approximately every six months.
- *Five Owls,* Five Owls, v. bimonthly.
- *Horn Book Guide to Children's and Young Adult Books,* Horn Book, 1990, v. semiannual.
- *Horn Book Magazine: About Books for Children and Young Adults,* Horn Book, 1924, v. bimonthly.
- *Instructor: Primary,* Instructor Publications, 1891, v. 8 nos. per year.
- *Language Arts,* National Council of Teachers of English, 1924, v. 8 nos. per year.
- *Library Talk: The Magazine for Elementary School Librarians,* Linworth Publishing, 1988, v. 5 nos. per year.
- *Multicultural Review: Dedicated to a Better Understanding of Ethnic, Racial and Religious Diversity,* Greenwood, 1992 v. quarterly.
- *New Advocate,* Christopher Gordon, 1988, v. quarterly.
- *Reading Teacher,* International Reading Association, 1957, v. 8 nos. per year.
- *School Library Journal: For Children's, Young Adult, and School Librarians,* Bowker, c/o School Library Journal, v. 12 nos. per year.
- *School Library Activities Monthly,* LMS Associates, v. 10 nos. per year.
- *Science and Children,* National Science Teachers Association, 1963, v. 8 nos. per year.
- *Teaching Children Mathematics,* National Council of Teachers of Mathematics, 1994, v. 8 nos. per year.
- *Teaching K-8,* Early Years, v. 8 nos. per year.

Few public or school library budgets can afford all of these publications, so again, selection comes into play. If the school is a magnet school for science, the library should subscribe to *Appraisal* and *Science and Young Children;* if there is an emphasis on art, it should subscribe to *Arts and Activities*. Every school should have access to *School Library Journal* and either *Horn Book* or *Booklist* at the minimum.

Teachers need to read the periodicals to see what's new and what is just right for their students. If schools and libraries do not subscribe to the above publications, teachers are responsible for finding the "right" books for their classes just the same. They have to read widely and talk to each other. Book clubs among teachers have been very successful in certain parts of the country. Teachers each read the same book and discuss it, or they each read a different book, talk about the book, and then discuss all the books. Of course, we're talking about the ideal world here—the one in which teachers never have to worry about kids being left after school or having nosebleeds, or throwing chairs—all of which limit a teacher's time to read. However, if a book is assigned, the teacher is obligated to know the book, which means the teacher should have read it!

Other ideas for learning about as many books as one can include giving two-minute book talks about new books at faculty meetings and sending every teacher home at the end of the school year with a basket of books to read.

Challenge Procedures

Book challenges happen often, and the best advice we can give is the scout motto of "Be Prepared." When a challenge happens, a teacher or librarian is often taken by surprise, so make a plan the first day you walk into your classroom. Think ahead about general words that you will use and the general way in which you will handle the situation. First, remain calm. Second, remember that the parents are sending you the very best they have. Take the high road and believe that they are challenging because they care. You should be so glad that your students have caring parents. Contrast them with the parents that you don't hear from during the whole year.

At the beginning of the year, learn who the person in charge of challenges is and the school's policy on handling challenged materials. In most schools, the first line of defense will be the media specialist. In some, it will be the curriculum specialist or the assistant principal, or even the principal.

Every school should have a Library (Media Center) Advisory Committee that is representative of the school community. The committee should be comprised of teachers representing each grade or subject level and two parents from the community. In the high schools, a student should be on the committee. The committee should reflect the interests, beliefs, and cultures of the school population.

If a parent casually speaks to you about a book, never become defensive. Just listen—it's hard, especially if you love the book! Do not commit to doing anything about the book. Instead, send the parent to the person who responds to challenges. That person will have a challenge form to immediately present to the parent for the parent to fill out. This relieves the teacher from being the bad guy and gets the teacher out of the position of defending the book choice. Challenges can be very emotional and can quickly escalate into a situation that is not pleasant for anyone involved.

Once a challenge has been formally presented, each committee member should read the challenged book and reflect on it. The members should not see the actual challenge form, nor should they know what precise aspect of the book has been challenged. That way, they can read and reflect without any preconceived ideas. Once all committee members have read the material, a meeting is set for the Advisory Committee to attend. At the meeting, the book is discussed, the committee is made aware of the actual challenge, and a decision is made about whether the book should be removed or remain, depending on the committee's decision and the demand of the challenger.

After the decision, a letter should be sent to the person who challenged the material clearly stating what the committee's decision is. The committee chairperson and the principal sign the letter. The decision may go to a district committee if the challenger is unhappy with the outcome. The final level would be the superintendent.

Common Reasons for Book Challenges

During our many years of working with children and books, we've discovered that the most common reasons for book challenges are

1. offensive language
2. violence
3. racial stereotypes
4. gender stereotypes
5. witchcraft and Satanism
6. sexuality

Offensive language ranks as the first reason by a huge margin. Possibly, this is because a child reading a book might be startled and fascinated by a word that is considered off-limits in a household and will draw it to the parent's attention. It may be that the parent casually picks up the book and sees a word that is offensive. Whatever the reason, we have been involved in many challenges over words during our years in the classroom and library. One such instance occurred over an alleged four-letter word in a book for reluctant readers. The learning resource teacher had identified this as an appropriate book for a group of special education students. She required it for a Literature Circle. A parent objected to a word in the book. The committee read the book and discovered that the word never appeared in the text. However, they were amazed that the challenge was over the word and not about the abusive behavior of the father toward the son. The committee decided that the book should be a choice, but not a requirement. When the letter was sent to the parent, it was returned with a stamp saying the person was no longer at the address and had left no forwarding address.

Another challenge involved the very fine *Bridge to Terabithia* by Katherine Paterson. A parent mentioned to a fourth-grade teacher that she was unhappy with the book, and the teacher directed her to the media specialist. The parent made a phone call and the media specialist said that she would send home the challenge form. Nothing else was heard until the principal attended a neighborhood "get-acquainted" meeting and the parent stood up and unfurled a scroll with a litany of words on page numbers in the remarkable book that she did not like. She wanted the book banned from the media center. There was a large group of parents at the meeting, many of whom had read the book completely, and the informal discussion ended with the parent being urged to read the book in its entirety. The principal offered to again call the Advisory Committee together to address a formal complaint, but nothing more was heard.

Finally, one last interesting challenge was over the appropriateness of *View from the Cherry Tree* as a read-aloud for fourth-graders. The book by Willo Davis Roberts is what adults would call a "good read." It was one of the first really good mysteries for kids. Unfortunately, the cat's name is S.O.B. and in the beginning of the book, the author tells that the father called the cat a "son of a bitch" and that's how the name stuck. The teacher read the book aloud, but simply read the name as "cat." A student in the class borrowed another copy from the media center and was delighted to find the real name and shared it with her parents. The father wrote an angry note to the teacher and filled out the challenge form. The committee reviewed the challenge and decided that the book was not appropriate for an elementary school and the book was sent to the middle school for its collection. Interestingly enough, the committee decided that the book was inappropriate because of a grizzly murder and discussion of drugs, rather than the language. Again, the first rule for teachers and media specialists is to remain calm and listen to the challenger. Then send the challenger to talk with the appropriate person about the challenge. Do not remove the material. If you do, you are censoring the other students' rights to read it. In the meantime, you can do the following to prepare yourself:

1. Think through your own classroom decision-making processes, not just about text choices but about classroom experiences as well.
2. Give students access to primary sources.
3. Work hard to get the professional time needed to review materials carefully, prepare rationales, and so on.
4. Seek creative responses to unrealistic challenges.
5. Allow students access to materials and evidence so they can become independent thinkers and educated persons.
6. Begin thinking of challenges as part of the expected, ongoing process of renegotiating curriculum.[7]

I Have a Wonderful Idea: An Expedition

Guiding Questions

1. How do people think of wonderful ideas?
2. What are some wonderful ideas that people have thought about?
3. What do they do with their ideas? How do they share them?
4. What are some of my wonderful ideas?

Standards

Standards for this expedition are from National Standards for Arts Education and from the American Association for the Advancement of Science.

The students:

1. employ organizational structures and analyze what makes them effective or not effective in the communication of ideas.
2. use subjects, themes, and symbols that demonstrate knowledge of contexts, values, and aesthetics that communicate intended meaning in artworks. [8]
3. can learn about others from direct experience, from the mass communications media, and from listening to other people talk about their work and their lives.
4. can also sometimes imitate people or characters in the media.
5. make sketches to aid in explaining procedures or ideas
6. learn that science is an adventure that people everywhere can take part in, as they have for many centuries.
7. learn that scientific investigations may take many different forms, including observing what things are like or what is happening somewhere, collecting specimens for analysis, and doing experiments.
8. learn that investigations can focus on physical, biological, and social questions. [9]

Initial Reading Options for Teacher Read-Aloud, Shared, Guided, or Independent Reading

1. *Snowflake Bentley* by Jacqueline Briggs Martin (picture book biography—middle elementary)
2. *Michelangelo* by Diane Stanley (picture book biography—upper elementary)
3. *Love That Dog* by Sharon Creech (chapter book in poetic form—middle elementary)
4. *Frindle* by Andrew Clements (chapter book—middle elementary)
5. *Martin's Big Words* by Doreen Rappaport (picture book biography—middle elementary)
6. *Officer Buckle and Gloria* by Peggy Rathman (picture book—primary)
7. *The Dinosaurs of Waterhouse Hawkins* by Barbara Kerley (picture book biography—middle elementary)
8. *The Gardener* by Sarah Stewart (picture book—primary)

Fieldwork Options

1. Identify and interview someone who has had a good idea.
2. Read about inventors who have had good ideas.

3. Make a model or draw a picture of a "good idea."
4. Develop and test an idea.

Individual Projects

1. Read about inventors and participate in literature discussion groups.
2. Design individual projects for the inventors' fair.

Class Projects

1. Locate, read, and prepare displays of brainteasers to share with other classes.
2. Create poetry ideas with forms of poetry and put together books of poetry.
3. Prepare for inventors' fair.

Sharing Outlets

1. Inventors' fair.
2. Class book of poetry.

Assessment Options

1. Rubric for assessing invention includes scientific inquiry and testing.
2. Drafting and final production of poetry.

Notes

1. http://www.elob.org/aboutel/principles.html

2. Margo Jefferson, "Harry Potter for Grown-Ups," *The New York Times Book Review,* January 20, 2002, 23.

3. Frances F. Goforth, *Literature and the Learner* (Belmont, Calif.: Wadsworth, 1998), 111.

4. Susan Cooper, *Dreams and Wishes; Essays on Writing for Children* (New York: Simon & Schuster, 1996), 96.

5. Jefferson, "Harry Potter," 23.

6. Linda Homa, ed., *The Elementary School Library Collection* (Williamsport, Pa.: Brodart, 2000), vi.

7. Ellen Henson Brinkley, *Caught Off Guard: Teachers Rethinking Censorship and Controversy* (Needham Heights, Mass.: Allyn & Bacon, 1999), 47–48.

8. http://artsedge.kennedycenter.org/professional_resources/standards/natstandards_58.htm.l

9. http://www.sciencenetlinks.com/benchmark_index.htm

Chapter 6

Literature that Touches the Heart: Empathy and Caring

"You know, my eyes ain't too good at all. I can't see nothing but the general shape of things, so I got to rely on my heart. Why don't you go on and tell me everything about yourself, so as I can see you with my heart."

And because Winn-Dixie was looking up at her like she was the best thing he had ever seen, and because the peanut-butter sandwich had been so good, and because I had been waiting for a long time to tell some person everything about me, I did.

—Kate DiCamillo, *Because of Winn-Dixie*, 2000

The design principle from Expeditionary Learning that is targeted in this chapter is "Empathy and Caring."

Learning is fostered best in small groups where there is trust, sustained caring, and mutual respect among all members of the learning community. Keep schools and learning groups small. Be sure there is a caring adult looking after the progress of each child. Arrange for the older students to mentor the younger ones.[1]

Realistic Fiction

Realistic fiction is a term used to describe imaginative tales about people who could be real, doing things that really can be done. Readers identify with the characters in realistic fiction and allow their hearts to be touched. Through this genre, more than any other, children learn about caring for each other, the importance of relationships, and the traits of character they will emulate with their lives.

In Kate DiCamillo's warm and wonderful *Because of Winn-Dixie*, Opal Buloni moves to Naomi, Florida, adopts a miscreant dog in the local Winn-Dixie and makes some unusual friends. One of the most unusual is Gloria Dump, the town "witch." Winn-Dixie leads Opal right to this kindly old lady "with crinkly brown skin" and a "big floppy hat with flowers all over it, and she didn't have any teeth, but she didn't look like a witch."[2] Not only does Gloria Dump see 10-year-old Opal with her heart, but she also listens to Opal's heart and helps Opal shed some of her loneliness and pain.

Contemporary realistic fiction takes place in the now—nothing in the story places it in a different time. Historical realistic fiction, on the other hand, takes place in a clearly identified time period—one before now. The identifiers could be as simple as a description of clothes worn by the characters or language used by the characters. The actual settings of times of war or other significant historical periods, such as pre-historic times, medieval England, or the Civil Rights movement in the United States, places the story squarely as one of historical fiction.

Contemporary realistic fiction has been around for a very long time. In 1868, Louisa May Alcott wrote about the March sisters and their daily struggles and triumphs in *Little Women*. Mark Twain (pseudonym for Samuel Clemens) entertained audiences with his tales of Tom's mischief in *The Adventures of Tom Sawyer* in 1876. Twain's classic, *The Adventures of Huckleberry Finn* followed in 1884. Frances Hodgson Burnett's 1910 classic, *The Secret Garden*, is still a favorite read-aloud in many elementary classrooms. Kids identify with Mary and her cousin Colin, and their reawakening to life and joy.

However, the 1970s witnessed an explosion of contemporary realistic fiction for children. Judy Blume led the way with her stories that delved into awakening sexuality, sibling rivalry, and the problems within peer groups. Both reviled and revered by adults and the young, Blume provided books that spoke to kids of the 70s and of today. In *Are You there God, It's Me, Margaret?* (1970) she discussed physical maturity and menstruation. Librarians and booksellers couldn't keep the book on their shelves. Three of the books that followed were *Then, Again, Maybe I Won't* (1971), *Deenie* (1973), and *Blubber* (1974). *Then, Again, Maybe I Won't* is the story of a boy who is disturbed with his family's changing attitudes and his own new sexual stirring. *Deenie* tells about a beautiful girl who discovers she has a curvature of the spine and will have to wear a brace for several years. The story touches upon masturbation. *Blubber* is an exploration of the viciousness of the young toward one of their own who is overweight. Blume's books are not known for their literary merit and are less popular than they once were, but in 1996 Judy Blume was the deserving recipient of the Margaret Edwards award for her lifetime contribution to literature for young adults. Ms. Blume made it impossible for parents to turn away from issues confronting their children and children made it impossible for authors to return to the simplicity of earlier books of realistic fiction.

Not all contemporary realistic fiction books are overwhelmed with angst. Ms. Blume also introduced us to the hilarious antics of the Hatcher family with *Tales of a Fourth Grade Nothing, Superfudge,* and *Fudge-a-Mania.* Sibling rivalry and parental approval are issues dealt with in these books, while readers laugh their way through them. Readers will never forget Mrs. Hatcher's horror when she discovers that Fudge has swallowed Peter's pet turtle. They snicker with the occupants of the elevator when she frantically announces why Fudge is being taken off on a stretcher. The popularity of these books has continued for two reasons. The characters are much stronger than in most of Blume's books, and the Hatcher stories have the element that all kids are looking for when they read for pleasure—humor.

Betsy Byars, writing at the same time, also explored issues that seemed taboo before the seventies. She introduced young readers to the mentally handicapped Charlie, in her 1977 Newbery Medal winner, *Summer of the Swans.* Charlie's sister, Sara, is a perfect study in character growth. In the book she changes from a whining, self-conscious preteen in puce-colored sneakers to a confident and determined young woman, coming to terms with what is and what is not important in life. Mrs. Byars writes with humor and intelligence and has introduced us to many other memorable characters over the years.

Katherine Paterson took a hard look at foster care. In *The Great Gilly Hopkins* (1978), readers are introduced to the tough-talking, bubble-gum-chewing Gilly who has resided in numerous foster homes and is now with Mamie Trotter. Ms. Trotter is determined to make a home for the temperamental Gilly, who loves four-letter words and uses them throughout the book. The idea still seems to shock parents of young readers. A friend tells the story of an interesting incident on an airplane. A parent, noticing that our friend had a bagful of children's books, asked how the Newbery Committee dared choose *The Great Gilly Hopkins* as a Newbery Honor book. She had just read it and was troubled. She continued by letting everyone in the surrounding area know of her intentions to contact the Newbery Committee and suggest all the members resign. Our friend wasn't brave enough to tell her that the members of the committee changed yearly, that she was on the current year's committee (1993), and was on her way to the meeting at which the committee would select the 1993 Newbery winner. However, she did explain that the language that Gilly uses is one of the things that makes Gilly a strong and believable character.

Paterson also struck a controversial chord when she wrote about a child's death in *Bridge to Terabithia*. The powerful story about the friendship between a boy and a girl, two children from very different backgrounds, but with similar interests, won the Newbery Medal in 1978. It remains a favorite of teachers and children today. The idea of a child dying in a book was so horrifying that when a colleague's son realized Leslie had died, he threw the book over the front seat of the car, almost causing an accident and eliciting a severe tongue-lashing. When mother and son arrived safely at home, they read the chapter together and burst into tears. No matter how hard they wanted it to happen, Leslie did not come back to life. She really did plunge to her death in that ravine.

In 1986 Marion Dane Bauer wrote another book in which a child died. *On My Honor* is frightening because it points out how a child's irresponsible behavior can cause his death. It explores the whole idea of honor. In not very many words, Ms. Bauer gave us a book to think and talk about for years. Her insight into the minds of twelve-year-old boys is chilling. Tony urges his friend, Joel, to join him in a bike ride to the bluffs. Certain that his father will deny permission, Joel is shocked when his father gives it. On their way, Tony insists that the boys swim. Against his better judgment, Joel joins his friend and is frantic when he can no longer find Tony. After determining that Tony did drown, Joel slinks home and locks himself in his room. Finally, confronted by the police, he admits what happened. "We all made choices today, Joel. You, me, Tony. Tony's the only one who doesn't have to live with his choice," exclaimed Tony's father.[3] Without being didactic, Bauer reminds the reader that life is a series of choices and we need to make each choice wisely so that we can live comfortably with it.

Barbara Park is another author who writes about things that touch the heart. In *Mick Harte Was Here* thirteen-year-old Phoebe talks with humor and pain about her brother, Mick, who died in a bicycle accident. Park has a genuine gift for writing about strong, witty young girls. Junie B. Jones ("My name is Junie B. Jones. The B stands for Beatrice. Except I don't like Beatrice. I just like B and that's all.")[4] is one of the most engaging characters in children's literature. She is a kindergartner going through the process of being a kindergartner and experiencing very typical kindergarten days. The books are wonderful beginning chapter books for transitional readers. Junie B. encounters all those things that every child does. They are also terrific read-alouds (as long as one explains that the language is that of a typical five-year-old and not a model to be followed) and can engage the attention of students from preschool through high school as well as adults

Lois Lowry, an author of incredible talent, has given us stories about Anastasia Krupnik, a character a little older than Junie B. and different. In *Anastasia Krupnik*, Anastasia is a precocious ten-year-old who loves to keep lists. When she discovers that her mother is pregnant, she adds two things to the list—"my parents" and "babies." Lots of other kids in this predicament would add the same items. Fortunately, by the time the baby arrives, Anastasia is ready to welcome him. It would only be right to introduce Sam's own books, and Ms. Lowry complied. In 1989 *All about Sam* was published and some of the best humor in children's literature is found in the Sam books. The image of the moving men racing trucks up and down the upstairs hall with Sam is hard to forget!

There are lots of good contemporary books with broad appeal for both boys and girls. Jerry Spinelli made his mark with *Maniac Magee* (1990), the spellbinding story of the orphaned Jeffrey Lionel Magee who became a legendary hero in Two Mills, Pennsylvania. Maniac's greatest accomplishment was uniting the racially divided town. The tale provides lots of topics for discussion and elicits passionate responses from young and old readers alike. Spinelli went on to write *Crash* (1996), *The Library Card* (1997), and *Wringer*, a 1998 Newbery Honor book. In all three, there are Maniac-like characters but none have the heroic stature that Maniac achieved. *Wringer* is set in Waymer, a town in Middle America that celebrates a weeklong Family Fest each year. The evening that caps the week involves a frightening rite of passage in which ten-year-olds wring the necks of wounded pigeons. It is a privilege and honor to be chosen as a wringer, one that Palmer LaRue does not want. He is fast approaching his tenth birthday and will be chosen as a wringer. He has also just found friends in a group of boys that think being chosen as a wringer is the highest accolade. The book is a good study of the problem of peer pressure, but seems almost surrealistic in suggesting that such a rite of passage would go on in small-town America.

So thought many readers. After reading the novel, a junior high school librarian sent a message to a popular literature listserv saying that she thought Jerry Spinelli had quite an imagination to come up with this plot. Soon after she'd had the thought, there was an article from the Associated Press telling about a government unit checking out a pigeon hunt. It seems that there was a controversial, but legal, pigeon shoot under way on private land outside a small town and teenagers wrung the necks of the injured birds. Was this an example of life imitating art or art imitating life?

Picture books should not be left out of the discussion of realistic fiction. Mavis Jukes's *Like Jake and Me*, is a particularly fine example of a well-done realistic fiction story. It is an excellent example to use as an introduction to the genre as well as a story that touches the hearts of many. All of the literary conventions come together to make this a masterpiece. Alex lives with his mother, Virginia, and his stepfather, Jake. The story opens with Alex admiring his stepfather's strength and making bumbling, but sincere, efforts to help him. Jukes has let the reader know in a variety of ways that Jake and Alex are very different; Jake is a genuine cowboy and Alex takes ballet lessons and shows an interest in entomology. Through a series of humorous misunderstandings Jake and Alex realize that they do have much in common, and the book ends with jubilation and tenderness.

Historical Fiction

As with all works of fiction, good historical fiction combines all of the literary elements. The uniqueness of the genre is that books of historical fiction must be set in a specific time period in the past. The author must do an amazing amount of research to establish familiarity with the time and place of the novel.

In fact, one of our best pieces of historical fiction, *Johnny Tremain,* was actually an outgrowth of the wealth of material Esther Forbes collected for an adult novel that she was writing. The adult work, set during the American Revolution, has long since been forgotten; *Johnny Tremain*, remains a captivating and well-loved story. She made sure that her details were authentic and her characters held the beliefs and values of the time, and behaved and spoke in ways that were appropriate during that time period.

Fourteen-year-old Johnny is an apprentice silversmith and lives in quarters with two other apprentices. He has proven himself to be almost as fine a silversmith as the owner of the business. However, he is also arrogant and impatient and defies convention by insisting that the other two apprentices work with him on the Sabbath. The other boys play a mean trick and Johnny's hand is burned badly by molten silver, making it impossible for him to pursue his vocation. Wandering helplessly, he meets Rab, a young newspaperman who helps Johnny find work and propels him into the middle of revolutionary activity in Boston. Johnny becomes involved with John and Samuel Adams, John Hancock, and James Otis, powerful forces in the American Revolution. He takes part in the Boston Tea Party and even finds himself at the Battle of Lexington, when the first shots for American freedom rang out.

This is historical fiction at its best. What better way could a student find out information about an important historical event, especially one so basic to our current way of life?

Linda Levstik claims "historical fiction can create a sense of history so powerful that children enter imaginatively into the past."[5] Imagination and fact are the basis for good historical fiction. Authors must be steeped in the facts of the time and draw on their powers of imagination to write a good story.

The struggles of our pioneers and stories of the westward movement in this country provide good backdrops for historical fiction. Gary Paulsen's *Tucket* series tells of the adventures of fourteen-year-old Francis Tucket after he wandered from the wagon train carrying his family to Oregon. As with all Paulsen's characters, Francis is resourceful. The books provide lots of adventure as well as insight into the hardships of the times.

Sarah, Plain and Tall, the perfect little jewel that won the 1986 Newbery, tells of a father and his two small children who have already found a place to settle, but now need a mother and wife. Caleb and Anna's mother died at Caleb's birth and their father advertises for a new bride. Sarah, who is tall and rawboned, answers from Maine. She visits the family and gradually falls in love with them and accepts their way of life. During the story, children get a true sense of the times and delight in Sarah's strength and her sense of fun. No reader can forget the image of Sarah working on the roof or sliding "down, down into the soft hay," with the light of the lantern making Pa's eyes shine as he smiled up at her.

Laura Ingalls Wilder's Little House books are probably the best-known books about settling the American frontier. The books begin with Laura as a six-year-old and follow the Ingalls girls and Wilder boys until Laura and Manley marry in the final story, *The First Four Years* (1971). An in-depth look at the Little House books reminds us that settlers during the nineteenth century were usually frightened of "Indians." The following are passages from the Wilder books:

> The drums throbbed and the Indians went on yelling. The terrible war-cry came again and again. [6]
> She did not know why the government made treaties with Indians. The only good Indian was a dead Indian. The very thought of Indians made her blood run cold.[7]

> He said you never saw Indians unless they wanted you to see
> them. He had seen Indians when he was a boy in New York State, but
> Laura never had. She knew they were wild men with red skins and
> their hatchets were called tomahawks.[8]

When teachers discuss some of these historical fiction works with
their students, they need to talk about the fact that attitudes and circumstances of the times dictate the way the stories are written. In many
passages of fiction about early America, Native Americans are portrayed as needlessly cruel, as brutal savages.

Patricia Polacco's powerful *Pink and Say* is an ideal book to use as
an introduction to this genre. The book is a brilliant blend of illustration
and story. Pinkus Alley and Sheldon Russell Curtis are Union soldiers
who met during the Civil War. Pink is black; Say is white. Pink takes
the wounded Say home to his beloved mama to be nursed back to
health. The boys build a close friendship, during which Pink teaches
Say how to read. Marauders kill Moe Moe Bay, Pink's mother, and the
boys begin their trek back to the front lines. Unfortunately, they are
captured by enemy soldiers and sent to the grim Andersonville prison.
Say is eventually released but discovers that Pink was hanged the day
they had arrived at the prison.

Based on an incident that actually happened in Mrs. Polacco's
family, she wrote it so the story would continue to be told. Heartbreak-
ing images remain with the reader, as well as an understanding of the
term "Marauders" and an introduction to some of the complexities of
the time.

Carolyn Reeder set two novels in the time of the Civil War, *Shades
of Gray*, and *Across the Lines*. *Across the Lines* explores the relationship between Edward and his slave, Simon. The two have been lifelong
friends and are now separated by the war. More compelling is *Shades
of Gray*, the story of Will Page, a Virginia boy, who is now an orphan.
His uncle takes him to live on a hardscrabble farm. Will isn't used to
such a life, nor can he understand why his uncle was a conscientious
objector during the war. The book not only encourages the reader to
think about the Civil War, but further, to think about war itself. The
ending is very satisfying.

But, again, not all the fine children's literature is somber. In fact,
even the books that deal with issues that touch the heart are often filled
with humor. That's the aspect that keeps children reading them. Richard Peck, a wonderful writer of juvenile fiction, has written terrific
books that are full of humor.

In *A Year Down Yonder*, Mary Alice's visit to Grandma Dowdel will captivate the fiercest nonreader. Mary Alice has been sent to spend the summer with her feisty, terrifying, and good-hearted old grandma. In Peck's first book about these engaging characters, *A Long Way From Chicago*, Grandma's exploits were seen through the eyes of her grandson Joey. Now it's 1937 and Joey has gone off to work for the Civilian Conservation Group and Mary Alice is with Grandma alone. It's not easy—particularly since Grandma Dowdel is eccentric and not quiet about it. One funny part that will have the most sedate among us laughing out loud occurs when Mary Alice is entertaining her first date and a loud banging is heard from the attic. Shortly after the banging begins, the town's postmistress races downstairs and out the door wrapped only in a boa constrictor. She had been posing for the resident artist and suddenly a boa constrictor, which had been living in the rafters, found her extremely delectable. The book is marvelously funny and very moving.

Studying literature by genre is a way to talk about common patterns and structure among literary pieces. Again, it is always dangerous to try to stuff anything into tight boxes. Students will frequently discover that stories cannot be pigeonholed. However, by urging children to read around a wheel, which includes a variety of genres, we are encouraging them to broaden their knowledge of literature and life, and so many of these stories touch the heart.

The John Newbery Award

Several of the books we have mentioned so far have been labeled as Newbery Medal or Honor books. In 1921 Frederic Melcher, a bookseller, booklover, and editor of *Publisher's Weekly*, urged the Children's Library Section of the American Library Association (ALA) to give a medal to the author of the most distinguished contribution to American literature for children under fourteen. The ALA division agreed, and in 1922, the medal was given to Hendrik Willem van Loon for his book *The Story of Mankind*. The medal was named for John Newbery and has been awarded to a children's book author every year since then.

John Newbery was an English bookseller who recognized children as an audience for books other than instructive tomes. He published *A Pretty Pocket-Book* in 1744 to amuse children and other similar books after that.

At first the committee selecting the Newbery Medal winner had a twofold role. They also selected the Caldecott Medal winner. Finally, in 1978, ALA realized that the task was overwhelming and they separated the committee into two committees—one would be the Newbery Committee and the other would be the Caldecott Committee. The Newbery Committee is composed of fifteen members chosen from the American Library Association's Association of Library Service to Children. Seven of the committee members are elected, seven are appointed, and the chair is elected. Members meet at the ALA annual conference held in the summer and its midwinter conference usually held in January. They also communicate constantly during the year. E-mail has simplified communication among the members.

Only one medal winner is chosen each year. The books examined are published during the preceding year. For example, *Missing May,* published in 1992, was the 1993 Newbery Medal winner. The committee can select an unlimited number of honor books for each year; however, committees are extremely selective about choosing the honor books as well as the medal winner. Until 1958, no author could receive the Newbery more than once unless the committee voted unanimously for it. Since then, several authors have won the Newbery Medal and Newbery Honor awards more than one time.

The medal winner and the honor books are announced at the ALA Midwinter Meeting, which is held in January or February and always held on a Monday. This medal and the Caldecott Medal are considered the Oscars of children's literature. Actually, children's literature professionals like to say that the Oscar awards are the Newbery and Caldecott awards of the movie field.

The Newbery winning and honor titles have to have been first published in the United States and are chosen because they are distinguished or marked by excellence. This has nothing to do with popularity, and often the book chosen is not the book of the year that is the most popular one with the kids. All Newbery Committee members understand this at the outset, and are careful to select books that meet the criteria.

It's tempting for teachers to urge their students to read only Newbery books or to read only Newbery books aloud to their classes. However, as in all book choices, books need to be chosen to meet the needs of the readers or listeners. Sometimes a book, whether Newbery or not, is just not the right book for the class or the student.

Winning authors often appear on television interviews the day after the award is announced. The winning author receives a medal cast in bronze at the ALA Annual Conference banquet. The authors of honor books receive certificates and their books are announced in alphabetical order, which gives equal tribute to all. Gold seals are affixed to all of the Newbery Medal books and silver seals are attached to the honor books.

Many states have children's book awards which reward authors who have written books that are popular with students. In most cases, the books do not have to have been published during the prior year. These awards, as well as the Newbery award, are given to authors for individual books.

The Laura Ingalls Wilder Medal

In 1954, the Association for Library Service to Children gave the first Laura Ingalls Wilder Medal to its namesake, Laura Ingalls Wilder. The award is given to an author or illustrator who has had a lasting contribution to children's literature over a period of years. Between 1954 and 1980 the award was given every five years; since then it has been awarded every three years. The past winners are:

2001: Milton Meltzer
1998: Russell Freedman
1995: Virginia Hamilton
1992: Marcia Brown
1989: Elizabeth George Speare
1986: Jean Fritz
1983: Maurice Sendak
1980: Theodor S. Geisel (Dr. Seuss)
1975: Beverly Cleary
1970: E. B. White
1965: Ruth Sawyer
1960: Clara Ingram Judson
1954: Laura Ingalls Wilder

The Randolph Caldecott Medal

The Caldecott Medal was named in honor of nineteenth-century English illustrator Randolph Caldecott. It is awarded annually by the Association for Library Service to Children, a division of the American Library Association, to the artist of the most distinguished American picture book for children published in the United States. The criteria stipulate that picture books for children up to and including the age of fourteen are to be considered. The award guidelines state that the picture book must "provide the child with a visual experience," "has a collective unity of story-line, theme, or concept, developed through the series of pictures," and "displays respect for children's understandings, abilities, and appreciations." The committee is comprised of seven elected members and seven appointed members plus an elected chairperson. The committee members look at all the worthy picture books published during a year, and during the early part of the next year, the award winner is announced.

The process is exactly the same as that of the Newbery Committee explained above. One medal winner is chosen and several picture books can be chosen as honor books. Committees usually opt to keep the number of honor books to around three, for fear of watering down the impact of the Caldecott Medal.

The work for the committee is challenging and intense, but they consider the criteria carefully and responsibly. Readers need to always keep in mind that this is not a popularity contest. This award is given to the book that is most distinguished for its illustrations.

Learning to Care: An Expedition

Guiding Questions

1. Why should I care?
2. How do I learn to care?
3. What should I care about?
4. Do people of all cultures show they care in the same way?
5. Have people shown care for each other in the same way throughout history?
6. How does caring for an animal equate to caring for another person?
7. How do parents show that they care for their children?
8. How do siblings show they care for each other?
9. How does one show concern and caring for mankind?

Standards

Standards for this expedition are derived from the National Council for the Social Studies (NCSS) and the American Association for the Advancement of Science (AAAS).

The students:

1. learn that people tend to live together in groups and therefore have to have ways of deciding who will do what.
2. understand that different groups have different expectations for how their members should act.[9]
3. describe how people create places that reflect culture, human needs, current values and ideals, and government policies.
4. compare and evaluate the impact of stereotyping, conformity, acts of altruism, and other behaviors on individuals and groups.[10]

Initial Reading Options for Teacher Read-Aloud, Shared, Guided, or Independent Reading

1. *Because of Winn-Dixie* by Kate DiCamillo (chapter book—middle elementary)
2. *Missing May* by Cynthia Rylant (chapter book—middle elementary)
3. *Thank you, Mr. Falker* by Patricia Polacco (picture storybook—primary)
4. *The Single Shard* by Linda Sue Park (chapter book—upper elementary)
5. *Dragon's Gate* by Laurence Yep (chapter book—upper elementary)
6. *Number the Stars* by Lois Lowry (chapter book—upper elementary)
7. *Wind in the Willows* by Kenneth Grahame (chapter book—upper elementary)
8. *The Wanderer* by Sharon Creech (chapter book—upper elementary)
9. *Sweet Clara and the Freedom Quilt* by Deborah Hopkinson (picture storybook—elementary)

Fieldwork Options

1. Visit fire stations, police departments, and health care facilities to find out job requirements and reasons for choosing these occupations.
2. Observe interactions of families.

3. Interview senior citizens to determine their interests and things they care about.
4. Interview members of families from other cultures to see what they consider appropriate ways to show caring.
5. Discuss with senior citizens ways that their families showed each other empathy and caring.
6. Visit a veterinarian, an animal shelter, or a zoo to see animal care.
7. Interview animal caretakers and find out what the most common problems are between pets and their owners.
8. Examine case studies of animals helping people.
9. Research appropriate cultural forms of caring.

Individual Projects

1. Interview a senior citizen and write a biography.
2. Keep a log of incidents when members of your family (including you) demonstrated care for other family members.

Class Projects

1. Compile biographies of senior citizens.
2. Find homes for Humane Society pets.
3. Create a classroom book of culturally appropriate responses of various cultures on social interactions such as greetings, eye contact, meal etiquette, and interactions between children and adults.
4. Distribute fliers for missing children.
5. Collect canned goods for the needy.
6. Collect books for preschools and pediatric departments of hospitals.
7. Make sound recordings of books for the blind.

Sharing Outlets

1. Celebration of lives of senior citizens.
2. A display of a graph showing how many pets have been adopted.
3. Biographies on display in library and/or published.

Assessment Options

1. Self checklist.
2. Teacher- and student-made rubric.
3. Contract completion.
4. Portfolio assessment of standards.

Notes

1. http://www.elob.org/aboutel/principles.html

2. Kate DiCamillo, *Because of Winn-Dixie* (New York: Candlewick, 2000), 63–64.

3. Marion Dane Bauer, *On My Honor* (New York: Houghton Mifflin, 1987), 88.

4. Barbara Park, *Junie B. Jones Loves Handsome Warren* (New York: Scholastic, 1996), 1.

5. Janet Hickman and Bernice Cullinan, eds., *Children's Literature in the Classroom: Weaving Charlotte's Web* (Needham Heights, Mass.: Christopher-Gordon, 1989), 136.

6. Laura Ingalls Wilder, *Little House on the Prairie* (New York: Harper, 1973), 295.

7. Ibid., 211.

8. Ibid., 55–56.

9. http://www.sciencenetlinks.com/benchmark_index.htm

10. http://www.ncss.org/standards/teachers/vol1/people.shtml

Chapter 7

Meeting Life's Challenges:
Successes and Failures

Just before Wilma turned five, she got sicker than ever. Her sisters and brothers heaped all the family's blankets on her, trying to keep her warm.

During that sickness, Wilma's left leg twisted inward, and she couldn't move it back. Not even Wilma's mother knew what was wrong.

The doctor came to see her then. Besides scarlet fever, he said, Wilma had also been stricken with polio. In those days, most children who got polio either died or were permanently crippled. There was no cure.

—Kathleen Krull, *Wilma Unlimited,* 1996

The design principle from Expeditionary Learning that is targeted in this chapter is "Success and Failure."

All students must be assured a fair measure of success in learning in order to nurture the confidence and capacity to take risks and rise to increasingly difficult challenges. But it is also important to experience failure, to overcome negative inclinations, to prevail against adversity, and to learn to turn disabilities into opportunities.[1]

Growing up is filled with meeting life's challenges. That's why adults don't want to do it again. However, the majority of us don't have to face the incredible challenges that Wilma Rudolph did in order to become "the world's fastest woman."

Earlier in this book, we've seen some wonderful examples in children's literature of kids going through difficult times and finding their ways through them. Stanley Yelnats fought and suffered in *Holes* as he dug his daily five-foot holes and then carried his best friend over the mountain. Sara in *Summer of the Swans* was desperate for a real family. Her father had left Sara and her sister and brother with an aunt. Sara felt the huge burden of responsibility for her mentally challenged little

99

brother, but she realized that he was worth every moment she spent on him.

Maniac Magee's life is a daily challenge. He has to sneak into a large family's home so he can eat dinner. He sleeps in a pen in the zoo. Maniac is a legend and gives kids hope that they can make a difference. Then there are all the folks dressed in fur. Henkes writes about Lilly in *Lilly and the Purple Plastic Purse,* who met her challenge and failed. She was so excited about her purple plastic purse filled with quarters that she could not keep them to herself, no matter how many times her teacher told her to wait. In *Owen,* the little mouse Owen met the challenge over his blanket. Mrs. Tweezers actually helped him find a solution, a success.

Look at Jack Gantos's *Joey Pigza Swallowed the Key.* Joey interprets his family tree:

> I am how I am because Grandma was born wired and my dad, Carter Pigza, was born wired, and I followed right behind them. It's as if our family tree looks like a set of high-voltage wires strung across a field from one steel tower to the next.[2]

Joey's plight breaks your heart as you read his story. He's a sweet kid who suffered abuse and neglect in his early years while living with his grandmother. Now his mother has returned, and Joey is learning what it's like to be loved. He is a hyperactive child with attention deficit disorder and this, coupled with aberrant behavior, results in his spending more time in the nurse's office and the principal's office than in the classroom. By the end of the book we are led to believe that Joey has found the right kind of help and he is on the way to success. A balanced medical dosage and behavior modification plus several caring, concerned adults are helping Joey. Those who know him always see the "naturally good kid," the kid with the "good heart."

Andrew Clements's books are filled with upper-elementary-aged students who face intriguing challenges and find success. In *Frindle,* fifth-grader Nick decides to introduce a new word, "frindle," into the English language. He did this as a smart-alecky sort of thing in response to a punishment from his teacher, Mrs. Granger. He thinks she makes it as difficult as possible for Nick to succeed, but all along she was actually spurring him on. Nick's plan is a success. "Frindle" does become an accepted word in the dictionary. It's a synonym for pen.

Twelve-year-old Natalie Nelson has written a powerful school story in Clements's book, *The School Story.* Although her mother is an editor of children's books at a large publishing house, Natalie knows that she would never be taken seriously if she submitted her manuscript in her own name. With the help of her determined friend and some advice from sympathetic adults, Natalie assumes a pen name, submits the manuscript, and her dream comes true. She had a wonderful idea, and it becomes a published book. She met the challenge successfully.

Sarny met the challenge of learning to read in the book by the same name. Lydia Grace Finch in *The Gardener* was sad when she had to visit her uncle during the depression. When she saw his sterile environment, she was even more desperate. She met the challenge and by the time she left, colorful flowers exploded all over her uncle's shop, his apartment, the street, and the roof of the apartment building.

One of the greatest challenges of all time is having to leave a well loved home during a time of war. In *Gleam and Glow* Eve Bunting tells such a tale, based on a true story about a family in Bosnia-Herzegovina. In her story, a father leaves to join the Liberation Army. Mama and the two children are left behind. Many villagers leave in fear and several from other villages pass through and spend a night with the family. One night a man came "carrying a bowl with water and two fish in it. He put the bowl on our table, and it seemed to me that all the light of the world was trapped inside that glass bowl." The visitor asked that the family keep the fish and, reluctantly, Mama agreed. Little sister, Marina, named the fish Gleam and Glow. Soon Mama, Viktor and Marina had to escape also and Viktor released the fish into their pond. After some time the family was reunited with the father and began the journey back home. When they got there, although no houses or barns were left in the village, the pond was as shimmery and dazzling as melted gold. It was filled with countless fish.

Mama pressed her hands to her heart. "Gleam and Glow and their children and their children's children," she said.

"They found their own nourishment," Papa said.

. . . *Like us*, I thought. *They lived.*[3]

Young readers can find examples of challenges in all genres of literature. However, what more perfect place is there to look than in biographies and autobiographies?

Biographies and Autobiographies

Authentic, Factual Biographies

Biographies and autobiographies examine the lives of real people, documenting their successes and failures. Today we are fortunate to have editors and authors focusing on, in fact, demanding, authenticity and accuracy when they tell these stories. Because of the new focus, coupled with imaginative insight and the emphasis on adding illustrations and photographs to spark children's interest, biographies have become a popular genre.

One thing readers need to understand is that every author has a point of view when writing about a subject. No author is purely objective. However, authors have a huge struggle examining the subject's life and putting it into some sort of order without losing the life of the story.

Readers identify with this new type of biography because the subject is presented in a balanced way. The subjects are real people with real-life concerns. Stories about people and their lives give the readers insight into the culture and the times. Authentic and accurate illustrations add to the validity of the story.

Jean Fritz was the first to make biographies for young people into something that they would want to read, but at the same time, stories that were soundly researched. When asked why she liked to write biographies, Ms. Fritz said,

> Sometimes I think it's because I enjoy research so much. For every book I write, I have to read a great deal and usually travel to the place where that person lived. It's like being a detective. I want to find the truth, so I never make up anything in these books, not even conversation. If you see quotation marks, you can be sure I have a source for them.
>
> The research often turns up surprises. (Who would think that young Patrick Henry was remembered for wearing clean underwear?) And it often leads to adventures. When I wrote about King George III, I went to London where there was an exhibit of his personal belongings, including his clocks of which he was so proud.[4]

Until Jean Fritz came along, most authors of children's biographies gave us fictionalized accounts of their subjects, inventing conversations and imagined situations that moved the story along. In *And Then What Happened, Paul Revere?* Fritz sets the scene by telling what Boston was like in 1735. There were

42 streets, 36 lanes, 22 alleys, 1,000 brick houses, 2,000 wooden houses, 12 churches, 4 schools, 418 horses (at last count) and so many dogs that a law was passed prohibiting people from having dogs that were more than 10 inches high.[5]

Ms. Fritz adds refreshing wit to her biographies as evidenced by the next lines.

But it was difficult to keep dogs from growing more than 10 inches, and few people cared to part with their 11- and 12-inch dogs, so they paid little attention to the law. In any case there were too many dogs to count.[6]

Fritz set the standard for biographies and went on to supply the children's book world with a number of fascinating and funny biographies about powerful figures, particularly those involved in the building of the United States. She told of the frustration and mental illness of King George in *Can't You Make Them Behave, King George?*, the brilliance and eccentricity of Ben Franklin in *What's the Big Idea, Ben Franklin?*, and the famous speech of Patrick Henry in *Where Was Patrick Henry on the 29th of May?* She also told about Sam Adams's preference to be an inciter rather than a fighter or soldier in *Why Don't You Get a Horse, Sam Adams?*, about the foppish John Hancock in *Will You Sign Here, John Hancock?*, and the brave fight of Elizabeth Cady Stanton in *You Want Women to Vote, Lizzie Stanton?* All of her subjects faced challenges; most were successful. Poor King George died from his overindulgences and Lizzie Stanton died before she saw her dream of seeing the passage of the nineteenth amendment. At least Lizzie was successful in meeting her challenge. On the other hand, King George failed in his effort to keep the colonists in line.

Jean Fritz wrote several more challenging biographies about well-known figures and was soon joined by Russell Freedman. Freedman likes to be thought of as a "factual writer" because he's afraid that too much emphasis on the word nonfiction will make children think he does uninteresting stuff. Freedman's honest, tough look at Abraham Lincoln in *Lincoln: A Photobiography* was awarded the Newbery Medal in 1988, which did much to assure that nonfiction children's literature deserved literary merit. The author has written many more outstanding works of nonfiction, including several other biographies. *Eleanor Roosevelt: A Life of Discovery* examines the life of one of the world's most admired female figures. Eleanor's challenges were constant, beginning with her difficult childhood, traversing her uncertain married years, and ending with her determination to make the world a better place. All of Freedman's books are carefully researched as is this one, which was named a Newbery Honor book in 1994. In *Babe Didrikson Zaharias: The Making of a Champion*, Freedman tells the courageous story of a woman who changed the world's idea of female athletes forever. Once again, he gives a balanced view of his subject, showing Babe as bossy, sometimes petulant, but generous and persistent. Mr. Freedman's biographies give us full-length portraits of admirable people. He does not veer from the truth, nor does he patronize his readers by minimizing the subject with simple vocabulary. His books are written for the upper elementary and middle school readers.

However, with the new attention to the importance of illustrations and photographs in nonfiction literature, there has been a flood of spectacular biographies for the younger set. Diane Stanley has interwoven strong text with lush illustrations in her series of biographies. Among her finest is *Leonardo Da Vinci,* one of the most amazing people who ever lived. Da Vinci, born in Italy in 1452, grew up to be a great painter, sculptor, architect, scientist, and inventor. In this overview of his life, Stanley also acknowledges the other side of his success— abandoned and unfinished projects, the limitations of working under patronage, and the losses of his renowned notebooks.

After her successful portrayal of the great Leonardo da Vinci, it seems fair for Ms. Stanley to tell us of Michelangelo Buonarroti, known to the world as Michelangelo. The two great painters were not friends, although they lived in Florence, Italy, during the same period, the age we call the Renaissance. The world saw Leonardo da Vinci as a courtly and charming man, but at heart, he was a solitary man. The world saw Michelangelo as a solitary man, living life like a hermit, but also as troubled and quarrelsome. Stanley draws vivid portraits of the two in words and paintings. In her biography of da Vinci, she states

> The two men disliked each other. Michelangelo, best known as a sculptor, had received much attention for the remarkable *David* he had carved out of marble. Leonardo resentfully described the art of sculpture as a "mechanical exercise." It was "often accompanied with much sweat and this combines with the dust and turns into a crust of dirt. . . . [The sculptor's] lodgings are dirty and filled with stone splinters and dust. In the case of the painter," he added, "he sits at great ease . . . well dressed, moving a light brush with agreeable colors. . . . His dwelling is clean and filled with beautiful paintings. He often has himself accompanied with music . . . which he may hear with great pleasure, undisturbed by the pounding of hammers."

For his part, the quarrelsome Michelangelo had once insulted Leonardo in public. "You made a model of a horse you could never cast in bronze," he said, "and which you gave up, to your shame. And the stupid people of Milan had faith in you!" So the battle of the artists began.[7]

Both artists struggled with the challenges of their successes and failures. After the *David* established Michelangelo as the greatest sculptor in all of Italy, he discovered that success came with a high price. From then on "he was hounded by patrons."[8]

Fictionalized Biography

Fictionalized biography is based strongly on research and facts. However, the author creates imaginary conversations in order to make the story a better one. Jean Fritz talks about her childhood in China in *Homesick, My Own Story.* She tells us in her forward,

> Since my childhood feels like a story, I decided to tell it that way, letting the events fall as they would into the shape of a story, lacing them together with fictional bits, adding a piece here and there when memory didn't give me all I needed. I would use conversation freely, for I cannot think of my childhood without hearing voices. So although this book takes place within two years—from October 1925 to September 1927—the events are drawn from the entire period of my childhood, but they are all, except in minor details, basically true.[9]

Edith Schaeffer, known as Mei Fuh in China, also shared some memories of her years in China in *Mei Fuh: Memories from China.* The daughter of American teachers in China, she spent her first five years there. The little book gives a lively account of her experiences, including a lengthy convalescence during which she raised silkworms, watched them spin silk, and later wore a dress made from the same silk. This is a pleasant memoir and introduces the reader to life in China in the early 1900s. Each of the stories about the girls in China has validity because they give us a flavor of the culture during that time, and they are both strongly based on truth.

Biographical Fiction

Sometimes writers of biographies cannot find enough factual information about their subjects to make a full story. Biographical fiction gives the author license to invent incidents and dialogue while telling the story of the biographee. The basic facts are true, but in order to make the subject come alive, the author feels it necessary to add something to the known facts. Unlike the Pinkneys' *Duke Ellington: The Prince of the Piano*, that is factual and looks at the entire life of Duke Ellington, Robert Burleigh only looks at a small part of Miles Davis's life in his picture-book biography, *Lookin' for Bird in the Big City*. In the beginning, Mr. Burleigh states, "This is the story of what might have happened when young Miles first arrived in the 'land of bebop,'" and in the afterword, he writes, "the story is loosely based on a time in the life of trumpeter Miles Davis." [10] The author writes about what he imagines Miles Davis did during the years he was a teenage music student in New York City and spending many hours trying to find Charlie Parker, whom everyone called Bird. The book is a pure pleasure to look at with its richly detailed impressionistic paintings and its bouncy text, and could be used as an introduction to the world of bebop. However, it is clearly a fictionalized biography.

The classic example of biographical fiction is *Minty: A Story of Young Harriet Tubman* by Alan Schroeder. The author writes in the preface:

> While Minty is a fictional account of Harriet Tubman's childhood, and some scenes have been invented for narrative purposes, the basic facts are true. [11]

Scholastic was clever in their origination of the Dear Diary series, a series of books that give insightful accounts of what life was like for girls throughout American history. The books are written in diary form "with each book extensively researched and inspired by real letters and diaries of the time." [12] These books sound so real that many students reading them think they are the diaries of real people.

In *A Coal Miner's Bride: The Diary of Anetka Kaminska, Littimer, Pennsylvania, 1896*, author Susan Campbell Bartoletti tells the story of a thirteen-year-old Polish girl who comes to America as a promised bride to a Pennsylvania coal miner. Joyce Hansen gives a very real view of the hardship and pain of a freed slave's life at the end of the Civil War in *I Thought My Soul Would Rise and Fly: The Diary of Patsy, a Freed Girl, Mars Bluff, South Carolina, 1865*. Because they sound so realistic, we need to be very careful about defining the difference between these and actual diaries, such as *The Diary of Anne Frank*.

Autobiographies and Memoirs

When people write about their own lives, we consider the writings as autobiographies. Ruby Bridges tells of her childhood memories of that fateful day in November 1960 when, surrounded by federal marshals, she became the first black student ever at the all-white William Frantz Public School in New Orleans, Louisiana. The whole world watched that tiny six-year-old in her courageous walk through a mob filled with hatred. Ruby's story has been told in other books but she tells it best in simple language.

Tomie de Paola, long known for his picture books, has given us some very enjoyable autobiographical accounts of his growing up years. One day his longtime assistant said,

> "I have an idea for a chapter book for you—in fact, for a series of chapter books. Why don't you write about all the things that you talk about from your childhood, but can't put into a single picture book." DING—the bell went off—the light bulb lit. "That's it!" I said.
>
> Then the work began. It wasn't hard for me to conjure up all the clear memories I have (and have had for years) of my immediate family and all the friends—and "characters" that surrounded me during my growing up years. Those memories were also reinforced by hours of home movies that my father and mother took—from little one-year-old Tomie all the way up to movies of me and my dancing partner Carol Morrissey, with various family/friend outings and siblings along the way.[13]

The author has made his story every bit as charming and wonderful as he remembers it. The family began building their house at 26 Fairmount Avenue just as the 1938 hurricane hit the town of Meriden, Connecticut. He tells of the funny, but unfortunate experience, of eating chocolates with his grandmother. The chocolates turned out to be chocolate laxatives. He tells of seeing "Mr. Walt Disney's Snow White" and his disappointment when he realized that "Mr. Walt Disney didn't read the story right!"

> . . . when "The End" appeared on the screen, boy, was I mad! I couldn't help it. I stood up and hollered, "The story's not over yet. Where's the wedding? Where're the red hot iron shoes that they put on the Evil Queen so she dances herself to death?"[14]

However, Tomie's biggest challenge of the year was going to kindergarten. He insisted that his mother let him go by himself. Of course, she watched him the entire way. When he arrived at the school, he walked in the wrong door. When a woman asked him who he was, he told her and asked, "Who are you?" It was an unfortunate beginning because she was the principal. This was the first day of many that he spent with her over the next seven years!

When Tomie finally arrived at the kindergarten room, it was filled "with kids crying and hanging onto their mothers." This was another bad omen, but the worst was yet to come. He asked the teacher, "When do we learn how to read?" She replied,

> "Oh, we don't learn how to read in kindergarten. We learn to read next year, in first grade."
> "Fine," I said. "I'll be back next year." And I walked right out of the school and all the way home.[15]

This is the first in Tomie de Paola's series of easy-to-read autobiographies.

Quang Nhuong Huynh wrote about his life, a very different life from de Paola's. He basically writes memoirs rather than a full-fledged autobiography, because he merely touches upon a few experiences in his life. He grew up in the highlands of Vietnam before the Vietnam conflict and wrote about his adventures in *The Land I Lost* and its companion volume, *Water Buffalo Days: Growing Up in Vietnam.* His tales of encounters with wild animals are amusing, and sometimes terrifying. One time, Mr. Huynh was in the fields with his cousin and suddenly realized that a giant horse snake was following him. He was so startled that he couldn't speak. Fortunately, his cousin had stopped in the path to pick up a fish and Huynh stumbled over him.

> Surprised at my unusual clumsiness, he looked back and saw the horse snake behind me. He was terrified too, but instinctively he swung his knife and struck the snake in the head. We dropped everything and ran home as fast as we could, more frightened than ever by the great noise the snake made behind us.[16]

In *Where the Flame Trees Bloom* by Alma Flor Ada, the author tells eleven stories about her experiences growing up in rural Cuba. Through these memoirs, she gives insight into a way of life that most youngsters in the United States are unfamiliar with, but she also enlivens her tales with wonderful characters, all members of her family.

Collective Biographies

Collective biographies are filled with stories about different people. The subjects collected in one book are linked by something: possibly themes, character traits, or occupations. Each person is featured in a paragraph, a page, a few pages, or a chapter. This format is ideal for those students looking for a few important facts on a subject.

As with all other nonfiction books, readers need to look carefully at the authority for the book, making sure that the information is factual. Kathleen Krull did a wonderful Lives series. In *Lives of the Artists: Masterpieces, Messes and What the Neighbors Thought* we can once again visit with Leonardo da Vinci and Michelangelo Buonarroti in the first two chapters. Diane Stanley took forty-eight pages to tell her readers about each of the two famous artists; Kathleen Krull tells about each of them in five pages. Naturally the reader doesn't get the wealth of detail in the Krull book. However, after reading the five pages, you do understand the important facts about each life and the basic personalities of each genius.

There are collections about sports figures, musicians, presidents, race car drivers, spies, persons of courage, gunfighters of the Old West, inventors, and numerous others.

Picture-book Biographies

More and more picture-book biographies are making their way into libraries and bookstores and, eventually, into young hands. When we choose pieces of literature from this vast selection, we need to keep in mind the standards we have set for choosing picture books and the standards we set for biographies. Because of space constraints, the biographical information in picture books is fairly slight. The illustrations give depth to the story.

The well-known biographer, James Cross Giblin, writes,

Whatever the reasons . . . picture-book biographies are obviously here to stay. This makes it even more imperative for authors to master the technique of compressing vast amounts of complicated material into no more than 10 or 12 manuscript pages. For example, Benjamin Franklin's autobiography takes more than seven pages to cover his surreptitious departure from Boston at the age of seventeen, and his journey first to New York and then to Philadelphia in search of work as a printer. In my picture-book biography, *The Amazing Life of Benjamin Franklin,* I had to condense these decisive events into just three short paragraphs, while at the same time attempting to retain the spirit and flavor of Franklin's original.[17]

A stunning example of a picture-book biography is Kathryn Lasky's *Vision of Beauty: The Story of Sarah Breedlove Walker*. Madame C. J. Walker was born in 1867 to former slaves, but was orphaned at an early age. She was an entrepreneur at a time when African Americans were denied many basic freedoms, and women of all colors were unable to vote or own property. The illustrations and text combine to give a mesmerizing account of why she first became interested in, and later developed, hair care products. The book also tells how she tried to lend her strength to other African American women in their struggle to survive and prosper.

Duke Ellington: The Piano Prince and his Orchestra, written and illustrated by Andrea and Brian Pinkney, was named a Caldecott Honor book in 1999. Brian Pinkney adds a feeling of energy and rhythm with his scratchboard paintings that are full of curlycues and swirls of color to give a sense of the music. The Pinkneys conceived the book because of Brian's love of jazz, and the fact that the Duke's music has often been described as painting. They carefully researched their subject in the Carnegie Hall Archives and the Museum of the City of New York and they give the reader a nice bibliography at the end, so the reader can learn more about one of the greatest composers of the twentieth century.

David Adler has written numerous picture-book biographies about people from different walks of life. He lives in New York and is an avid Yankees fan. For him, writing *Lou Gehrig: The Luckiest Man*, was a labor of love. In the attractive book, Mr. Adler gives an overview of the fine first baseman who lived his life with remarkable dignity and courage. Gehrig never missed a day of school, and during fourteen years of playing for the New York Yankees, he never missed a single baseball game, earning himself the nickname of Iron Horse. The New York fans, who cheered wildly whenever he came on the field, adored Lou Gehrig. Even though on his thirty-sixth birthday he was diagnosed with a deadly disease that affected the central nervous system, Lou Gehrig thought of himself as the" luckiest man on the face of the earth."[18] Facing his greatest challenge, he continued to display grace and humility.

Teaching Strategies

Children need to connect with the figures of history. They need to be given a background within which to understand the subjects they are reading about. After providing opportunities for students to understand the historical context within which the biographical subjects have lived, teachers need to encourage the students to interact with the information. Following is a way to do this.

Students can:

1. dress up as their subjects and tell a bit about them before the class in a live presentation or on videotape.
2. make biography cubes to share their information about their subjects. This involves a cubed box, made from a paper model. On each side of the cube an important fact about the subject is written or illustrated.
3. make biography posters. On them, they can draw a picture of their subject and state some significant information such as size, hair and eye color.
4. make a chain. In each piece of the chain, a significant event in the subject's life is linked to the one that occurs before it.
5. make ladders for accomplishments for their subjects. They make rungs in a ladder and write the person's accomplishment on each rung of the ladder.
6. make a cluster of characteristics. The subject's name is the center of the cluster and characteristics that describe the person surround the name.

Who Am I?: An Expedition

Guiding Questions

1. What do I know about myself?
2. What are some of the challenges that I have faced in my life?
3. What do I consider my successes?
4. What are some of my failures?
5. What are biographies?
6. What are autobiographies?
7. How can I find heroes and role models through literature?

Standards

These standards have been derived from the National Council on Social Studies (NCSS), The American Association for the Advancement of Science (AAAS), and The National Council of Teachers of English/ International Reading Association (NCTE/IRA).

The students:

1. analyze group and institutional influences on people, events, and elements of culture in both historical and contemporary settings.
2. apply an understanding of culture as an integrated whole that explains the functions and interactions of language, literature, the arts, traditions, beliefs and values, and behavior patterns.[19]
3. think about what caused a situation and then consider whether to seek out or avoid similar situations.
4. understand that communicating the different points of view in a dispute can often help people to find a satisfactory compromise.[20]
5. adjust their use of spoken, written, and visual language (e.g., conventions, style, vocabulary) to communicate effectively with a variety of audiences and for different purposes.[21]

Initial Reading Options for Teacher Read-Aloud, Shared, Guided, or Independent Reading

1. *Shoeless Joe & Me: A Baseball Card Adventure* by Dan Gutman (chapter book—upper elementary)
2. *Langston Hughes, American Poet* by Alice Walker (picture book—middle elementary)
3. *Joan of Arc* by Diane Stanley (picture book—middle elementary)
4. *Starry Messenger: A Book Depicting the Life of a Famous Scientist, Mathematician, Astronomer, Philosopher, Physicist: Galileo Galilei* by Peter Sis (picture book—middle elementary)
5. *Story Painter: The Life of Jacob Lawrence* by John Duggleby (picture book—upper elementary)
6. *My Life in Dog Years* by Gary Paulsen (chapter book—upper elementary)

7. *The Life and Death of Crazy Horse* by Russell Freedman (photographic essay—upper elementary and middle school)
8. *Under My Nose* by Lois Ehlert (picture book—middle elementary)
9. *Small Steps: The Year I Got Polio* by Peg Kehret (chapter book—upper elementary)

Fieldwork Options

1. Take the Myers-Briggs Personality Inventory online at http://www.personalitytype.com/quiz.html.
2. Assess your own personality with preferences and styles.
3. Identify a living hero—someone you would like to emulate— and research that person's life.
4. Write a letter to solicit additional information on your hero.

Individual Projects

1. Read one fiction and one nonfiction book about your selected "hero" or role model.
2. Examine health issues for the studied character, if appropriate.
3. Create a Venn diagram to compare the literary and informational texts.
4. Dress up as subject of biography and tell about the person.
5. Write your autobiography and bind it into a book for display.

Class Projects

1. Role Model Day when everyone dresses and acts according to research on that person's life.
2. An information display (shoe box diorama, trifold display board) should be prepared for each character in this study.
3. Recognition Day for each person's display of autobiography.

Sharing Outlets

1. School library may be used for Recognition Day with a section designated for autobiographies to be displayed.
2. Role Model Day event may be held in school cafeteria during lunch break so larger groups of other classes may hear and see the characters.

3. Bulletin board may be designated for posting of responses to letters for additional information or personal contacts with the heroes and role models.

Assessment Options

1. Checklist for participation.
2. Rubric for Venn Diagram.
3. Rubric with evaluation criteria for autobiography.
4. Evaluation criteria for the character (hero, role model) study project.

Notes

1. http://www.elob.org/aboutel/principles.html.

2. Jack Gantos, *Joey Pigza Swallowed the Key* (New York: Farrar, Straus & Giroux, 1998), i.

3. Eve Bunting, *Gleam and Glow* (San Diego: Harcourt, 2001), 27.

4. http://www.cbcbooks.org/html/jeanfritz.html.

5. Jean Fritz, *And Then What Happened, Paul Revere?* (New York: Coward, 1973), 5.

6. Ibid., 5.

7. Diane Stanley, *Leonardo Da Vinci* (New York: HarperCollins, 1996), 31.

8. Diane Stanley, *Michelangelo* (New York: HarperCollins, 2000), 20.

9. Jean Fritz, *Homesick: My Own Story* (New York: Dell, 1982), i.

10. Robert Burleigh, *Lookin' for Bird in the Big City* (San Diego: Harcourt, 2001), v.

11. Alan Schroeder, *Minty, A Story of Young Harriet Tubman* (New York: Dial, 1996).

12. http://www.scholastic.com/dearamerica/books/timeline/index.htm.

13. Tomie de Paola, *26 Fairmount Avenue* (New York: Putnam, 1999), 58.

14. Ibid., 23.

15. Ibid., 35.

16. Quang Nhuong Huynh, *The Land I Lost: Adventures of a Boy in Vietnam* (New York: HarperCollins, 1982), 91.

17. James Cross Giblin, "Biography for the 21st Century," *School Library Journal* (February 2002): 45.

18. David Adler, *Lou Gehrig: The Luckiest Man* (New York: Gulliver, 1997), 32.

19. http://www.ncss.org/standards/teachers/vol1/individuals.shtml

20. http://www.sciencenetlinks.com/benchmark_index.htm

21. www.ncte.org

Chapter 8

Learning to Grow Together: Collaboration and Competition

Bellini stepped out onto the wire and saluted the crowd. He took a step and then froze. The crowd cheered wildly. But something was wrong. Mirette knew at once what it was. For a moment she was as frozen as Bellini was.

Then she threw herself at the door behind her, ran inside, up flight after flight of stairs, and out through a skylight to the roof.

She stretched her hands to Bellini. He smiled and began to walk toward her. She stepped onto the wire, and with the most intense pleasure, as she had always imagined it might be, she started to cross the sky.

—Emily Arnold McCully, *Mirette on the High Wire*, 1992

The design principle from Expeditionary Learning that is targeted in this chapter is "Collaboration and Competition."

Teach so as to join individual and group development so that the value of friendship, trust, and group endeavor is made manifest. Encourage students to compete, not against each other, but with their own personal best and with rigorous standards of excellence.[1]

Growing with Picture Books

"Picture books! Those things. They're for babies!" said a kindergartener as he yanked out one book after another, looking for the perfect book to borrow from the school library.

"Why do you say that?" asked the media specialist.

"Well, because babies need all those pictures; I just want real words 'cause I can read."

This isn't an unusual response from the little guys, the youngest of the crowd of elementary schoolchildren. The smart teacher and media specialist will encourage him and others like him to choose exactly what they want. Eventually, through the tutelage of savvy teachers, those children will realize that picture books are truly for everybody.

Barbara Kiefer maintains, "In the best picture books, the illustrations extend and enhance the written text, providing the reader with an aesthetic experience that is more than the sum of the book's parts."[2]

The History of Picture Books

Picture books as we know them are fairly new phenomena. Most historians consider the first picture book for children to have been Johann Amos Comenius's *Orbis Pictus* (*The World in Pictures*) published in 1658. Comenius, a forward-looking educator from what is now the Republic of Slovakia, wanted children to become knowledgeable about nature. His purpose was to educate, but he added pictures to increase enjoyment. During the eighteenth century, John Newbery, an enterprising British bookseller, published *A Little Pretty Pocket Book.* Instead of using just any old woodcuts as others did before him, he actually tried to line up interesting and attractive illustrations that would complement the text. During the nineteenth century three remarkable English illustrators provided the children's book world with a standard for excellence in illustrations for picture books.

Walter Crane, illustrator of *The House That Jack Built,* was greatly influenced by Japanese color prints and much of his work reflects this. His toy books are credited with marking the beginning of a new era in color illustrations.[3] Kate Greenaway's drawings of happy children in the English countryside were a result of the somewhat sentimental idea of childhood expressed in the Victorian era. Her exquisite paintings overflowed with flowers, gardens and "precious" children. Today there is a Kate Greenaway award, sponsored by the British Library Association, given to the illustrator of the most distinguished work in illustration in a children's book first published in the United Kingdom during the preceding year.

Randolph Caldecott was the third British illustrator who had enormous influence on the future path of picture books. He was a careful observer of Walter Crane's work and believed completely in having his illustrations complement and enhance the text of the book. Even today readers enjoy his humorous and vital illustrations. The Caldecott Medal, sponsored by the Association for Library Service Division of the American Library Association, is named for Randolph Caldecott and is given to the illustrator of the most distinguished picture book for children published during the preceding year. Embossed on the medal is a picture from Caldecott's *The History of John Gilpin.* It shows Gilpin galloping through an English village. As the twentieth century rolled around, we began to see more picture books specifically made to entertain children. The market for the didactic moral treatise was dying, and people were beginning to see children as something different from little adults. Beatrix Potter wrote her warm stories about her neighborhood animals for herself, but they are still well loved. Her exquisite miniature paintings fit nicely into the size of her books, which she insisted should fit easily into children's hands.

By the 1930s the American picture book was no longer a phenomenon. The first hardcover edition of Wanda Gág's *Millions of Cats* was published in September 1928. We have entertained hundreds of children with this book over the past thirty years of our teaching careers. Truly it has stood the test of time, still popular after seventy-five years. Why is that? It's illustrated in black and white. No color. However,

> Gág was the first to take art beyond conventional illustrations: Her pictures helped to tell the story by using negative space to indicate the passage of time, varied page layouts, and illustrations that broke out of their frames to extend across two pages. These innovations were immediately imitated and refined by other artists creating books for young children, and very soon they were considered conventions of the art itself.[4]

After Gág opened the door, the art of making picture books began to flourish. Dr. Seuss's first book, *And to Think That I Saw It on Mulberry Street,* was published in the 1930s. Margaret Wise Brown entered the scene and gave us the beloved *Good Night Moon* and *The Runaway Bunny,* both illustrated by Clement Hurd. Robert McCloskey joined the arena with *Make Way for Ducklings* and *Blueberries for Sal* along with many others. Lynd Ward wrote and illustrated *The Biggest Bear,* and Robert Lawson wrote *The Story of Ferdinand,* which was illustrated by Munro Leaf. All of these picture books continue to be read and enjoyed by youngsters today.

During the years before the 1980s, illustrating in color imposed an arduous task on picture-book artists. Artists could work with up to four colors, depending on the publisher's budget. If more than just black and white, artists would have to separate the colors by hand. They'd prepare all the parts of the illustration that used black first. This was the keyplate. Then they'd have to paint the other colors in the appropriate places—a separate sheet for each color. The sheets, called overlays, were then placed on top of each other to make the finished product. The process was not easy and often the illustrator finished before the product was finished!

Changes in technology in the 1980s made color illustrations much easier. Thanks to computers, high-speed presses, and scanners, the beauty of the illustrations dazzles readers of picture books. We still feel warmly about those earlier classics, however.[5]

What are Picture Books?

Picture books include all books in which the illustrations are essential to the book. A picture book can include baby books, interactive books, toy books, alphabet books, counting books, concept books, wordless books, and informational books in which illustrations accompany the expository text, and picture storybooks. Usually when we refer to picture books, we are referring to picture storybooks in which the narration is found in both the text and the illustrations. For these to be effective, the two parts need to blend effortlessly. The text must incorporate the elements that make a good story: compelling plot, believable characters, appropriate setting and theme.

In most picture books, the pictures stay close to the text. For example in a favorite Margaret Wise Brown picture book, *The Runaway Bunny,* Clement Hurd's very first illustration shows baby bunny running, and the text below the picture proclaims, "Once there was a little bunny who wanted to run away. So he said to his mother, 'I am running away.'" Mother Bunny responds that if he runs away, she will run after him "For you are my little bunny."[6] Page after page alternating between the ways little bunny will run away and how his mother will catch him fill this tender story of mutual love. The illustrations faithfully follow the text.

However, in other picture books, pictures and text deviate markedly, still creating a unified whole, but demanding that the readers follow the narration in the pictures as well as in the text. In *Officer Buckle and Gloria,* for example, the hilarity would be missed if the readers were not reading the illustrations. Gloria, that clever dog, dupes Officer Buckle into believing that he has the rapt attention of his audiences as he provides safety tips. Officer Buckle admonishes the audience,

"'NEVER leave a THUMBTACK where you might SIT on it!' The audience roared. Officer Buckle grinned. He said the rest of the tips with *plenty* of expression."[7]

Behind his back, Gloria was performing antics that illustrated each of his tips. Readers can see what's happening all the time, but Officer Buckle only realizes it when he sees himself on the ten o'clock news on TV. The text never let's this cat (or dog!) out of the bag. Officer Buckle is certain that Gloria is collaborating with him and she thinks she is also. But readers see that she's really competing with her policeman friend. Eventually, they learn what collaboration really means.

Picture books display the artistry and craftsmanship unique in the field of literature. In the best picture books, illustrations need to be true to the plot, whether following along in lockstep fashion or embellishing the tale. They need to set the mood of the story and help delineate the characters. To do this successfully, illustrators of children's picture books have to be gifted artists with a true understanding of how the author envisioned the story.

Picture books are usually thirty-two pages and include about two thousand words or fewer than sixty words per page. Picture books for younger readers can be twenty-four pages, and occasionally picture books will be as long as sixty-four pages. Even in the longer picture books, the author's number of words is limited. Therefore, the pictures need to provide much of the excitement.

When readers look at illustrations in picture books, they usually "just know" if they like them or not. Let's discover some of the reasons that make the pictures "likeable."

Artistic Media

The artistic medium is quite simply the material used to make the illustration. Illustrators use a variety of media to create their images for picture books. Using a tool, they apply medium directly to canvas, paper, or whatever surface they are using. Blocks or plates that are inked and then imprinted on paper produce a variety of graphic techniques.

Trying to identify the medium used in children's picture books is often like solving a puzzle—it's frustrating but when you hit upon the answer, it enriches the entire experience of the book. While you are on the hunt for the answer, be sure to look at the dust jacket, the introductory material, and definitely look at the verso, which is the back of the title page. The answer is often found in one of those places. Following

are some brief definitions of media with examples of picture books in
which each has been used.

Painting

Paint comes from pigments, which are powdered colors that come
from a variety of natural elements: rocks, earth, plants, insects, fruit,
and shellfish. The pigment is then ground into a fine powder and mixed
with liquid such as oil or water.[8]
Watercolor is probably the most popular of the paints. Water is
used to apply the paint, and the effect ranges from translucent to
opaque, depending on the amount of water mixed with the paint. It provides a wide range of expression. Helme Heine's *Pig's Wedding* is a
wonderfully humorous example of very translucent watercolor paintings. Jerry Pinkney combines watercolors with pencil in his work, such
as *Sam and the Tigers* and *John Henry*. Kevin Henkes's winsome characters, Owen, Chrysanthemum, Lily, and Sheila the Brave, all take
amusing shape through Henkes's skillful use of watercolor and black
pen. Some extraordinarily rich examples of the use of watercolors can
be found in many of Ted Rand's works, such as *Barn Dance,* John
Steptoe's gorgeous illustrations in *Mufaro's Beautiful Daughters*, and
John Schoenherr's paintings for Jane Yolen's *Owl Moon*. Barry Moser
is another illustrator who does remarkable paintings with watercolor in
his warm and funny stories about his dog, Rosie, and his granddaugh-
ters. Now he's introduced us to a new dog, Truman, in *Sit, Truman* by
Dan Harper.
Gouache is an opaque watercolor in which the pigment is thick-
ened by white chalk. Lloyd Moss used it for his illustrations in *Zin!
Zin! Zin! A Violin* by Marjorie Priceman. Sharleen Collicott used it in
Judi Barrett's *Which Witch is Which?* Vera Williams used this medium
for her *"More More More," Said the Baby.* Not only did she do the
paintings in gouache, but she managed to do the lettering within the
paintings in gouache as well. Several illustrators mix gouache with
other media. Paul Meisel used gouache and watercolors in Anne Rockwell's *Morgan Plays Soccer*. Paul Goble combines his usual pencil,
India ink, and watercolor illustrations with gouache in his 2001 *Storm
Maker's Tipi*.
Acrylics are synthetic polymer or plastic paints with a water base.
They can be used either transparently or opaquely. They've only been
around for fifty or sixty years, and painters are just beginning to use
them instead of oils because they are so much more durable than oils.
They are water soluble, so there are no health hazards involved with

paint thinner. It's difficult even for the most experienced person to tell whether someone has painted with oil or acrylic paints. Acrylics cover with lush, brilliant colors. Their flexibility is their most important characteristic. Often, as in oils, you can see the brush strokes. Leo and Diane Dillon have given readers a visual feast in Virginia Hamilton's *The Girl Who Spun Gold.* The illustrations are done with acrylics and overpainted with gold paint. Borders around the illustrations are created using gold leaf. Reynold Ruffins's handsome acrylic illustrations accompany Judy Sierra's Indonesian version of the Cinderella story, *The Gift of the Crocodile.* James Ransome works in both oils and acrylics. His vibrant acrylic illustrations in Eve Bunting's *Peepers* make the reader feel a part of the brilliant fall scene, peeping at the changing leaves. In Eve Bunting's *Smoky Night,* David Diaz uses acrylics to paint strong, evocative images showing the powerful emotions characters are experiencing. Acrylics are also used by Lynn Curlee to accompany the grand visual history of the Brooklyn Bridge in *Brooklyn Bridge.* Barbara Cooney uses acrylics to paint her lovely pictures in *Miss Rumphius* and she adds accents with colored pencils.

Oil paint has linseed oil as a base, instead of water. Oils have been around for centuries and carry with them a certain prestige. They are extremely forgiving and the painter can fool with the painting, making changes, even up to three weeks before the paint dries. The problem with oil paintings is that they need maintenance and crack and chip over time. As a result many illustrators are moving to acrylics. However, Caldecott medal winner Paul O. Zelinsky has done a great deal of work in oil. He retold and illustrated both *Rapunzel* and *Rumpelstiltskin* and for Anne Isaacs's *Swamp Angel,* he surprised the book world by painting with his oils on maple, cherry, and birch veneers. Thomas Locker's illustrations in children's books have become well known as fine examples of oil paintings. Joe Cepeda has worked with a number of authors and uses oil paints—*Daring Dog and Captain Cat* by Arnold Adoff, and the controversial *Nappy Hair* by Carolivia Herron, to name two. His lively illustrations for Marisa Montes's *Juan Bobo Goes to Work* clearly portray that foolish and lucky popular Puerto Rican folktale hero.

Drawing

Pastels and charcoals can be used in stick or pencil form. They are made of dry powdered pigments mixed into a paste with a water-soluble binding medium. The paste is then formed into sticks and dried. (The name "pastel" comes from this paste.) Charcoal and pastel sticks are suitable for broad strokes, for painting large areas and they are applied with fingers. For more finely detailed drawings, charcoal and pastels can be compressed and coated with either wood or rolled paper to form pencils. These are called contè or pastel pencils. Chris Van Allsburg uses pastels in the *Wreck of the Zephyr* and *The Polar Express.* In *Sister Anne's Hands* by Marybeth Lorbiecki, Wendy Popp and K. Wendy Popp draw incredibly moving portraits of Sister Anne and her young charges using pastels. The exquisite pastel drawings in Jim LeMarche's *The Raft* make it possible for the reader to drift down the river with Nicky.

Ed Young is another artist who enjoys using pastels, often in combination with watercolors. In *Lon Po Po,* the Chinese Little Red Riding Hood story, Young deftly shows the terror of the children as they deal with the wolf. You will also find good examples of pastel illustrations in *The New Baby* by Robert Harris, illustrated by Michael Emberley and *Subira, Subira* written by Tolowa M. Mollel and illustrated by Linda Saport.

Finally, if you want an all-out hearty laugh, take a look at the Olivia books written by Ian Falconer. They are a combination of charcoal and gouache paintings. Pastel pencils are used by Stephen Gammell in *Song and Dance Man* by Karen Ackerman and by Thomas B. Allen in Louise Borden's, *Good-bye, Charles Lindbergh.* Gammell's pencil work shows the exuberance of the grandfather and the soft colors exude warmth. Mr. Allen's illustrations, although using the same colors, are more serious and misty. Chris Van Allsburg used a contè pencil for *Jumanji* and *The Garden of Abdul Gasazi.* Lynne Cherry used colored pencils and watercolors in many of her books: *The Shaman's Apprentice, River Ran Wild,* and *The Great Kapok Tree.* Patricia Polacco used pencils and acetone markers to illustrate her moving story, *The Keeping Quilt.*

Crayons are used infrequently in picture books. Wax crayons are water resistant, light resistant, and nontoxic. John Burmingham shows us an older example in *Come Away from the Water, Shirley.*

Graphic Techniques

Woodcuts were the earliest technique of printmaking. They were first used in China in the ninth century and arose in Europe around 1400. They were mainly used as stamps for fabrics, but by 1600 they were looked upon as an important art form. After sketching the picture on a block of wood, the artist uses gouging tools to carve away pieces of the wood. The raised portion of the wood is inked and then a paper is pressed upon the wood. The raised areas on the block of wood are printed on the paper. If more than one color is used, separate blocks are used for each color. Ed Emberley's woodcuts for *Drummer Hoff*, retold by Barbara Emberley, are fine examples of woodcuts. The "boom" at the end is full of flashing color. Jacqueline Martin's recent Caldecott Medal winner, *Snowflake Bentley*, illustrated by Mary Azarian, is a fine example of woodcuts.

Scratchboard is a technique in which the artist first paints a heavy, black ink over a smooth, white surface of a board (called a "scratchboard") and then scratches the design onto the surface with a sharp instrument. Color can be added by applying it to the white surface before the black ink is painted on, or the color can be applied afterwards. Good examples of the technique are *Lucy's Summer* by Donald Hall, illustrated by Michael McCurdy, and Brian Pinkney's illustrations in most of his work, including *The Faithful Friend* and *Mim's Christmas Jam*.

Photography

Tana Hoban's photographs hang in the Museum of Modern Art in New York and in galleries around the world. We are very fortunate that she has chosen to use her talents in the realm of children's literature for the very young. With full-color and black-and-white photographs in books such as *Count and See, So Many Circles, So Many Squares*, and *Is it Red? Is it Yellow? Is it Blue?* Hoban challenges children to stretch their minds and notice that wherever you are there are exciting things to discover.

Sandra Markle has joined several other children's authors of nonfiction books who use gorgeous photography to make science discovery accessible and fun for kids. Her *Outside and Inside* series gives intriguing looks at a variety of creatures, including bats, alligators, dinosaurs, sharks, snakes, and spiders—all animals that inspire curiosity in kids.

Composite Techniques

The following techniques all involve some sort of assembling of materials and placing them on paper.

Collage is a technique that involves cutting and pasting materials to create a picture or a part of the picture. Master children's illustrators such as Leo Lionni, Ezra Jack Keats, and Molly Bang have used it for some time. A favorite of children is Keats's *Jennie's Hat*, in which a little girl desperately wants a fancy hat and receives, instead, a plain straw hat with a little bow. She sees hats everywhere—all sumptuously made (in the illustrations) by extravagant wallpapers. She ends up with a magnificent hat that is topped with a bird's nest and includes baby birds—all made from cutout wallpaper. David Diaz startled the children's book world with his collage images of the Los Angeles riots in *Smoky Night.* Materials for the collages included pieces of cellophane, newspaper, and breakfast cereal.

Fabric art can be seen at its best in Margaret N. Hurst's *Grannie and the Jumbie,* a Caribbean tale. Hurst writes the following about the art in her book,

> I like to think of all cloth as "story fabric."
> Some pieces are older and already have a story. Other pieces are new, waiting to create stories. Most of the fabrics I have used are from St. Thomas. Some of the older pieces saved from dresses I remember my mom wearing; some from dresses that she made.
> . . . The new fabrics I used are now sewn together with the older pieces to create yet another new story.[9]

Cut paper is used brilliantly by David Wisniewski. He cuts layers of colored paper with an X-Acto knife to create his pictures. He will use nearly one thousand blades for each book. *Golem,* the legend of a giant who is molded from clay by a sixteenth-century rabbi, earned Wisniewski the Caldecott Medal in 1997. Beni Montresor uses sharp-edged paper-cutout silhouettes of the children in his 2001 version of *Hansel and Gretel.* Amy Walrod illustrates her *How Hungry are You?* with large cut-paper illustrations that will captivate her readers.

Computer graphics have become a technique of some illustrators. Audrey Wood was one of the first to use this technique when she illustrated *The Red Racer* in the mid-1990s. She allows readers a glimpse of the way she did it in a very frank author's note. Her son challenged her and, in one night, she completed the illustrations for the book. A note for the 2001 *Lookin' for Bird in the Big City* by Robert Burleigh and illustrated by Marek Los reads: "The illustrations in this book were done in pencil, oil paint, and watercolor and were scanned and finished in Photoshop and Painter on Macintosh 7100."[10] It looks like children's book art is "going digital" as is everything else. In Janie Bynum's *Altoona Up North,* the third story about Altoona Baboona, a paragraph states "The illustrations in this book were done in digital pen-and-ink and watercolor."[11]

Mixed Media

Many illustrators use a variety of media in their illustrations as we've already seen. Jerry Pinkney uses pencil and watercolor in most of his work. The most common format of mixed media is a pen-and-ink drawing with color painted over it. Joan Cottle uses watercolor, colored pencil, and ink in *Miles Away from Home,* and Leslie Tryon uses pen and ink with watercolor in Alma Flor Ada's *With Love, Little Red Hen.* However, recently illustrators are often combining a number of other media for their mixed media illustrations as well. Stephen Gammell uses colored pencils often, and in Jim Aylesworth's *The Burger and the Hot Dog,* he uses colored pencils, watercolors, pastels, crayons, and even coffee for his illustrations. Gerald McDermott uses gouache, colored pencil, and colored ink for his dazzling illustrations in the 2001 trickster tale from the Amazon, *Jabuti the Tortoise.* Heather Solomon combines watercolors, collage, acrylics, and oils for Margaret Willey's tall tale, *Clever Beatrice,* a tale from Michigan's Upper Peninsula that tells about a very clever little girl who outsmarts a giant. In *Ashanti to Zulu,* Leo and Diane Dillon used pastels, watercolors, and acrylics. Victoria Chess uses a combination of acrylics, watercolor, pastels, and colored pencil in *Teeny Tiny Tingly Tales* written by Nancy Van Laan, and Glin Dibley used acrylics and colored pencils in Margie Palatini's *Tub-Boo-Boo.*

Artistic Styles

Another dimension of children's literature lies in the various artistic styles used to complement the story or information. As was true with artistic media, the perfect match between style and content usually signals an outstanding book.

Styles used most frequently in children's books are: realism, impressionism, expressionism, and surrealism.

Realism is artwork that represents life as it really is. Artists who use this style are faithful to the nuances of life. Some illustrators try to be absolutely true to detail and their illustrations are almost photographic. *Alphabet City* by Stephen T. Johnson was a Caldecott Honor book in 1996. Readers express amazement when they realize that Mr. Johnson painted the pictures in the book; he did not photograph them. Alan Say's illustrations for *Grandfather's Journey,* and James Ransome's paintings for *The Wagon,* are other examples of nearly photographic reality. Judith Viorst's black-and-white drawings for *Alexander* *and the Terrible, Horrible, No Good, Very Bad Day* are clear and precise. No mother could question the reality of these illustrations.

Impressionism originated as a term of abuse. It was applied to an exhibit that appeared to have paintings that were sketchy and unfinished. Masters, such as Edgar Degas, Claude Monet, August Renoir, and Camille Pissaro rebelled against the realistic style. They were trying to use the effects of light and dark in their paintings and paint from nature. Impressionism is artwork that captures fleeting looks at nature and objects. It prioritizes light, movement, and color over the definition of detail. In other words, the artist captures the image of an object as someone would see it if they just caught a glimpse of it. Maurice Sendak's illustrations for the charming *Mr. Rabbit and the Lovely Present* are a classic example of Impressionism. Another example is *Where the Buffalos Begin* by Olaf Baker, illustrated by Stephen Gammell. Not many illustrators of children's books use this style exclusively in their books. You'll find bits of it in many books.

Expressionism in its broadest sense is a style that promotes distorted shapes and brilliant colors and uses those characteristics to elicit an emotional response from the reader. Expressionism was a movement that developed simultaneously in several northern European countries at the beginning of the twentieth century. Expressionist paintings attempt to reflect the artist's mind rather than the reality of the outside world. Chris Raschka's *Yo! Yes?* is an extreme example of the style as it's used in a children's picture book. There are actually several other styles that fit under expressionism: cartoon art, folk art, abstract, and cubism. Betsy Everitt's *Mean Soup* is another superb example of an artist giving free expression to her feelings.

Cartoon art is full of wiggly, squiggly characters that urge readers to laugh. It is art which is characterized by bright, bold strokes, movement, and humor. James Marshall's illustrations in his folktale retellings are excellent examples. Comic characters enrich the well-loved, tongue-tying tales of Dr. Seuss. And who could ever forget the characters in William Steig's *Sylvester and the Magic Pebble?* James Stevenson is another wonderful example of an artist who delights us with his cartoon characters.

Folk art is art characterized by simplicity and little regard for perspective or real space. It resembles naïve, childlike drawings. There is a simplification of line, color, and space. The illustrations are flat and lack proportion. Barbara Cooney's work in *Ox-Cart Man* is an excellent example of this style. Folk art also represents cultures around the world. You'll find motifs, symbols, and decorative patterns of the specific culture in Tomie dePaola's *The Lady of Guadalupe* and in Gerald McDermott's *Arrow to the Sun.*

Cubism was a movement developed by Picasso and Braque in the early twentieth century. Artists that use this style use geometrical forms, decorative shapes, and bright colors in their work. Lois Ehlert's work is a perfect example of this movement. Look at her illustrations in *Chick Chicka Boom Boom* and *Red Leaf, Yellow Leaf* for examples of geometric shapes, and bright colors. Gerald McDermott's work is also a fine example. Look at his *Arrow to the Sun* and *Raven: A Trickster Tale from the Pacific Northwest.*

Abstract art is typified by a broad show of feelings and emotions, huge gestures, and little direct representation of the object. Betsy Everitt's work in *Mean Soup* and *TV Dinner* provides good examples of a clever artist using an abstract style.

Surrealism is art which skews realism in its attempt to mingle the subconscious with dreamlike qualities of the imagination. *The Grey Lady and the Strawberry Snatcher* by Molly Bang is a wordless picture book that tells the story of an elderly lady who loves strawberries. Unfortunately, the strawberry snatcher also loves strawberries and follows her, trying to snatch the strawberries. The ugly thing looks very peculiar, and his attempts at getting the strawberries are always thwarted. He follows the lady by foot and by skateboard into the swamp where he finds blackberries! *Jumanji* by Chris Van Allsburg is replete with startling images that just could not be—a huge snake wrapped up on the mantel, lions in the living room. Judy and Peter brought their jungle adventure into the house.

Design Elements

If a book is not visually appealing from the moment the reader sees it, it has little chance of being borrowed, purchased, or read. Following are some of the crucial items in making a good-looking picture book.

Cover and dust jacket are the first things seen. In fact, their primary purpose is to call attention to the book. We used to see a gorgeous dust jacket covering a cloth cover that was a single color. Now publishers often copy the illustration from the dust jacket onto the book cover. Wrap-around covers carry the picture in a continuous way between front and back covers. A good example of this is the cover for *Hush! A Thai Lullaby.* If a teacher or librarian reads the book aloud with the cover facing the audience, they will see a double-page spread focusing on a mother holding her sleeping baby. Behind the mother and baby is a cat sprawled on its back, lying off the bamboo mat and close to large pots. Lots to look at and think about there.

Endpapers are often a glorious expression of illustrators' talents. The endpapers comprise the first and last page of the book, and the other half of the paper in the front and the back is glued to the cover of the book. The paper is sometimes stiffer than that used for the other pages of the book. Often the reader will get hints of what's to come in the story from the endpapers, or will be reminded of what has been. Endpapers usually harmonize with the colors used in the cover and throughout the book. They provide foreshadowing and an invitation for reading pleasure.

In Jamie Lee Curtis's delightful, *Tell Me Again About the Night I was Born*, Laura Cornell includes cartoons on her endpapers, which indicate that the reader is in for a rollicking good time! The front endpapers have cartoons of a funny baby and dime-store photos of the mom; the back endpapers have pictures of the same baby and strip photos from a booth in a dime store of the dad. The scene was set and the story completed—perfectly, I might add. The endpapers in Jerry Pinkney's *The Ugly Duckling* are certainly significant. The ugly one is trailing behind Mama and her ducklings and a showboating father in the front endpapers. The back endpapers are devoted to a magnificently beautiful swan.

Front Matter follows the endpapers. These are the pages of the book that lie between the front endpapers and the first pages of the text. Often they prepare the reader for what is to come. The title page can be simply a page of text or it can be an illustrated scene that relates to the story that follows. In Judy Sierra's *Monster Goose*, Jack Davis illustrates the double-spread title page with a twenty-first-century Monster Goose working on her computer under the moon and stars. Readers understand instantly that this is NOT the traditional Mother Goose, especially when the first rhyme finds her typing on her laptop computer.

There Was an Old Lady Who Swallowed a Fly by Simms Taback has a title page that prepares readers for the hungry animals in the old folk song. The cow tells us all about the artwork. John Steptoe has a page before the actual text of the story begins in *Mufaro's Beautiful Daughters*, telling that the story was inspired, "by a folktale collected by G.M. Theal and published in 1895 in his book, *Kaffir Folktales.*"[12]

In the front matter of *Flight*, Robert Burleigh includes a note from Jean Fritz about her feelings as a child in India when she heard about Lindy's daring flight. Petra Mather draws symbols on the beginning pages of Verna Aardema's *Borreguita and the Coyote: A Tale from*

Ayutla, Mexico. There is also a glossary on the page before the beginning of the story.

Back matter is another place for additional information about a picture book. Back matter includes the leaves following the main body of the book and before the endpapers. However, they can often contain the following information: source notes, supplemental information, review or summary of the book, visual glossary, index, extension of reading, or related readings. Back matter can include related material like the recipe for Thunder Cake in the book, *Thunder Cake*, by Patricia Polacco. Sorche Nic Leodares, the reteller of *Always Room for One More*, provides readers with notes about the source story as well as the folk song and its music that inspired the retelling.

In *Mirette on the High Wire* the page after the story shows a little girl looking longingly at a poster advertising Mirette and Bellini in an upcoming show. Is that little girl dreaming of becoming another Mirette? The reader is left wondering. However, the reader is not left wondering in *Click, Clack, Moo: Cows That Type*. The typing cows skillfully manipulate Farmer Brown into giving them electric blankets. The trade-off is that they will give Farmer Brown back his typewriter. They'll send it via duck the next day. It's obvious that the typewriter never arrived at Farmer Brown's doorstep because the last page of the story reads,

> The next morning he got a note:
> Dear Farmer Brown,
> The pond is quite boring.
> We'd like a diving board.
> Sincerely,
> The Ducks
> Click, clack, quack.
> Click, clack, quack.
> Clickety, clack, quack.[13]

Turn the page and you'll see a duck half in the water after diving off the new diving board!

Borders add visual appeal to picture books. They often include additional information as Jan Brett does in her picture books. Ms. Brett's trademark is using detailed borders in her pictures. Within those she can add lots of details, and has said that the borders hold her "overflow of thoughts." David Small uses borders in *The Library*, a book written by his wife, Sarah Stewart. Stewart's librarian, Elizabeth Brown, LOVES to read. Ms. Stewart tells how she "even read while exercising, and standing on her head."[14] Mr. Small shows this by breaking the border surrounding the text with a book. The small illustration of the book the librarian is reading within the outer border shows the Eiffel Tower as Elizabeth Brown sees it—upside down. Vera B. Williams uses borders in *My Mother's Chair*, many of which use the fabric that covers the chair. In Chris Van Allsburg's *Polar Express*, white borders surround the illustrations. This serves to distance the reader from the fantasy. The borders Faith Ringgold uses at the bottom of her illustrations for *Tar Beach* provide an unusual story themselves. Ms. Ringgold is a storyteller, painter, and quiltmaker. As she became more interested in the three crafts, she began using quilts as vehicles for her stories. The *Tar Beach* story quilt is now hanging in the Guggenheim Museum in New York City. The picture book

> . . . shares many elements with Ringgold's story quilt. The text, originally written on fabric strips around the border of the quilt, has been altered slightly for stylistic and textual reasons. Ringgold created entirely new paintings for the book, using acrylic on canvas paper, similar to the canvas fabric she used in the original quilt painting. The page border is reproduced from the original story quilt.[15]

Artistic Elements

Color is the artistic element that most of us react to immediately. When we discuss color, we usually are referring to the hue, the actual name of the color, such as "red." However, the value and the brightness or intensity also needs to be taken into account. Value refers to the lightness or darkness of any color. The value is what frequently projects the mood of the story. When color artwork shows no variation in value, it is described as flat. Colors project feelings. Table 8.1 relates colors to feelings in our culture.

Look at the effect that color has on the entire book in *When Sophie Gets Angry—Really, Really Angry*. Bright deep red and yellow endpapers scream at the readers as they open the book. And Sophie is soon screaming on the inside of the book. "Oh, is Sophie ever angry now!" is the text under a double-page spread of Sophie, wildly looking out. The page is full of brilliant yellow and red. The tiny blue dots for the eyes are even furiously brilliant.[16] As Sophie begins solving her own problem, blues and greens creep in as the predominant colors on the pages. Finally "And Sophie isn't angry anymore,"[17] and the facing page is a calm blue.

Patricia Polacco uses color with extraordinary effect in *The Keeping Quilt.* Throughout the book, she uses a contè pencil—except when she draws any of the fabric that went into the quilt or the quilt itself. Then she uses acetone markers. When Anna arrives in the new world, "The only things she had left of back home Russia were her dress and the babushka she liked to throw up into the air when she was dancing."[18] When her dress became too small, Anna's mother made a quilt from the dress and babushka, Uncle Vladimir's shirt, Aunt Havalan's nightdress, and an apron of Aunt Natasha's. The neighborhood ladies "cut out animals and flowers from the scraps of clothing." "The border of the quilt was made of Anna's babushka."[19]

Table 8.1. Relationship of Colors to Feelings in Our Culture

Color	Examples of Opposing Feelings	
Orange	Striking. Warm. Fire in the East, religious overtones—Buddhist monk wears orange robes.	Sharp, fire
Blue	Tranquility, feeling of space and height, truth, divinity, spirit. Water, air, and heaven.	Ice, cold
Yellow	Warm, renewal and growth. Spring and summer.	Bright
Green	Rebirth, spring, restfulness, and serenity.	Poison, jealousy, decay
Red	Strongest color, love and passion, can be warm and positive. Royal color for China.	Provocative, angry
Black	Traditional symbol of evil, death, and the unknown.	Sophisticated
White	Good, purity, innocence, cleanliness.	Cold, unemotional
Violet	Royalty.	Enigmatic

Perspective is another convention through which the illustrator can control the response of the reader. Look, for instance, at the clasped hands in Patricia Polacco's *Pink and Say*. The image on the page is simply of two hands, one black and one white. Pink wants to touch the hand that has touched the hand that has touched the hand of Abraham Lincoln—just one more time. As the final note in the story, the image is incredibly moving. No words could have said it better.

Perspective in a story can change as it does in *Polar Express*. Sometimes we feel as though we're going through the tunnels on the train, other times we are looking down upon Santa and his sleigh or upon the elves in the North Pole. We look up at Santa and the boy when Santa is holding the first gift of Christmas, and we look from afar at the boy when he waves good-bye to Santa. On the final page, the reader sees the boy and his sister up close as they prepare to open the package from under the Christmas tree.

In *Flight: The Journey of Charles Lindbergh,* Mike Wimmer takes over the first page of the story and makes it a double-page spread with Charles Lindbergh's legs in the foreground—one is firmly planted on each page. Through his legs, we see his plane, the Spirit of St. Louis, in the distance. Perspectives vary in this story also, but the first pages establish that Charles Lindbergh is in control of this story!

Texture is an effective visual element in picture books. Although the reader cannot, in most instances, feel anything other than a flat surface, there are ways the illustrator can encourage a tactile response communicated through the medium used to create the picture or to receive it. For example, the oils used to create the marvelous rich, thick paintings in Ezra Jack Keats's books about Willie encourage readers to rub their hands over the full-page illustrations. The wood veneer that Paul O. Zelinsky paints his illustrations on for Anne Isaacs's *Swamp Angel* tells us that those pictures feel hard.

Readers will feel the softness of pictures that are made with fabrics. The feeling does not come from their hands, but their minds. Denise Fleming uses cotton and rag fiber beaten to a fine pulp and suspended in water to create her brilliant images in such books as *Count* and *In a Small, Small Pond*. Chemicals and pigments are added to the pulp to make it paint. Then Ms. Fleming builds layer upon layer of this unusual paper technique. The overall tactile feeling is one of roughness.

Competition and Collaboration in Picture Books

Picture books provide a wealth of visual and literary experiences for all children, even for that little guy who wanted a "real book." Teachers of older students will often introduce new units with a picture book. For example, several teachers we know use Polacco's *Pink and Say* to introduce the Civil War with a power that a written text alone cannot provide. Middle and high school teachers have been known to use Van Allsburg's *Mysteries of Harris Burdick* to provide illustrations for writing.

Picture books provide a unique opportunity for students to hone their visual literacy as well as their knowledge of story and of good writing. They also provide wonderful opportunities to discover how characters can collaborate to reach a goal as the sisters do in *Sheila Rae, the Brave,* as John Roebling did with others in *Brooklyn Bridge* by Lynn Curlee, and as Fannie Farmer did when she helped Marcia make the perfect golden cake for her mother.

Competition is also evident in picture books. Just think of Alice in Barbara Cooney's *Miss Rumphius.* As a tiny girl, she told her beloved grandfather that she was going to go to faraway places and live by the sea. He said that was all "very well" but "You must do something to make the world more beautiful." Alice Rumphius grew up, and she did go to faraway places and live by the sea. She thought and thought about the third thing: how to make the world more beautiful. One summer she planted a little garden full of lupines, the flowers she loved best. Miraculously, they began to appear all over and

> "Miss Rumphius had a wonderful idea!"
> . . . She scattered seeds along the highways and down the country lanes. She flung handfuls of them around the schoolhouse and back of the church. She tossed them into hollows and along stone walls.
> . . . The next spring there were lupines everywhere.
> . . . Miss Rumphius had done the third, the most difficult thing of all![20]

Miss Rumphius has set high standards for herself and has met them.

In Patricia Polacco's *Thank you, Mr. Falker,* we see another youngster striving to attain her personal best. Teased and humiliated at her struggle to read, little Trisha tries and tries to do it right. Finally, with the help of Mr. Falker and other adults, she attains her goal.

And then one spring day—had it been three months or four months since they had started?—Mr. Falker put a book in front of her. She'd never seen it before. He picked a paragraph in the middle of a page and pointed at it.

Almost as if it were magic, or as if light poured into her brain, the words and sentences started to take shape on the page as they never had before, "She . . . marched . . . them . . . off . . . to . . . Slowly, she read a sentence. Then another and another. And finally she'd read a paragraph. And she understood the whole thing.[21] "

What a triumph for little Trisha! She has accomplished her personal best.

Be the Best You Can Be: An Expedition

Guiding Questions

1. How can I be the best that I can be?
2. How can I work with others?
3. How can I compete with my own record to be better?
4. How can I collaborate with others to accomplish goals?
5. What can I learn from stories about how characters become their best?
6. What can I learn from stories about how characters help each other?
7. When I look at pictures in books, how can I understand the characters or the stories better?

Standards

The standards for this expedition are from the National Council of Teachers of English/IRA (NCTE/IRA); National Center for History in Schools (NCHS); and American Association for Advancement of Science (AAAS).

The students:

1. read a wide range of literature from many periods in many genres to build an understanding of the many dimensions (e.g., philosophical, ethical, aesthetic) of human experience.
2. develop an understanding of and respect for diversity in language use, patterns, and dialects across cultures, ethnic groups, geographic regions, and social roles.

3. use a variety of technological and information resources (e.g., libraries, databases, computer networks, video) to gather and synthesize information and to create and communicate knowledge.[22]

4. compare the dreams and ideals that people from various groups have sought, some of the problems they encountered in realizing their dreams, and the sources of strength and determination that families drew upon and shared.[23]

5. write instructions that others can follow in carrying out a procedure.

6. make sketches to aid in explaining procedures or ideas.

7. use numerical data in describing and comparing objects and events.[24]

Initial Reading Options for Teacher Read-Alouds, Shared, Guided, or Independent Reading

1. *My Rotten Redheaded Older Brother* by Patricia Polacco (picture storybook—primary)

2. *Fire in the Forest: A Cycle of Growth and Renewal* by Laurence (nonfiction chapter book—middle elementary)

3. *Hatchet* by Gary Paulsen (chapter book—upper elementary)

4. *Brian's Return* by Gary Paulsen (chapter book—upper elementary)

5. *Walk Two Moons* by Sharon Creech (chapter book—upper elementary)

6. *The Wanderer* by Sharon Creech (chapter book—upper elementary)

7. *My Name is Georgia: A Portrait* by Jeanette Winter (picturebook biography—primary)

8. *Martha Graham: A Dancer's Life* by Russell Freedman (chapter-book biography—middle school)

9. *Langston Hughes, American Poet* by Alice Walker (picturebook biography—middle elementary)

Fieldwork Options

1. Conduct Internet searches under the guidance of the teacher or parent to identify information and addresses for figures whom you admire for "being the best."

2. Write letters or e-mails to someone you admire and ask "How did you accomplish your goals?"

3. Collect picture-book biographies and bring them to class for a display on people who are models of excellence.

Individual Projects

1. Collect and read picture-book biographies.
2. Compile a chart for comparing the biographies that includes the following cells for information: name of character, name of book, author, colors used in illustrations, emotions noted in illustrations, events that made character strong, ways traits were shown in illustrations, how character collaborated, how character competed with self.
3. Read a chapter book biography and compare to the picture book.
4. Prepare to dress as a character and give a book talk on a biographical character.
5. Assemble a book about yourself and illustrate it.
6. Make a poster highlighting your outstanding characteristics. Use specific colors to designate emotions or characteristics.
7. Create a collage of the important events in your life.
8. Write a bio poem.

Class Projects

1. Plan and present "Biography Day" to another class or to the school. Each student will dress as a character and present a book talk on that character.
2. Create a bulletin board of the characters studied.
3. Compile a book of one-page biographies of all characters studied and present to the library.
4. Determine a class project, such as cleaning up the beach, and give each person a task.

Sharing Outlets

1. Invite community members to "Biography Day" activities.
2. Write a letter to the local education columnist for the newspaper and invite the columnist's participation in events.
3. Prepare display for library or school entrance sharing materials developed in this study.

Assessment Options

1. Rubrics for biographical book talks and written products.
2. Checklists for participation.
3. Assessment of letters, e-mails and other communications for form and accuracy.

Notes

1. http://www.elob.org/aboutel/principles.html.
2. Charlotte S. Huck, *Children's Literature in the Elementary School*, 7th ed., rev. Barbara Z. Kiefer (New York: McGraw-Hill, 2001), 168.
3. Donna E. Norton, *Through the Eyes of a Child: An Introduction to Children's Literature*, 2d ed. (Columbus, Ohio: Merrill, 1987), 55.
4. Kathleen T. Horning, *From Cover to Cover: Evaluating and Reviewing Children's Books* (New York: HarperCollins, 1997), 88.
5. Ibid., 89.
6. Margaret Wise Brown, *The Runaway Bunny* (New York, HarperFestival, 1991).
7. Peggy Rathmann, *Officer Buckle and Gloria* (New York: Putnam, 1995), 10–11.
8. Elizabeth Waters, *Painting* (New York: Dorling Kindersley, 1993).
9. Margaret N. Hurst, *Grannie and the Jumbie* (New York: Laura Geringer, 2001), back matter.
10. Robert, Burleigh, *Lookin' for Bird in the Big City* (San Diego: Harcourt, 2001), verso.
11. Jane Bynum, *Altoona Up North* (San Diego: Harcourt, 2001), verso.
12. John Steptoe, *Mufaro's Beautiful Daughters: An African Tale* (New York: Lothrop, Lee & Shepard, 1987), v.
13. Doreen Cronin, *Click, Clack, Moo: Cows that Type* (New York: Simon & Schuster, 2000), 27.
14. Sarah Stewart, *The Library* (New York: Farrar, Straus & Giroux, 1995), 15.
15. Faith Ringgold, *Tar Beach* (New York: Scholastic, 1991), back matter.
16. Molly Bang, *When Sophie Gets Angry—Really, Really Angry* (New York: Scholastic, 1999), 5–6.
17. Ibid., 31.
18. Patricia Polacco, *The Keeping Quilt* (New York: Simon & Schuster, 1988), 4.
19. Ibid., 7.
20. Barbara Cooney, *Miss Rumphius* (New York: Puffin Books, 1982), 19--24.
21. Patricia Polacco, *Thank You, Mr. Falker* (New York: Scholastic, 1999), 31.

22. www.ncte.org
23. http://www.sscnet.ucla.edu/nchs/standards/standardsk-4-1.html
24. http://www.sciencenetlinks.com/benchmark_sub.cfm?Grade=3-5&
BenchmarkID=12

Chapter 9

Joining Communities and Cultures: Diversity and Inclusivity

Once in a while someone asks me, "What are you?" I usually answer, "Human." When one kid at school asked me, that's what I said. Then I asked him, "What are you? Alien?" I've always wondered, why do I have to be anything? We're all part of the human race. So far as I know, no one has proven that aliens exist.

—Bethany Kandel, *Trevor's Story*, 1997

Once in the history of our country, it was believed that the many cultures and peoples of the world who were settling in the United States would become a melting pot. They would become part of the society of the United States, regardless of their heritage, and there would be one large culture. That vision might have been fulfilled except that the immigrants to this country were survivors, looking for a better life, but not willing to forego the rich backgrounds of their former lives. They lived their cultures; they lived their histories at the same time they were being acculturated into mainstream United States of America. And so this country's population has become a people of dichotomies: People who contribute to the current contemporary culture in our country while maintaining pride in the old one also; people who have pride in their roots and view themselves as the populace of the greatest country on earth—the United States of America.

The shortcomings of our history also have to be recognized as we note that not all of the people in our country today and their ancestors came here as immigrants, searching for a better life. In particular, we have to acknowledge that Native Americans were here before the European Anglos settled. We also have to feel shame for the reality of our treatment of the Native Americans and for the history of African Americans, who were subjected to capture, slavery, poverty, and are still, in many cases, suffering from those atrocities.

We must also recognize and value the diversity of ethnicities, cultures, religions, and traditions while accepting the differences and likenesses of our people as a key to our strength. As a result of a broad, but sometimes distorted, view of our citizens' rights, along with a fierce defense of our privileges as individuals, this country—not without growing pains—has adopted a unique view of multiculturalism.

Against the backdrop of the rich history of the various cultures that make our country great, it is also important to realize that writers about those cultures have unique viewpoints. Students can be assisted in evaluating these viewpoints against their own perspectives and backgrounds. Through the eyes of authors who have lived a culture or who have had insightful experiences to share about a culture, students will grow in their own global perspectives

With literature that is powerful enough to change attitudes and steer readers toward mind-sets and opinions that could last a lifetime, how can teachers guide students toward the evaluation of the literature? An ongoing debate asks readers to determine the authenticity of the experiences of the writer. One might think that having lived the experiences is the highest degree of telling a true tale, but even with this level of accuracy, there may be distortions due to perspective and biases. Even so, many believe that literature written by one who has lived in the culture has a better chance of validity than if written by an outsider. A strategy that teachers may use as a guide to help students examine the level of genuineness and lack of propaganda is to have them ask these questions:

- Is the subject appropriate for the intended audience?
- Is the content valid and objective?
- Does the voice ring true as having authority to make the statements or tell the story?

Along with answering these questions, students may decide where books fall on a continuum of appropriate voice and message, ranging from the high validity of one who has lived through an experience, to a lesser degree with an author who belongs to the culture but still needs to research the facts, all the way to a low level of understanding when the author is completely outside the culture and who may or may not include researched information.

As teachers share examples of literature from authors representing these levels, they may direct students to someone who has "lived the experience, " such as Francisco Jimenez's *The Circuit: Stories from the Life of a Migrant Child.* They may also show students how an author's cultural background could provide the foundation for research into a culture, but if they are writing about the culture in a different time period, extensive research may still be required. Frederick and Patricia McKissack have authentic understandings of African American culture, but they had to complete extensive research into an earlier time period to write about Frederick Douglass. Teachers could provide insight for intermediate-level students by sharing with them Scholastic's website,[1] *Writing with Writers,* in which the McKissacks provide a step-by-step process for researching and providing validity to the message.

When showing students a continuum of authentic voices and messages, other points on the scale could include the writings of Linda Sue Park, 2002 Newbery Medal recipient, who was born in the United States, studied in Ireland, taught in England, and whose parents and grandparents were from Korea. It was through their lives that she understood much of the Korean culture. *A Single Shard* is set in twelfth-century Korea, thus requiring extensive research into the historical period as well as the values and attitudes of the Korean culture.

Further down the scale of experience are those authors who, at first glance, may be considered totally outside of a culture. For an example, one could cite Ezra Jack Keats, a white man, whose stories were illustrated with African American characters, such as *The Snowy Day* and *Peter's Chair.* It can easily be argued in this case that the authenticity comes from the fact that these books are about childhood experiences and reflect all cultures across many time periods. It is clear that in some cases, familiarity with the culture may or may not be a criterion of authority.

As students read literature representing diverse settings, time periods, political perspectives, and human interactions, it is clearly the responsibility of adults to guide them toward awareness and methods for determining the appropriateness of the voices and the messages in the texts. Recognizing where an author falls on a continuum of authenticity from "lived through" to completely "outside" will help students make those decisions.

Defining Diversity and Inclusivity

Most of us recognize the meaning of diversity as being related to the acceptance and celebration of differences. The actual definition in the *Merriam-Webster Collegiate Dictionary* simply states: "the condition of being diverse." Further clarification of the word "diverse" leads to two specifics: "differing from one another" and "composed of distinct or unlike elements or qualities."[2]

Inclusivity, a derivative from the word "inclusive" refers to broad acceptance of diversities. The design principle from Expeditionary Learning that is targeted in this chapter is "Diversity and Inclusivity."

> Diversity and inclusivity in all groups dramatically increase richness of ideas, creative power, problem-solving ability, and acceptance of others. Encourage students to investigate, value, and draw upon their own different histories, talents, and resources together with those of other communities and cultures. Keep the schools and learning groups heterogeneous.[3]

Principles of Multiculturalism

The goals of this Expeditionary Learning design principle in the elementary classroom include the sharing of literature that enables students to recognize, accept, and celebrate the diversities in our world. Multicultural education has been influenced by several principles, as discussed in depth by Bennett.[4] These principles are synthesized here into four areas: learning about cultures, cultural pluralism, social justice, and empowerment and reform.

Learning about Cultures

Information leads to understanding. It is with this thought that books may be presented to children for the purpose of learning about cultures.

Currently, there is much interest in cultures from the Middle East. In Khadijah Knight's book, *Islamic Festivals,* readers learn about the beliefs of the Muslims and the life of the Prophet Muhammad, all of the holidays, and special places of worship. Color photographs follow two children as they practice their faith.

Diane Hoyt-Goldsmith has gained acclaim for her excellent books about other cultures. In her book, *Buffalo Days,* she focuses on ten-year-old Clarence Three Irons, Jr. and the heritage of the Crow Indians of Montana. In *Day of the Dead: A Mexican American Celebration,* she describes the Dia de los Muertos celebration of Latinos living in the Sacramento area of California. She includes the creation story of how the Aztecs came to be. Another of her collaborations with Lawrence Migdale is *Celebrating the Chinese New Year,* in which she introduces us to Ryan, a young Chinese-American boy living in San Francisco. We join Ryan and his family as they prepare for the coming Chinese New Year. Hoyt-Goldsmith explains the origins of the holiday, the symbolism of the rituals, the significance of the Chinese zodiac, and the ingredients of special meals, while Migdale covers the pages with his colorful photographs showing the family shopping for symbolic foods and flowers, taking a trip to the cemetery to honor ancestors, and more.

Book Selections from Various Cultures

It is in the spirit of learning about cultures that we are listing book selections from various cultures. It is important to include a range of levels of reading in your classroom collections, so we have noted picture books at early and middle levels, and chapter books at middle and upper levels.

Selections from Hispanic Literature
1. *Friends From the Other Side/Amigos del Otro Lado* by Gloria Anzaldua (picture book—primary)
2. *My Very Own Room/Mi Propio Cuartito* by Amada Irma Perez (picture book—primary)
3. *Amelia's Road* by Linda Jacobs Altman (picture book—middle elementary)
4. *The Golden Flower: A Taino Myth from Puerto Rico* by Nina Jaffe (picture book—middle elementary)
5. *Roberto Clemente* by Thomas W. Gilbert (chapter book—middle elementary)
6. *Under the Royal Palms: A Childhood in Cuba* by Alma Flor Ada (chapter book—middle elementary)
7. *An Island Like You: Stories of the Barrio* by Judith Ortiz Coffer (chapter book—upper elementary)
8. *Baseball in April and Other Stories* by Gary Soto (chapter book—upper elementary)
9. *Circuit: Stories from the Life of a Migrant Child* by Francisco Jiménez (chapter book—upper elementary)

Selections from Asian Literature
1. *Halmoni's Day* by Edna Coe Bercaw (picture book—primary)
2. *Everybody Cooks Rice* by Norah Dooley (picture book—primary)
3. *I Live In Tokyo* by Mari Takabayashi (picture book—middle elementary)
4. *Tea with Milk* by Allen Say (picture book—middle elementary)

5. *Dragon New Year: A Chinese Legend* by David Bouchard, (picture book—middle elementary)
6. *Grandfather's Journey* by Allen Say (picture book—middle elementary)
7. *A Single Shard* by Linda Sue Park (chapter book—upper elementary)
8. *Goodbye, Vietnam* by Gloria Whelan (chapter book—upper elementary)

Selections from Native American Literature
1. *A Picture Book of Sitting Bull* by David Adler (picture book—primary)
2. *A Boy Called Slow* by Joseph Bruchac (picture book—middle elementary)
3. *Iktomi and the Boulder: A Plains Indian Story* by Paul Goble (picture book—middle elementary)
4. *Birchbark House* by Louise Erdrich (chapter book—middle elementary)
5. *Anpao: An American Indian Odyssey* by Jamake Highwater (chapter book—upper elementary)

Selections from Jewish Literature
1. *The Borrowed Hanukkah Latkes* by Linda Glaser (picture book—primary)
2. *Miriam's Cup: A Passover Story* by Fran Manushkin (picture book—primary)
3. *Let the Celebrations Begin!* by Margaret Wild (picture book—middle chapter)
4. *Hershel and the Hanukkah Goblins* by Eric Kimmel (picture book—middle elementary)
5. *Surviving Hitler: A Boy in the Nazi Death Camps* by Andrea Warren (chapter book—middle elementary)
6. *The Key Is Lost* by Ida Vos (chapter book—upper elementary).

Selections from African American Literature
1. *Something Beautiful* by Sharon Dennis Wyeth (picture book—primary)
2. *All the Colors of the Race* by Arnold Adoff (picture book—primary)
3. *The Palm of My Heart* by Davida Adedjouma (picture book—middle elementary)

4. *Momma, Where Are You From?* by Marie Bradby (picture book—middle elementary)
5. *Osceola: Memories of a Sharecropper's Daughter* by May Osceola and Alan Govenar (chapter book—middle elementary)
6. *Through My Eyes* by Ruby Bridges and Margo Lundell (photobiography-middle elementary)
7. *Let It Shine: Stories of Black Women Freedom Fighters* by Andrea Davis Pinkney (picture book—middle elementary)
8. *Only Passing Through: The Story of Sojourner Truth* by Anne F. Rockwell (picture book—middle elementary)
9. *Second Cousins* by Virginia Hamilton (chapter book—middle elementary)
10. *Bluish* by Virginia Hamilton (chapter book—middle elementary)
11. *Tears of A Tiger* by Sharon Draper (chapter book—upper elementary)
12. *Forged by Fire* by Sharon Draper (chapter book—upper elementary)

Selections from Eastern European Literature
1. *Joseph Had a Little Overcoat* by Simms Taback (picture book—primary)
2. *Zlata's Diary: A Childhood in Sarajevo* by Zlata Filapovic (chapter book—middle elementary)
3. *Freya on the Wall* by T. Degens (chapter book—upper elementary)

Selections from Middle Eastern Literature
1. *The Day of Ahmad's Secret* by Florence Parry Heide Judith and Heide Gilliland (picture book—middle elementary)
2. *Muslim Child: Understanding Islam Through Stories and Poems* by Rukhsana Khan (chapter book—middle elementary)
3. *Shabanu* by Suzanne Fisher Staples (chapter book—upper elementary)
4. *Haveli* by Suzanne Fisher Staples (chapter book—upper elementary)
5. *Shiva's Fire* by Suzanne Fisher Staples (chapter book—upper elementary)

Multicultural Children's Literature Awards

A remarkable source for books that gives insight into selected cultures is the American Library Association.[5] They have created several awards to recognize and promote multicultural children's literature. These awards have reflected ideas from the principles of multicultural education as they open unknown worlds to children.

Coretta Scott King Award

Named after the wife of Dr. Martin Luther King, Jr. this award recognizes writers and authors of African descent whose writing values and appreciates American efforts. The award commemorates the life and accomplishments of Dr. King and honors Mrs. King's tireless work toward peace and common goals for humankind.

The 2002 award went to Mildred Taylor's *The Land*, a prequel to *Roll of Thunder, Hear My Cry*, which tells the life story of Cassie Logan's grandfather, a man of mixed races, who was constantly caught between the black and white worlds. Set during the Reconstruction period right after the Civil War, the book is a study on race relations and on the intense determination of a man to own his own land.

An award winner for middle school students is Sharon Flake's *Money Hungry*. This stark story reveals poverty and Raspberry Hill's philosophy about what a girl could do with money. She and her mother have left her drug-addicted father and find themselves in the projects. Her mother works two jobs and is going to school while Raspberry does every odd job she can find to build up her bankroll. It's a tough look at life, but full of tender moments between Raspberry and her new friends and Raspberry and her mother. Raspberry is a commendable role model for adolescents.

Two picture-book award-winners for 2002 for outstanding art are Patricia McKissack's *Goin' Someplace Special*, illustrated by Jerry Pinkney, and Doreen Rappaport's *Martin's Big Words*, a book of Dr. King's quotes, illustrated by Bryan Collier. Interestingly, both books talk about the same time period. Rappaport's story tells of Martin Luther King, Jr.'s entire life from 1929–1968. Rappaport writes,

> The courage and determination of the southern black Americans who confronted violence with nonviolence transformed my life and ideas. I went to the March on Washington in 1963 to support this inspirational movement. I went South to teach in a Mississippi freedom

school during the summer of 1965. In Mississippi I saw firsthand the fragility of being black in white America.[6]

McKissack's *Goin' Someplace Special* is a poignant account of the same time period, the 1950s and 1960s when Dr. King was trying to change the situation for African American families. Although McKissack's work is fictionalized, the author says,

> The events are taken from my own childhood growing up in Nashville, Tennessee. Nashville, like most southern cities in the 1950s, was segregated. The doors of hotels, restaurants, churches, and amusement parks were posted with Jim Crow segregation signs that barred African Americans, who also had to endure the further indignities of riding in the backs of buses, attending separate schools, sitting in the last rows of the balcony, and drinking from separate water fountains. But, in the late 1950s, Nashville's public library board of directors quietly voted to integrate all their facilities. The downtown branch was one of the few places where there were no Jim Crow signs and blacks were treated with some respect.[7]

The "Someplace Special" that Tricia Ann is heading for throughout the book is the public library, the place that Mama Frances called a "doorway to freedom." The final page is powerful. "Before bounding up the steps and through the front door, Tricia Ann stopped to look up at the message chiseled in stone across the front facing: PUBLIC LIBRARY: ALL ARE WELCOME."[8]

Coretta Scott King/John Steptoe New Talent Award

This award recognizes black authors and illustrators who have published no more than three books. The award is not given every year, but is given when appropriate talent is published. In 1995 Sharon Draper's book, *Tears of a Tiger*, received the award. The book is at the high end of children's literature, appropriate for seventh to twelfth graders. It's potent in its exploration of alcohol abuse and teenage suicide. Four friends celebrate after winning a ball game. One of the boys is killed in an automobile accident and Andy, the driver, can't forgive himself. The story is revealed through journals, letters, and homework assignments and ends in his suicide. Racism is also addressed in the book.

Pura Belpré Award

Two awards are given biennially for books written and illustrated by Latino/Latina authors and illustrators that celebrate the Latino culture. Pura Belpré was a librarian in New York City who enriched the lives of many Puerto Rican children through the preservation of Latino literature.

Pam Munoz Ryan's *Esperanza Rising* won the 2002 award for the narrative. Susan Guevara illustrated Gary Soto's *Chato and the Party Animals*, the winner of the award for illustrations.

Esperanza, the Spanish word for hope, is symbolic of the story of a young girl in Mexico during the 1930s. Her father is killed, and she and her mother are forced to leave their affluent lifestyles and emigrate to the U.S. Esperanza witnesses all of the desperation of the Depression and the deep resentment toward the Mexicans. However, hope is truly the message for upper elementary and middle students who read this story.

For the younger children, Chato is up to his old tricks. He plans a birthday party for his best friend, but forgets to invite the guest of honor! Whatever the culture, young readers are bound to identify with the birthday plans and to enjoy the fun. *Chato's Kitchen,* a 1995 winner of the Pura Belpré award, has been a winner with kids ever since its publication.

Another winner of the award for illustrations in 2002 was *Juan Bobo Goes to Work.* Marisa Montes retells this Puerto Rican folktale in the tradition of Pura Belpré. Cepeda's stunning illustrations show the simple pleasure that Juan Bobo gets from life!

Mildred Batchelder Award

This award given annually recognizes books that are first written in another language and then translated into English. It is through these books that we gain authentic insights into cultures through books written by authors who are native to that culture. Some recent titles include: Karin Gündisch's *How I Became an American,* told from the perspective of a ten-year-old German boy whose family migrated to the United States in 1902. James Skofield translated the book.

Another Batchelder winner takes place on the West Bank. Two boys, who have seen too much war, meet in a hospital; one is Palestinian, the other is Jewish. The book, *Samir and Yonatan,* was written by Daniella Carmi and translated from Hebrew by Yael Lotan.

More information about all of these awards is available at www.ala.org, the home page for the American Library Association.

Cultural Pluralism

Another concept noted by Bennett[9] and applied to multicultural teaching is the theory of cultural pluralism, which asserts the rights of each ethnic group to retain its heritage. This principle is recognized in many works of children's literature as exemplified in George Ancona's *Barrio: Jose's Neighborhood*, in which the family life, schools, holidays, and traditions found in a San Francisco barrio are explained along with Spanish words and terms. Another picture book that champions the rights of an ethnic group is the unique holiday story, *Gracias, the Thanksgiving Turkey* by Joy Cowley. Miguel's father, a truck driver, sends a turkey named Gracias back to Miguel with instructions to fatten the bird up for Thanksgiving. The bird becomes a beloved pet and Miguel can't imagine him as Thanksgiving fare for the family. Joe Cepeda's magnificent oil paintings of the urban setting and Spanish words are used throughout the story. Readers will become familiar with the landscapes and traditions of Hawaii when they read *Luka's Quilt* by Georgia Guback. Tutu (the Hawaiian word for grandmother) promises her granddaughter a quilt. Luka dreams of a multicolored gift, but is disappointed when she receives a quilt that is only green and white. Two-colored quilts are traditional in Hawaii. Lush cut-paper collage illustrations accompany the story.

Susan Kuklin writes nonfiction books that serve a variety of ages and cultures. In *How My Family Lives in America,* for example, she looks at three different families. "Because Sanu, Eric, and April each have at least one parent who did not grow up in the United States, their family heritage is an interesting mixture. Some traditions, remembered from a parent's childhood in another place, are kept alive in America."[10]

The three children share experiences that they are enjoying with their families. Sanu's father is from Senagal and she is learning to braid her hair in a Sengalese twist and make the same African meal that her father makes. Eric's family speaks two languages in their home, English and Spanish. He tells the reader about the delicious Spanish meals he helps his mother prepare, gives us the words to a Spanish healing poem and tells how he likes to dance the *merengue* with family and friends. Finally, April, whose Spanish name is Chin Lan gives us a lesson in writing and speaking Chinese. Her parents both came to this country from Taiwan and speak Mandarin. She also tells about the Chinese school she attends on Saturdays and the game, *Chi chiao banc* that the family plays at night.

Laurence Yep, known as a premier Asian American author, writes about Chinese culture within the confines of the American city in several of his novels for upper elementary and middle school students. *Child of the Owl* is set in the Chinatown of the 1960s, and although many things have changed since, it is easy to see how powerful a culture within a culture can be. Twelve-year-old Casey, a Chinese American girl, has been raised by her father outside of Chinatown and has little knowledge of her Chinese background. Her father, an inveterate gambler and liar, has engaged in both activities once too often and is beaten to a pulp. Cassie, reluctantly, goes to stay with her grandmother in Chinatown, where she learns about her ethnic heritage for the first time. Along with Cassie, readers learn much about Chinatown in San Francisco, a culture within a culture.

Just as Laurence Yep writes from his own experience growing up in San Franciso's Chinatown, Kam Mak relies on his experience of growing up in New York City's Chinatown. In his picture book of poems, *My Chinatown: One Year in Poems*, he examines this extraordinary place of two cultures, one within the other.

> My favorite shop is dark inside,
> Warm and quiet.
> Near the ceiling,
> Dragons, birds, butterflies
> Soar on paper wings.
> Masks watch me from the walls.
> On the shelves are
> Bowls and chopsticks,
> Paper finger traps,
> Bamboo snakes.[11]

The 2001 Newbery Medal was granted to Linda Sue Park's *A Single Shard*, a distinctive book of historical fiction. Set in twelfth-century Korea, the lifestyle of orphaned Tree-ear is starkly contrasted to the youth of today in many ways, and yet we hope that contemporary youngsters will have the same kind of inner strength evidenced by Tree-ear. We learn of the culture of his country and his era through one of themes of the book: Tree-ear's arduous journey to learn the trade of pottery-making. In addition to the cultural understandings, much of the book's appeal comes from the challenge of understanding the thinking of this twelve-year old, who lives with Crane-man under a bridge and who has been taught by word and deed to be an honorable person. Tree-ear's thoughts throughout the book exemplify his ongoing process to determine what is right and honorable while he struggles with daily living.

Social Justice

Another concept for development through multicultural literature represents our beliefs in social justice with efforts to end racism, sexism, ageism, and other discriminations. Teachers may use the following books to explore these situations and help children make judgments about their own biases. Hopefully, children can see the hurt and harmfulness of the injustices throughout the centuries and plan ways for the coming generations to eradicate inequities.

Nina Aamundsen writes in *Two Shorts and One Long* about two Norwegian friends who face their own prejudices when an Afghanistan family becomes part of the neighborhood. In Barbara Cohen's excellent tale, *Molly's Pilgrim,* a young Jewish Russian immigrant learns about the first Thanksgiving and teaches her classmates a lesson about pilgrims. Molly and her classmates have been asked to make a pilgrim doll. Molly's mother takes over the task and sends Molly to school the next day with a beautiful pilgrim doll, but not the kind the other children expect. Molly's afraid that she will never fit in, but the teacher introduces the class to the real meaning of the word "pilgrim."

Upper elementary readers will be deeply moved by Mildred Taylor's *Mississippi Bridge.* In the 1930s black people could not ride the bus if there wasn't enough room for the white passengers. Jeremy Sims watches as his friend, Josias Williams, is cruelly thrown from the bus when white passengers arrive at the last minute and need his seat.

Most of us have heard the frightening story of the persecution of the Jews in World War II. Many have read *The Diary of Anne Frank.* Two other titles that deal with the same issue and provide a great deal of historical information and much "food for thought" are Lois Lowry's *Number the Stars* and Joanna Reiss's *The Upstairs Room.* Each of these books has a brave young woman as a protagonist, however, *Number the Stars* is a work of fiction and *The Upstairs Room* is based on the author's experiences. Ms. Reiss writes, "This book is about my life, or rather part of my life, the part that took place in Holland during the Second World War. In this book I have gone back to those years, when I was a child, and Jewish, and therefore undesirable, when I had to hide from the Germans."[12]

In recent years, the stories of the Japanese incarceration by Americans during World War II have been a topic of discussion. It was an embarrassing time in our history, but was precipitated by the events that began with the Japanese bombing of Pearl Harbor. Recent events surrounding the conflict in the Middle East and discussion of Muslim terrorists have reminded Americans that they need to be judicious in their responses to people living in our country, but who look different or worship differently. *Journey to Topaz* by Yoshiko Uchida is a shattering story of an eleven-year-old child whose father is taken by the FBI in the wake of the attack on Pearl Harbor. Then she and her mother and older brother are taken to the horse stall of Tanforan Racetrack and then to the desert where they are incarcerated in the concentration camp called Topaz.

In the prologue, Yoshiko Uchida wrote,

> I would ask readers to remember that my characters portray the Japanese Americans of 1942 and to recall that the world then was totally different from the one we know today. In 1942 the voice of Martin Luther King had not yet been heard and ethnic pride was yet unborn. There was no awareness in the land of civil rights, and there had yet been no freedom marches or demonstrations of protest. Most Americans, supporting their country in a war they considered just, did nothing to protest our forced removal, and might well have considered it treasonous had we tried to resist or protest.
>
> . . . I hope by reading this book young people everywhere will realize what once took place in this country and will determine never to permit such a travesty of justice to occur again.[13]

Racism

We know that racism is an ugly part of the world's history. To better understand how it has affected people over the decades, children can read about these injustices. Following is a selected list of books that deal with racism toward African Americans in our country during the last century.

1. *Sister Anne's Hands* by Marybeth Lorbiecki is a story of a nun who endures racist attitudes from her students and attempts to show them the African American history (picture book—middle elementary)

2. *White Socks Only* by Evelyn Coleman is a story of a little girl who tries to drink from a fountain labeled, "Whites Only," (picture book—primary)

3. *Listening to Leroy* by Betsy Hearne is a chapter book set in the 50s, with the story of a white girl who gets to know an African American boy and changes her attitude. She also has the strength to stand up for her beliefs (chapter book—upper elementary)

4. *Dangerous Skies* by Suzanne F. Staples. Racism emerges as white and black characters are treated differently; prejudice and mistreatment are so widespread that life can never return to normal (chapter book—upper elementary)

Discussion must follow the reading of these books, so it is recommended that the books be read aloud by the teacher or scheduled in small discussion groups. There must be time allowed for questions and reflections. Writing time following reading and talking is a good outlet for both questions and emotions.

Empowerment and Reform

As students read these stories of injustices, they will learn of inhumanities that have been forced on some segments of our society. Beyond the horrible inequities, though, they will read of characters whose struggles have resulted in reform. They will read of characters who would not accept injustice, such as Rosa Parks, who tells, along with James Hoskins in *Rosa Parks: My Story*, how she would not give up her seat on a bus—just because of her skin color. Through her strength, other African Americans have been empowered to seek reform and to rectify the injustices to her race that began with slavery.

In *Martin's Big Words: The Life of Dr. Martin Luther King, Jr.* by Doreen Rappaport, we hear the strength of his commitment to free his race from the chains of racism, prejudices, segregation, and iniquitous treatment. Children will slowly realize that humans suffer often to turn a wrong into a right for a future generation. That knowledge is empowering, and it makes way for the courage for continued reforms.

When we think of societal reforms, we think of many unanswered injustices that brew today. Native Americans have suffered since the colonization of this country. Even today, many are struggling with the conflict of living on reservations or in the mainstream culture. *Eagle Song* by Joseph Bruchac explores what happens to a child when the family moves from the reservation to the city. In this story, Danny has to find the courage to follow his convictions and his heritage even in the face of contemporary issues, such as gangs. This story does not provide an answer to the societal problems but will leave children knowing that the strong family is the real key to survival.

This Land is My Land, written and illustrated by Plains Cree Nation artist George Littlechild, explains through his vivid pages of art his position on his people's loss of their land. Children may get an authentic glimpse of a thoughtful Native American perspective that could impact non-Native Americans as well.

For today's children, the horrors of the Holocaust seem many lifetimes away from theirs. For this reason, it is important for them to read and to know of the horrific results of one regime's prejudices. Compensation is not possible to the Jewish culture for all they have had to bear and are still bearing today. Their hope must lie in the younger generations who must never let such atrocities happen again. Several books about the Holocaust have been previously noted. Another one for intermediate level readers is Natalie Babbitt's *The Devil's Arithmetic*. The book has a fantasy element with a contemporary Jewish child being transported to the 1940s and finding herself in a death camp. The realities of the fight for survival and the insight into the strategies to protect oneself from the dehumanizing tactics of the Germans are enough to call on today's reader to feel this horror. When young readers realize that these stories came from historical facts that are more sickening than the fiction depicts, they will find it hard to shrug off these events and their consequences.

Today's world brings more challenges for social justice reform. Although children's books are sometimes published on contemporary inequities, they lag behind the actual events. During the last decade, books have been published on the events in Haiti that led to military tyranny and exiles to the United States. *Tonight by Sea* by Frances Temple vividly depicts the struggles and fears of a group of Haitians who must leave their homes and run for their lives. *Zlata's Diary: The Life of a Child in Sarajevo*, an authentic diary by Zlata Filapovic gives insight into life under fire in Bosnia-Herzegovina within the last decade also.

Teachers only have to pick up a newspaper, however, to read the daily conflicts throughout the world. Books on those clashes from the eyes of children will be coming also. Through reading about characters who have faced adversities in the multicultural world and have been a part of changes in our society, students will begin to recognize possibilities for personal empowerment.

Characters of Mixed Races

In Bethany Kandel's *Trevor's Story*, Trevor describes his life as a biracial child. Readers get a glimpse of what it's like to be a child of mixed race. It's a story that can be shared with young children, but they won't be able to read it by themselves. *Black, White, Just Right!* on the other hand, is a happy, positive story for younger children that celebrates the fact that Mom and Dad are different. Author Marguerite Davol tells us that Mom's face is "chestnut brown"; Dad's face gets pink in the sun. But more important is the difference in the parents' taste in food, in dance, and in other things. Best of all is their alikeness.

Mildred Pitts Walter tells a wonderfully candid story in *Ray and the Best Family Reunion Ever*. Ray, a Los Angeles boy, is excited about visiting his family roots far away in Louisiana at the family reunion. Unfortunately, there will be family turmoil because his father's estranged father will be there. Ray has heard often that he reminds his own Papa of Ray's Gran-papa and he thinks he's discovered the reason. They are both very dark-skinned, whereas much of the family of African, French, and Creole descent is light-skinned. Ray wrestles with the discovery and eventually confronts his father. The ending gives emotional satisfaction.

Students who read these books or have them read to them, and are allowed to ask questions and respond, are likely to come to the conclusion, as Trevor did, that, "There is really only one race—the human race."[14]

Cross-Cultural Relationships

A formidable aspect of becoming empowered to face life's challenges—not to mention making a difference in the world—is learning to interact across cultures and other man-made boundaries. There are some excellent models for youngsters to read, depicting characters whose plights have driven them to find some successful strategies for cross-cultural relationships.

When going out to the larger world, it may be comforting to have an imaginary friend. That's what Leon did in Simon James's *Leon and Bob*. As most children do, however, Leon realized when he could trade in the imaginary Bob for a real Bob. Early understandings of crossing cultures are subtly depicted in this picture book.

Another picture book with a subtle message of cultural interactions is Eve Bunting's *Smoky Night*. With the background of the Los Angeles riots in the 1980s, the characters show hesitancy to mingle with those from another culture. "My mama and I don't go in to Mrs. Kim's market even though it is close. Mama says it's better if we buy from our own people. Mrs. Kim's cat and my cat fight all the time . . . "[15] The events, including the riots and the fire, along with the cats that ultimately lick from the same bowl, lead the characters from different races to make some small commitments to future interactions.

For older readers, glimpses into the lives of children who are living with cross-cultural conflicts are possible in *I Hadn't Meant to Tell You This* by Jacqueline Woodson. Two best friends, one white and one African American, have both lost their mothers and are having trouble at home because they have a friend of another race.

In Walter Dean Myers's, *Slam*, a book for middle school level, a kid from Harlem going to a white high school finds that he is better on the basketball court than in other parts of his life. He struggles for ways to conquer cross-cultural obstacles and find answers for his life.

Through the solutions that the characters in these books seek and sometimes find, and through their personalities and courage to persist, models are clear for young, contemporary readers.

Strategies for Multicultural Literature

Word Walls for Unfamiliar Terms

Word walls are welcome sights to children when reading multicultural literature because unfamiliar terms can interfere with comprehension. Words that are associated with various books being read independently or in literature discussion circles should be written in large letters on cards in a special area of the classroom. If attached with Velcro, they can be replaced with other cards easily. Although the teacher may place some cards on the word wall, children enjoy the task of making a card for new and unfamiliar vocabulary as they are reading.

Venn Diagrams for Showing Likenesses as Well as Differences

A clear message to children who read multicultural literature should be that there are many likenesses among the different cultures. The focus of insights and discussions should be on celebrating uniqueness while noting that like traits run across humankind. When children look for likenesses for the two overlapping circles in the Venn diagram, they recognize how people are alike.

Criteria Charts for Good Literature

It is important for children to start evaluating literature with a critical eye at an early age. Self-selection of literature is a privilege that children enjoy. Helping them determine some criteria for good books will give them confidence in their selections. As the class is exposed to a genre and has heard the teacher share ideas about what makes a good book, the class may brainstorm a list of criteria they believe make a good book from a selected genre.

Multicultural Folktale Collections and Displays

Multicultural folktales provide a fascinating unit of study. Every culture has a Cinderella tale, and it is easy to find similarities in many other tales across various groups of people. The Oryx Multicultural Folktale Series has compiled Cinderella stories and Beauties and Beasts. Students may read these variations in the tales and display their collections.

We, the People: An Expedition

Guiding Questions

1. Who are the people who make up our country?
2. Why did so many people leave their homelands to migrate to the United States in the 19th and 20th centuries?
3. What traditions did they bring with them?
4. Why are many people still coming to this country to live? How many immigrants come to this country each year? From what countries do the migrations come?
5. What do they expect to find here and how does that compare with what they experience? What jobs are they holding here? How are they becoming "citizens" of this country? What is the naturalization process?
6. How does immigration of today compare to that of a hundred years ago?
7. How are we alike and different?
8. What is the status in our country on equality for ethnicities and gender?
9. How do music and art vary by culture?

Standards

From the areas of U. S. history, music, and language arts, these standards are from the National Council of Teachers of Math (NCTM), National Council of Teachers of English (NCTE), and from National Standards for United States History (NCHS).

The students:

1. describe regional folk heroes, stories, or songs that have contributed to the development of the cultural history of the United States.
2. draw upon a variety of stories, legends, songs, ballads, games, and tall tales in order to describe the environment, lifestyles, beliefs, and struggles of people in various regions of the country.
3. examine art, crafts, music, and language of people from a variety of regions long ago and describe their influence on the nation.
4. analyze the dance, music, and arts of various cultures around the world to draw conclusions about the history, daily life, and beliefs of the people in history.[16]
5. solve problems that arise in mathematics and in other contexts.
6. apply and adapt a variety of appropriate strategies to solve problems.
7. monitor and reflect on the process of mathematical problem solving.[17]
8. participate as knowledgeable, reflective, creative, and critical members of a variety of literacy communities.
9. develop an understanding of and respect for diversity in language use, patterns, and dialects across cultures, ethnic groups, geographic regions, and social roles.[18]

Initial Reading Options for Teacher Read-Alouds, Shared, Guided, or Independent Reading

1. *Dreaming of America: An Ellis Island Story* by Eve Bunting
2. *The Land* by Mildred Taylor
3. *Esperanza Rising* by Pam Munoz Ryan
4. *Grandfather's Journey* by Allen Say
5. *Across America on an Emigrant Train* by Jim Murphy

6. *The Journal of Jasper Jonathan Pierce: A Pilgrim Boy* by Ann Rinaldi
7. *Duke Ellington: The Piano Prince and His Orchestra* by Andrea Davis Pinkney
8. *Richard Wright and the Library Card* by William Miller
9. *Dangerous Skies* by Suzanne Fisher Staples

Fieldwork Options

1. Interview recent immigrants and ask questions on their stories.
2. Find statistics to answer questions through reference books, nonfiction sources, and Internet sites.
3. Visit music stores and identify popular music for each culture discussed in class.
4. Listen to the radio or MTV and tally music associated with each culture. Share information with class.
5. Call local museums and see if there are any museums in your area that recognize specific cultures. Make a list and select one of them to visit.

Individual Projects

1. Read about a specific culture or ethnicity and prepare a display of your information for the class.
2. Research a sport, such as basketball, played by Michael Jordan.
3. Make a list of the rules of the games to share with the class.
4. Create a PowerPoint or Hyperstudio presentation on a figure from one of these cultures: African American; Asian; Hispanic; Mideast; Eastern Europe.
5. Use technology to prepare features for presentation on factual cases, statistics, or accomplishments of immigrants.

Class Projects

1. Read books on refugee children and make a display of the books in the library.
2. Share PowerPoint or Hyperstudio presentations with another class.
3. Research immigration laws and current status of ethnic groups that are immigrating to this country. Compile the research and place data on a bulletin board.

4. Adopt a local immigrant and help in the immigration process.
5. Create a handbook for immigrant children who move into this school.

Sharing Outlets

1. Share displays and materials in the classroom, hallways, and library for the school to see.
2. Schedule information from the class research to be shared with a local radio talk show.
3. Create web page for information found on immigration and cultures.
4. Present technology programs to school or to another class.
5. Create a bulletin board mural with a time line reflecting characters from books.

Assessment Options

1. Rubrics for projects.
2. Participation checklists including a self-evaluation checklist.
3. Portfolio artifacts from this expedition.
4. Contract completion.

Notes

1 http://teacher.scholastic.com/writewit/biograph/biography_own.htm

2. http://www.m-w.com/cgi-bin/dictionary?book=Dictionary&va=diverse

3. http://www.elob.org/aboutel/principles.html

4. Christine Bennett, "Genres of Research in Multicultural Education," *Review of Education Research* 71 no.2 (2001): 171–217.

5. www.ala.org

6. Doreen Rappaport, *Martin's Big Word* (New York: Hyperion, 2001), iv.

7. Patricia McKissack, *Goin' Someplace Special* (New York: Simon & Schuster, 2001), 32.

8. Ibid., 31.

9. Bennett, "Multicultural Education," 172.

10. Susan Kuklin, *How My Family Lives in America* (New York: Aladdin, 1998), 1.

11. Kam Mak, *My Chinatown: One Year in Poem* (New York: Harper-Collins, 2002), 23.

12. Johanna Reiss, *The Upstairs Room* (New York: Harper, 1972), i.

13. Yoshiko Uchida, *Journey to Topaz* (Berkeley, Calif.: Creative Arts Book Company, 1985), viii.

14. Bethany Kandel, *Trevor's Story* (Minneapolis, Minnesota: Lerner, 1997).

15. Eve Bunting, *Smoky Night* (San Diego: Harcourt, 1994), 7.

16. http://www.sscnet.ucla.edu/nchs/

17. http://standards.nctm.org/document/chapter5/prob.htm

18. www.ncte.org/

Chapter 10

Relating to the Universe and Fostering Stewardship: The Natural World

When his mother gave him an old microscope,
he used it to look at flowers, raindrops, and blades of grass.
Best of all, he used it to look at snow.
While other children built forts
and pelted snowballs at roosting crows,
Willie was catching single snowflakes.
Day after stormy day he studied ice crystals.

—Jacqueline B. Martin, *Snowflake Bentley*, 1999

Curiosity about the natural world is an inherent motivator found in most children. As Willie Bentley, also known as "Snowflake," was drawn to the uniqueness of each snowflake and spent untold time studying and recording his findings, so can other children be drawn into the world of nature. Watch a child with a bug on the sidewalk or a leaf floating through the air, and it is clear how the objects of nature can be a driving force in students' understanding of the natural world. Their interest is already there and the opportunities for learning about scientific principles and the workings of the world are easy for teachers and parents to provide.

In this design principle, teachers are encouraged to support students' efforts in using the world of literature as they relate to the universe, discover the meaning of stewardship, and become stewards of our natural world. The encouragement and support of this principle of growth may develop gradually through exposure to nature and many opportunities to enjoy the outside environment.

A direct and respectful relationship with the natural world refreshes the human spirit and reveals the important lessons of recurring cycles and cause and effect. Students learn to become stewards of the earth and of the generations to come.[1]

163

Literature and Science Connections

Reading about characters living and playing in the outside world leads students to value those experiences. From Janice Udry's classic of nearly fifty years ago, *A Tree is Nice* to Henry Cole's *I Took A Walk*, a contemporary book about observing nature, children have had opportunities to appreciate the natural world. Attitudes about nature are developing in the young years and are strongly influenced by the books to which children are exposed. Some books that promote a positive attitude about the wonders of the natural world and our need to preserve its ecology include:

1. *The Berenstein Bears Don't Pollute (Anymore)* by Stan and Jan Berenstein (picture book—primary)
2. *The Little House* by Virginia Lee Burton (picture book—primary)
3. *Letting Swift River Go* by Jane Yolen (picture book—middle elementary)
4. *Welcome to the Ice House* by Jane Yolen (picture book—primary)
5. *And Still the Turtle Watched* by Sheila Magill-Callahan (picture book—middle elementary)
6. *Endangered Animals* by Faith McNulty (chapter book—easy-to-read)
7. *The Gift of the Tree* by Alvin Tresselt (picture book—primary)

Debates are currently raging over the vigor with which we need to work to preserve our environment.[2] Ultimately, that preservation is in the hands of the children who are reading children's books today and will be making environmental policy decisions tomorrow. Mark Galan has clarified some of the ecological issues for children in his *There's Still Time: The Success of the Endangered Species Act*. His book explains nineteen examples from 1973 to the present of recovery of species and gives the reader a view of the importance of this environmental act.

Phyllis Stanley's *American Environmental Heroes* in the Collective Biographies series provides inspiration from the lives of ten environmentalists. Children's awareness of the importance of the ecological debate will be heightened with the reading of this book.

Principles of Science

When children begin to recognize the principles of science, their attitudes about the world and the interdependent connections are supported. The American Association for the Advancement of Science (AAAS) has identified twelve areas from science for curriculum development. Selected areas that specifically relate to the natural world and its stewardship are provided here with recommendations for literature in the classroom.

The Nature of Science

This area of study includes an understanding that through studies and through sharing information, scientists are learning how the world works. The role of children in this area is to learn to observe and to be aware of likenesses, differences, and changes in the world about them. Promoting this theme is Charlotte Zolotow's *When the Wind Stops*. In this book, a mother and her son deliberate on what happens to the wind when it stops. She helps him see that in nature things do not end but go on to other beginnings. It is a calming book for young children to begin knowing the world around them.

Scientific inquiry and the scientific enterprise are both related to the use of the scientific method. The AAAS emphasizes that scientific method is more than testing theories. It is embedded in collaborative sharing when there is a mixture of strict organization of scientific information along with innovation and inventiveness. A book that supports such inquiries is *What is a Scientist?* by Barbara Lehn. The scientific method of inquiry is shown to be part of the natural curiosity of first-grade students in the book. Another book, Virginia Wright-Frierson's *An Island Scrapbook: Dawn to Dusk on a Barrier Island*, takes the reader on an exploration of an ecosystem, learning about the sketches and field notes that scientists use in discovering information.

The Physical Setting

Physical setting content includes concepts related to the universe, the earth, processes that shape the earth, matter, energy transformations, motion, and forces of nature. *The Kingfisher Young People's Book of Space* by Martin Redfern is a good place to start with basic information on the universe. The forces of nature with their changes are clear in Jane Kurtz's *River Friendly, River Wild* and in Sherry Garland's *The Summer Sands*. The magnified photographs and simple experiments explain the concepts of the water cycle in *A Drop of Water: A Book of Science and Wonder* by Walter Wick, showing children, very clearly, one of the processes of this wonderful earth.

The Living Environment

Study in this area requires students to delve into the diversity of life, heredity, interdependence of life, flow of matter and energy, and evolution of life. *Sweet Magnolia* by Virginia Kroll provides a story of a young girl visiting her grandmother, who is a wildlife rehabilitator in Louisiana. In this story, Denise learns firsthand about environmental stewardship. Another fascinating book to use with the study of the environment is Jan Thornhill's *Before and After: A Book of Nature Timescapes*. In this book, readers get a glimpse of nature's changes occurring over various time spans.

From preschool to high school, students seem to have an attraction to birds of prey or raptors. In Caroline Arnold's *Hawk Highway in the Sky: Watching Raptor Migration,* readers can see photographs and information on how hawks live and migrate. The detailed ways they are studied give students a view of the importance of these raptors to the environment. A study of the living environment would not be complete without a view of *The Most Beautiful Roof in the World: Exploring the Rainforest Canopy* by Kathryn Lasky. In this beautiful book, scientist, Meg Low shares her world of canopies, while Christopher Knight photographs them for the world to see.

The Human Organism

This study involves human identity, human development, basic functions, learning, physical, and mental health. Seymour Simon's many books on the human body are important additions to the classroom to promote understanding of these human development principles. Two books of particular interest to young readers are Simon's *Bones: Our Skeletal System* and *The Brain: Our Nervous System*. Both books have illustrations and photographs showing details of the systems of the body. A book about the body that will keep readers glued to the pages is Mike Janulewicz's *Yikes! Your Body, Up Close* in which body parts are shown through a microscope. It is often hard to believe they are really human parts. For the mature readers, Jenny Bryan's *Genetic Engineering* blends ethics into the science issues of human genetic research. Also for middle and high school students, Michael

Ford's *The Voices of AIDS* gives insight into this tragic disease through personal stories and well-researched facts.

Common Themes

Students examine themes as ways of thinking and they cross many fields of study, including science. These themes are identified as systems, models, scales, and ways of viewing constancy and change. A book that will help open the minds of students and teachers to the inclusivity of science in all realms of living is *Good Earth Art: Environmental Art for Kids* by Mary Ann F. Kohl. The organization of scientific information is a theme that is exemplified in much of children's literature in terms of classification and comparison. Steven Jenkins's *Biggest, Strongest, Fastest* provides organizational charts that help children classify the records of various animals. Size, speed, and other items related to characteristics and habitats are provided. Two more examples of such organization are *Close, Closer, Closest* by Shelley Rotner and Russell Ash's *Incredible Comparisons*. Another way of organizing themes across science is to teach children to search for patterns in nature. *Echoes for the Eye: Poems to Celebrate Patterns in Nature* by Barbara Esbensen is a delicately illustrated picture book that encourages the celebration of patterns. Similarly, nature's patterns of camouflage are found in beautiful colors in Susan Stockdale's *Nature's Paintbrush: The Patterns and Color Around You.*

These principles constitute major ideas in the study and appreciation of our natural world. As students have experiences with literature that guide them in their pursuit of these concepts, they will be developing the processes of thinking, speaking, and writing as they are integrated across the curriculum. These skills lead to the writing, drawing, building, and other manifestations of the developing processes.

Processes for Understanding the Natural World

Through the integration of science concepts with children's literature, time may be carved out of the daily schedule for observing, reading about observations, and representing ideas through manipulating objects, drawing, and creating symbols with graphics.

Observation and Experimentation

Literature that will promote observation and experimentation includes *Buried Treasure: Roots and Tubers* by Meredith and Tom Hughes. The simple experiments are explained for young scientists to watch and follow. In Leila Ward's *I Am Eye—Ni Macho*, a young Kenyan girl opens her eyes to the world around her as a model for children who read this book. Another book, which takes readers on a tour and guides observation is *Autumn Leaves* by Ken Robbins, while a chapter book that promotes observation is Jim Arnosky's *Secrets of a Wildlife Watcher*.

Discussion

For science comprehension and meaningfulness, many opportunities for discussion are vital. Some of these books may be read as a group or a whole class, much as they would read and talk about a fictional narrative.

Picture books that may be read aloud to students or shown on an overhead display for them to read and discuss include:

1. *The Wump World* by Bill Peet (picture book—elementary)
2. *Each Living Thing* by Joanne Ryder (picture book—primary)
3. *Just A Dream* by Chris Van Allsburg (picture book—upper elementary)
4. *Turtle Spring* by Deborah Turney Zagwyn (picture book—primary)
5. *Trashy Town* by Andrea Zimmerman (picture book—primary)

Chapters or sections may be assigned for reading, followed by "literature circles," sometimes called "literature discussion groups." Listed below are some books that allow readers to get caught up in stories that promote scientific principles as well as encourage thinking. These chapter books for intermediate readers provide opportunities for students to read about science and discuss their insights and have their questions discussed by group members.

1. *How to Really Fool Yourself: Illusions for All Your Senses* by Vicki Cobb (nonfiction book—upper elementary)
2. *River Friendly, River Wild* by Jane Kurtz (nonfiction picture book—primary)

3. *Summer of Fire: Yellowstone 1988* by Patricia Lauber (nonfiction book—upper elementary)
4. *Dolphin Man: Exploring the World of Dolphins* by Lawrence Pringle (nonfiction book—upper elementary)
5. *To Space and Back* by Sally Ride (nonfiction book—middle elementary)

Vocabulary Growth

Many books have italicized vocabulary with meaningful ways to connect to the new words. Others have words that are italicized or in a bold font that make the new words stand out for the reader. Most informational books of merit have a glossary in which the reader can check any new word whose meaning is unfamiliar.

1. *Soaring with the Wind: The Bald Eagle* by Gail Gibbons (nonfiction book—primary)
2. *A Dinosaur Named Sue: The Story of the Colossal Fossil* by Pat Relf with the SUE Science Team of the Field Museum (nonfiction book—middle school)
3. *The Universe* by Seymour Simon (nonfiction book—middle elementary)
4. *Outside and Inside Dinosaurs* by Sandra Markle (nonfiction book—middle elementary)
5. *Australian Animals* by Caroline Arnold (nonfiction book—middle elementary)

Visual Literacy

Students need to be aware of the visual clues that authors and illustrators use to convey information. Authors use devices to promote visual as well as verbal literacy. Through the manipulation of white space on the page, sidebars of textual information, and changes in font sizes and shapes, authors and publishers are attempting to direct the eye to salient information. An example of this promotion of visual literacy is *Gentle Giant Octopus* by Karen Wallace. Look at this book and you will see interesting fonts and sidebars of information. A photographic device that encourages visual inquiry is that of limited views and unique angles in showing the pictures on the page. Henry Horenstein has done this remarkably in his *A is for . . . ? A Photographer's Alphabet of Animals.*

Representation

Children must have opportunities to represent their understandings through writing, drawing, building, art media, dramatizations, and real, hands-on experimentation. Cole[3] describes a class experience of examining sunflowers that were grown in the school garden and comparing one that had been damaged by a storm with one that had not. Through such an experience, children have opportunities to plant seeds, watch them grow, manipulate the growing environment with fertilizers, water, and care. Many opportunities would be available for drawing, researching, even bonding with the young blossoms as they grow and develop. Keeping observation records on a regular basis will give students an idea of how a scientist follows the development of plants and animals. Writing stories and poems or "how-to" gardening books are possible outcomes of such an experience. Whatever topic is being studied in science, the opportunity should be provided for students to develop skills of observation, discussion, and representation.[4]

Criteria for High Quality Books: Promote Thinking and Critical Assessment

Today's generation of young people will need to have read and understood enormous amounts of information by the time they are adults. Therefore it's crucial that these kids begin to read expository text early in their lives. With the quality of nonfiction books being published today for young readers, children have every opportunity to read factual information that is presented in an attractive format and in accessible language. Beverly Kobrin,[5] a nonfiction zealot, has inspired a generation of teachers to make reading nonfiction books the rage. Her enthusiasm is catching, and she urges teachers to have classrooms bulging with books and let the students choose what they want to read, never saying to a child, "That's too hard," or "That's too easy," and spoiling their fun of choosing a book that is of interest to them. Those ugly old factual series books are going away. Today's books are carefully designed and filled with eye-catching illustrations. Readers can pick and choose what they want to read and look at in each book.

However, "looks aren't everything." The purpose of informational books is to present facts. Two crucial aspects of informational books are authority and accuracy. As you look at a nonfiction book, ask who the author is. Whether the text is from a first- or third-person perspective, the authority to tell the story or give the information must be established. In nonfiction texts, the authority is often presented on the book jacket by giving the author's credentials, but students must be taught to realize that qualifications can be misleading. The fact that an author has written two books on a subject does not in itself make that author credible in the subject. Consideration must be given to background, training, and experience, all of which could qualify someone to write a book. Students can easily be taught to ask several questions to determine the veracity of the voice speaking in the text. These questions include:

- What are the author's credentials?
- Is there anything on the back flap that states whether or not this author has written other books on the subject or worked in the field?
- Is there anything about the author's education that would indicate knowledge of the subject?
- Is there evidence that the author's resources are up-to-date—acknowledgements or photo credits that will help the reader evaluate the book?
- Is the content balanced and unbiased?
- If the subject is controversial, are various perspectives explored?
- Does the author use recent resources and references to make points?
- Are there other books on the same subject that contradict content? If so, where can more information be found?
- Is the author presenting a voice of authenticity?

- As we guide these budding critical readers of expository text, it's good for teachers to remember that

Authenticity reigns supreme in nonfiction inquiry. Topics are chosen based on sincere questions and interest. Research involves real-world pursuits such as Web searches, interviews, and surveys. Professionals serve as mentors. Writing is modeled through authentic nonfiction text from magazines, trade books, billboards. If we adhere to this ideal of authenticity, we deliver added value throughout students' lives.[6]

National Geographic published *Zoo in the Sky: A Book of Animal Constellations* in 1998. The book is a visual delight and jam-packed with information. Who is the author? Jacqueline Mitton. The back flap tells us that she holds a master's degree in physics from the University of Oxford and a doctorate in astrophysics from the University of Cambridge. The asteroid 4027 was named Mitton for Simon and Jacqueline Mitton jointly by the International Astronomical Union in 1990.[7] Clearly this book has "authority," which basically means that the author has the knowledge or knows where to go and who to ask for the information necessary.

Stuart Murphy is the author of the very fine MathStart series of books for HarperCollins. The back flap of one of his most recent books gives the following information about him: "A visual learning specialist, and a graduate of the Rhode Island School of Design, he has a strong background in design and experience in the world of educational publishing."[8]

This does not really tell the reader anything about Mr. Murphy's abilities or expertise in math, so one needs to see if there is any other information to give validity to the book as a "math" book. The next place to look for information is the acknowledgements page. There it says, "The publisher and author would like to thank teachers Patricia Chase, Phyllis Goldman and Patrick Hopfensperger for their help in making the math in MathStart just right for kids."[9] This gives us more confidence in the accuracy of the math in the book.

Most of us who read a nonfiction book choose it because we are looking for information; therefore we aren't really in the position of judging the accuracy of the information supplied. Since it's a published book, we trust that the editors made certain that the facts were accurate. If we've verified the author's credentials, we're usually comfortable with the work. If there is any question about the accuracy, the reader could check a recent edition of an encyclopedia, other books on the same subject, or visit the library and look at reviews of the book.

Woolly Mammoth: Life, Death, and Rediscovery was written by Windsor Chorlton, "well known for his scientific writing, particularly in subjects dealing with geology, biology, evolution and paleontology."[10] Upon further examination, it is apparent that the book is full of detailed information about the 1999 excavation and airlift of the Jarkov mammoth from the permafrost and ice of the Taimyr Peninsula of Siberia. Replete with authentic photographs and original documents from the excavation, readers realize that this book is full of accurate details and factual data. In order to promote the importance of critical reading, it's always good to have students read two or three books on a subject. This way, they cannot only check for accuracy, but also see a subject from more than one perspective.

How do students get "hooked" on informational books? First the information has to be presented in such a way that they are immediately intrigued and want to read on. In most instances, if they aren't engaged within the first few minutes, they'll put the book back on the library shelf, or anyplace close. Trevor Day's *Youch! It Bites*, begins with "Watch your step!" Those words will immediately gain attention. The next paragraph will rivet most young readers (and old ones!),

If you go down to the woods today, you're sure of a scary surprise. Because the woods, and many other places, are crawling with all sorts of horrible little plants and creatures. If you get in their way they might bite, prick, or sting you. Some of them can even kill. And many of them are much more dangerous to you than any kind of big creature you might be frightened of.[11]

Mr. Day has established a distinct "voice" in the book, one with which readers can easily identify. He has clearly let his audience know that this book is going to be exciting, scary, fun, and factual. He has "hooked" his readers and now he will hold them by offering convincing details. Quotations, anecdotes, and significant and unusual facts captivate readers further.

Once inside a nonfiction book, readers should ask the following questions. Is the book well organized? Are there some visual clues such as different sizes or font types that scream, "Stop here; this is important!" Are there headings and subheadings that break up large blocks of text? Is the information presented in a logical way? Do the illustrations complement the text or are they just scattered throughout willy-nilly?

Challenges for Teachers

With the contemporary lifestyles of many families, children are involved in a compacted schedule that includes being transported to school, maneuvered through daily routines, picked up and taken to varied after-school activities, only to be followed by homework time to finish off the day. When does a child have time to study the shapes of a snowflake? How can teachers open the doors to the natural world for their students?

It is clear that a large part of the responsibility lies on the shoulders of teachers to find time for students to commune with nature, reflect on their observations, and respond to them in some way.

Teaching Strategies

Strategies that provide opportunities for interacting with the natural world include:

integrating science with language arts and other reading activities to provide the time for exposure to the science content. When a special block of time is required for science activities, it may be taken over by other curricular areas, especially if science is not tested on statewide assessments.

using nonfiction science trade books for guided reading, independent reading, and literature discussion groups will provide opportunities for students to explore the world of expository writing while gaining insights into science principles.

taking students on nature walks and giving them responsibilities for taking field notes, for sketching, and for reporting back to the whole class on their observations.

planning experimentations for small groups with share-back to the whole class describing findings of the group.

encouraging students to keep journals for recording observations from various perspectives. For example, watch a squirrel nibble a nut in a tree and imagine what other creatures may be watching the squirrel. Describe your view and that of another creature from a different angle.

balancing the writing program with personal narratives, fictional narratives, expository texts, including descriptions, letters, and persuasions.

Getting to Know Our World: An Expedition

Guiding Questions

1. What are some ways that people have learned to appreciate our natural world?
2. How have they traveled?
3. Why have they traveled?
4. What have they found out about their world?
5. How have their own worlds differed from those they found in their travels?
6. Did their lives change because of their travels? How?
7. How can we learn more about our world?

Standards

The standards in this expedition are from the National Society of Geographical Information,[12] the National Council of Teachers of English/International Reading Association,[13] and the National Council of Teachers of Math.[14]

The students:

know how to use maps and other geographic representations, tools, and technologies to acquire, process, and report information from a spatial perspective.

know how culture and experience influence people's perceptions of places and regions.

read a wide range of print and nonprint texts to build an understanding of texts, of themselves, and of the cultures of the United States and the world; to acquire new information; to respond to the needs and demands of society and the workplace; and for personal fulfillment. Among these texts are fiction and nonfiction, classic and contemporary work.

understand measurable attributes of objects and the units, systems, and processes of measurement.

Initial Reading Options for Teacher Read-Aloud, Shared, Guided, or Independent Reading

1. *Uncommon Traveler: Mary Kingsley in Africa* by Don Brown (picture book—elementary)
2. *Alice Ramsey's Grand Adventure,* by Don Brown (picture book—primary)
3. *Ruth Law Thrills a Nation,* by Don Brown (picture book—primary)
4. *A Voice from the Wilderness: The Story of Anna Howard Shaw* by Don Brown (picture book—primary)
5. *Rare Treasures: Many Anning and Her Remarkable Discoveries,* 1999 by Don Brown (picture book—primary)
6. *Across a Dark and Wild Se,* by Don Brown (picture book—middle elementary)
7. *One Giant Leap: The Story of Neil Armstrong* by Don Brown (picture book—middle elementary)

Fieldwork Options

1. Map the areas traveled in your book. Identify latitude and longitude for each destination.
2. Find a public library online near the destination in each of the Don Brown books and find local information on the characters and their travels.
3. Measure distances from your city to the destinations of the characters in the books. Determine travel time for various speeds and modes of travel.

Individual Projects

1. Read books as assigned for literature discussion groups and be prepared for each discussion.
2. Keep a log of information on where the characters went and what experiences they had.

Class Projects

1. Write Don Brown and communicate with him about his books.
2. Invite him to visit your classroom.
3. Raise money to pay an honorarium to the author.
4. Compare travel expenses for flying or driving to various locations.
5. Ask your local librarian for the names of people in your community who have been "uncommon travelers." Try to contact those people and invite them to your class. Develop questions to ask them based on where they have traveled and what they have experienced.
6. Study the geography of each area and recognize the natural world as experienced by each character in the books.
7. Conduct literature discussion groups at least two times a week until all students have read all of the travel books.
8. Design a mural to show all of the travels and the experiences of the characters.
9. Simulate a travel agency and prepare materials for each trip.

Sharing Outlets

1. Author Day to focus on the author of these books and others discovered during this expedition.

2. Mural depicting the sites and characters in the Don Brown books in the school entrance or in a hallway where others may see it.
3. Student created "Travel Agency" in the media center with travel logs and brochures made by students showing the sites studied in the books.

Assessment Options

1. Students should complete checklist of activities in which they participated.
2. Materials developed will be placed in individual portfolios (maps showing longitude and latitude).
3. Written responses to the literature discussion groups will be assessed for the literature standard.
4. Measurement data will be shown in portfolio.

Notes

1. http://www.elob.org/aboutel/principles.html
2. Michael Sanera and Jane S. Shaw, *Facts, Not Fear: Teaching Children about the Environment* (Washington, D.C.: Regnery, 1999).
3. Elizabeth S. Cole, "An Experience in Froebel's Garden," *Childhood Education* 67 (1990): 18–20.
4. Theodora Polito, "Frederick Froebel's Illuminations on Kindergarten Children's Relatedness to Nature," *Education* 116 (1995): 223–229.
5. Beverly Kobrin, *Eyeopeners II: Children's Books to Answer Children's Questions About the World Around Them* (New York: Scholastic, 1995).
6. Stephanie Harvey, *Nonfiction Matters: Reading, Writing, Research in Grades 3–8,* (York, Maine.: Stenhouse, 1998), 7.
7. Jacqueline Mitton, *Zoo in the Sky: A Book of Animal Constellations* (Washington, D.C.: National Geographic, 1998), back flap.
8. Stuart Murphy, *Safari Park* (New York: HarperCollins, 2002), back flap.
9. Ibid., iv.
10. Windsor Chorlton *Woolly Mammoth: Life, Death, and Rediscovery,* (New York: Scholastic, 2001), back flap.
11. Trevor Day, *Youch! It Bites* (New York: Simon & Schuster, 1999), 1.
12. http://www.nationalgeographic.com/xpeditions/standards/index.html
13. http://www.ncte.org
14. http://standards.nctm.org/

Chapter 11

Replenishing Energies: Solitude and Reflection

Sometimes, in a summer morning, having taken my accustomed bath,
I sat in my sunny doorway from sunrise till noon, rapt in a revery,
amidst the pines and hickories and sumachs, in undisturbed solitude
and stillness, while the birds sang around or flitted noiseless through
the house, until by the sun falling in at my west window, or the noise
of some traveller's wagon on the distant highway, I was reminded of
the lapse of time.

--Henry David Thoreau, *Henry David's House,* 2002

It is this kind of solitude and reflection that represents the design principle from Expeditionary Learning.

Solitude, reflection, and silence replenish our energies and open our minds. Be sure students have time alone to explore their own thoughts, make their own connections and create their own ideas. Then give them opportunity to exchange their reflections with each other and with adults.[1]

Henry David Thoreau, an American scholar and disciple of Ralph Waldo Emerson, sought solitude so he could return to a simple life. He lived alone on the shore of Walden Pond in Concord, Massachusetts, from July 4, 1845, until September 6, 1847. During this time, he wrote his most famous work, *Walden.* He spent each day carefully observing and recording experiences and thoughts in his journals. Nine years later it was published.

A small segment of Mr. Thoreau's journal provides the text for the lovely picture book that Steven Schnur has edited. Peter Fiore's luxuriant, impressionistic paintings evoke exactly the kind of peacefulness that leads to reflection.

Literature that Promotes Reflection

Readers can find books that inspire reflection in any genre. Nonfiction is a good place to start. We've seen an excerpt from Henry David Thoreau's journal. There is no question that this is an example of someone who is experiencing life in solitude and through reflection.

Thoughtful observations are a part of reflection. It is easy to assume that our lives are composed of usual routines and objects when those objects and daily routines may actually lead to unique, creative thinking. Have you ever examined the scales on a turtle's shell? Few of us would recognize the potential for such scrutiny. Joseph Bruchac, however, thought about them and tells a Native American moon legend for each scale. Just imagine how he was inspired to retell these tales. He must have studied the scales for some time, thinking about the beauty of each and connecting the patterns to the tales he wanted to tell. The poet, Jonathan London, joined forces with Joseph Bruchac to effectively mold the words to represent these Native American tales. Thomas Locker, the illustrator, must have contemplated each tale as he shaped the oil paintings. Such solitude and reflection for the three of them led to the creation of *Thirteen Moons on Turtle's Back: A Native American Year of the Moons*.

Jim Arnosky is an artist and a naturalist and, after many years of examining the natural wonders found around his home in northern Vermont, he and his wife decided to explore wildlife in different parts of the United States. *Wild and Swampy* reflects his fascination with "Southern swamplands and the creatures that live there."[2] His text and illustrations give the reader a sense of peace as he reflects on the magnificence of nature.

Jean Craighead George's books reveal her deep reverence for nature and living in accord with it. Quiet respect and honor of nature are encouraged, whether the setting is the Everglades of Florida in *The Talking Earth*, or the Catskill Mountains of New York, the setting for *My Side of the Mountain*. The characters take on the traits of Ms. George and her family, all of whom have a great love of nature and an interest in observing and preserving it. *The Everglades*, illustrated by Wendell Minor, with paintings that invite the reader to linger on in depth, begins with a Seminole storyteller poling a canoe through the river of grass, telling the five children with him about the natural evolution of the Everglades and then the man-made destruction of it. A child responds at the end of the story, "But this is a sad story." [3] The storyteller then tells another story—a happy story—about his hope for the children to grow up and restore the earth's natural resources.

There are some excellent Internet websites where children can read interviews with Ms. George that reflect not only her love of nature and the animals that she has cared for over the years, but also her encouragement to students to write about their own observations and experiences. A quick search of her name will produce many current sources of information.

Descriptive sequences, without characters or plot, lead the reader to appreciate the season, the month, or the aspect of nature. Cynthia Rylant's *In November*, depicts unrelated events of both animals and humans that give a thoughtful feeling to the month of November. Another book of descriptions, although wordless, is Peter Spier's *Rain*.

Books such as these call on readers to evoke their own reflections and memories. Many different themes are present in the books that look back on other days and other times. From *The Dust Bowl* by David Booth, readers are able to see the natural disaster brought on by nature's wrath when the drought in Canada turned the land into a dust bowl. Through the memories of his grandfather, Matthew gains respect for the "Big Dry" of the 1930s.

Another book that provides an excellent model for thinking about the past and reliving memories is Lois Lowry's autobiographical, *Looking Back: A Book of Memories*. Through the series of vignettes connected to photographs and excerpts from her books, Ms. Lowry gives the reader a personal tour of her life and memories. One could learn to reflect by studying this example.

Many intergenerational books with characters ranging through several generations reveal moments of looking back as the oldest of the characters reflects on lives and events. *The Memory Box* by Mary Bahr finds a grandfather and grandson preserving artifacts that will someday remind them of their times together. Sometimes these memories are passed on to the younger ones and sometimes they are trapped in the minds of the older generation, with only a glimpse of emotion to show that something is still there. *The Sunsets of Miss Olivia Wiggins* by Lester Laminack implies the presence of some good memories as shown by a quiver of a smile on the face of a grandmother with Alzheimer's disease.

Learning to Be a "Watcher"

In Mary Lyn Ray's *Basket Moon*, beautifully illustrated by Barbara Cooney, a boy wants to follow his father's footsteps in making baskets from black ash trees. His father tells him to be "a watcher," and through his watching and listening, he is able to understand the craft of his family and take pride in it, knowing that someday he will follow in this trade.

Becoming a watcher should be one of our goals for children. Any genre of literature can cause one to stop and think about what has been read or seen in the illustrations. Almost any topic can be the source for pondering. Very young children spend much time looking at illustrations. Their observation skills are much better than those of adults, whose superficial glossing over of pages can cause embarrassment when children have seen so much more in the illustrations. For example, how many adults have noticed the mouse on almost every page of Tomie de Paola's *Charlie Needs a Cloak* or who has noticed an unnamed troll in *Helga's Dowry* throughout the book? Most adults who read Arlene Mosel's *The Funny Little Woman* never realize that the black-and-white sketches at the top of the pages tell a story—not the one in the text. Chris Van Allsburg's spotted dog in his illustrations is rarely seen by adults without a prompt! Children, however, notice these visual teasers.

Children spend much time examining what they see and deciding if their observations match with previous ideas and information. Preserving that tendency from early into later childhood, to consider and wonder about what is in a book, should be a goal in the schools today. Books that provide details in words and pictures, such as Sharon Creech's *Fishing in the Air*, give children many reasons to spend time becoming "watchers." Through detailed questions and answers in the story and colorful, abstract illustrations by Chris Raschka, the little boy who went fishing caught " . . . a bubble of breeze and a sliver of sky and a slice of yellow sun and a small gray house with a crooked porch and tiny windows and a red roof and rolling green fields with red flowers waving and tall green trees and a river rippling cool and clear."[4]

Learning to be a Thinker

When teachers promote thinking time by waiting for children's answers, they are giving children a message on the importance of deliberation and thinking before they speak. When teachers ask higher order "thinking" questions, such as those beginning with "why," "how," "in what ways," or "what if," children learn to reflect on possibilities. In the computer age, when information is at one's fingertips, the skills of interpreting information and applying it will carry a learner much further than factual information. Teachers have great opportunities to support and extend those strategies in their students by giving them opportunities to think and plan around higher order questions and application assignments.

Judith Langer writes of strategies that we can teach students as they construct their own understandings of information as they read. The first strategy they use is to get an overview of what the text is all about and how the author seems to be envisioning it. Next the reader will connect what is believed about the author's vision with information already known about the topic. In this stance, the reader asks questions and tries to fit new concepts or ideas with existing ones. The third part of this model is for the readers to reflect on their own experiences and rethink what they already know, adapting and planning for application of the information. The last stance is to look critically at the content and the text and compare it to other pieces of information, other texts on the same subject, other fiction dealing with the same themes, and to ultimately construct their own way of thinking about this information or experience.[5] By providing students with opportunities to move through these stances, teachers are valuing the thought processes question.

Trickster tales often promote this kind of thinking when children in the elementary grades search for their understanding of characters and their behaviors along with their growing appreciation of humor. Gerald McDermott's *Coyote: A Trickster Tale from the American Southwest, Zomo the Rabbit: A Trickster Tale from West Africa,* and *Anansi the Spider: A Tale from the Ashanti* are good books for giving students opportunities to think about motivation, actions, and consequences.

When children have opportunities to think about situations that challenge their previous knowledge, they are forced to compare what they know to the new information. When they face this kind of disequilibrium, they work hard to find new understandings. In Nila Leigh's *Learning to Swim in Swaziland,* the eight-year-old author tells about moving south of the equator where the seasons are reversed. School begins in the winter, the constellations in the sky are totally different, and bathtubs drain clockwise instead of counterclockwise. With books such as these, teachers have an opportunity to model their own thinking and help children find strategies for reconciling new information with old and adapting it to their own understanding.

For mature readers in upper elementary and middle school, the Time Quartet by Madeleine L'Engle, composed of *A Wrinkle in Time, A Wind in the Door, A Swiftly Tilting Planet,* and *Many Waters,* challenges readers' knowledge of the physical world with science fiction while delivering wholesome stories of families growing up and growing together as they search for information, rescue each other, and have anxious moments in their struggle for good over evil. Thinking and comparing new information to the old are processes that automatically occur while reading these books. The books in this quartet are outstanding for read-alouds since they are written at fairly high levels but can be understood by most middle elementary students. If you, the teacher, fail to read these books to your students, they may never be exposed to this "classic" literature.

Poetry for Solitude and Reflection

Many forms of literature give children the motivation to think and reflect, and they appreciate the time to explore their thoughts and make connections. Poetry, though not exclusively reflective, often brings the reader to an introspective state. Eloise Greenfield's *Nathaniel Talking,* a compilation of a nine-year-old boy's remembrances, gives us a glimpse into the mind of a child trying to sort out what has been happening in his life.

> I remember
> walking down the street beside
> Uncle Eddie's legs
> taking a nap in Mama's lap
> talking to the pigeons in the park
> I remember
> my fuzzy hat, my yellow cat
> my potty pot
> I remember a lot
> but I wish I remembered
> what I forgot[6]

This poem is typical of the child mind, first describing in a reflective mode his memories of earlier days, memories of Mama, who is no longer with him, and then jumping abruptly to the humorous ending. Yes, poetry for children can be reflective; children can value solitude and time to think and ponder, but you can't keep them in that mind-set for very long. Kids are by nature emotional, but they are also prone to action, humor, sounds, images, and the rhythmical dance of the words. They move in and out of emotions and of solitude quickly.

Ralph Fletcher, author of fiction, nonfiction, and poetry tells us that poetry matters.[7] He identifies the components of poetry as emotion, image, and music. We will explore those areas as we look at poetry for children.

Emotions in Poetry

Mr. Fletcher says poetry must touch the soul.[8] Poetry seems to have a language of its own and children understand the language once they are exposed to it in a nonthreatening way.

Jim McKenna, a well-known story reader from New York was a speech teacher in an elementary school for many years. During his tenure, he decided that the most effective way to teach children how to speak correctly was to read aloud to them every single day. Mr. McKenna has shared his love for children's literature with thousands of students all over the country since then and, on a ride home from one of his story reader sessions, the following poem came, almost fully formed into his mind:

Reading with Mom and Dad

My mother always reads to me
Before I go to bed
But sometimes she is busy,
So my dad
will read instead.
My mom and dad both love to read,
I like it when they do.
Reading books that they pick out
And some of my books, too,
They sound just like they're talking
When they read those books with me.
The way they read the words out loud
Are pictures I can see.
My dad does all the voices,
Some are low and some are high,
And when my mom reads quiet books,
It almost makes me cry.
I asked them how they learned to read
Tiptoeing down the hall.
They said their parents read to them
When they were very small.
They sat around with lots of books

And did not watch TV
So when they got to go to school,
The words came easily.
Some day I'll read just like them
And make books come alive,
But I guess I'll have to wait awhile
'Cause gee! I'm only five!!!

—Jim McKenna, 1999[9]

Jim often shares this poem with his audiences and explains how important it is for parents to read aloud to children. Not only does it provide a time when listeners can develop a sense of language, but it also provides an emotional bond between the reader and the listener. This poem touches the soul.

Poems about animals are also safe for touching the emotions, motivating the child's interest, and when written in rhyme, they are likely to be enjoyed by children.

Mother Doesn't Want a Dog

Mother doesn't want a dog.
Mother says they smell,
And never sit when you say sit,
Or even when you yell.
And when you come home late at night
And there is ice and snow,
You have to go back out because
The dumb dog has to go.

Mother doesn't want a dog,
Mother says they shed,
And always let the strangers in
And bark at friends instead,
And do disgraceful things on rugs,
And track mud on the floor,
And flop upon your bed at night
And snore their doggy snore.

Mother doesn't want a dog.
She's making a mistake.
Because more than a dog I think
She will not want this snake.

—Judith Viorst

From the animal kingdom, what more attention-grabbing creatures are there than frogs, especially when *The Frogs Wore Red Suspenders*? This book of poetry by Jack Prelutsky with a poem by the same name as the title of the book is bound to captivate youngsters.

The frogs wore red suspenders
and the pigs wore purple vests
as they sang to all the chickens
and the ducks upon their nests.

They croaked and oinked a serenade,
the ducks and chickens sighed,
then laid enormous spangled eggs,
and quacked and clucked with pride.[10]

In this oversized book with large, colorful watercolor illustrations, animals abound along with a few places and people. This book is bound to be one that children will take to heart and read until they can recite some of the verses.

Beastly Banquet: Tasty Treats for Animal Appetites by Peggy Munsterberg is a good choice for poetry about feeding animals, birds, insects, and arachnids and the kinds of foods they like. Dogs, goldfish, and goats are the pets shown and then the eating habits of lots of wild animals are addressed in rhyming and rhythmic poetry.

For children (and adults) getting in touch with their own childhood interests and emotions, such as new babies, fears of the Boogie Man, and off-color subjects such as belly buttons and toe jam, a hilarious book for all ages is *Barking Spiders and Other Such Stuff: Poetry for Children* by C. J. Heck. As a read-aloud, teachers and parents can use this book to delight the children, and they can be assured that the book will be picked up later for browsing.

Here is a selected list of poetry that will touch the emotions of children and show them what a vivid pleasure poetry can be.

1. *You Come Too: Favorite Poems for All Ages* by Robert Frost
2. *My Kingdom for a Horse: An Anthology of Poems About Horses* edited by Betty Ann Schwarts
3. *From Daybreak to Good Night* : Poems for Children by Carl Sandburg
4. *Random House Book of Poetry for Children* by Jack Prelutsky

Image in Poetry

Ralph Fletcher's second descriptor of poetry is image.[11] It is important for children to be able to "see" in their minds' eyes the scenes depicted in the poetry. For this reason, it is vital that poetry for children be written about things they have experienced, dreamed about, or could possibly imagine. Younger children, with concrete cognitive development, delight in poems about topics they know. Collections have been published over the years, keeping in mind the developmental needs of children. One such book, still in print from 1969, is *Poems Children Will Sit Still for: A Selection for the Primary Grades* by Beatrice Schenk De Regniers. The poems are presented in sections that include the following topics: weather, spooky poems, animals, people, seeing, feeling, thinking, and nonsense. It is easy to see how children can relate to these poems and create wonderful pictures in their minds from them. Following is an example:

Dogs

The dogs I know
Have many shapes.
For some are big and tall,

And some are long,
And
some
are thin,
And some are fat and small

And some are little bits of fluff
And have no shape at all.

—Marchette Chute[12]

Who could deny the fun of reading and thinking about this poem by Rhoda Bacmeister:

Galoshes[13]

Susie's galoshes
Make splishes and sploshes
And slooshes and sloshes

As Susie steps slowly
Along in the slush.

They stamp and they tramp
On the ice and concrete,
They get stuck in the muck and the mud;
But Susie likes much best to hear

The slippery slush
As it slooshes and sloshes,
And splishes and sploshes,
All around her galoshes.

Although the previous poems are classics, poems from previous generations continue to be published, as they still strike a note of accord with children. One newly published book is Liz Attenborough's compilation of *Poetry by Heart: A Child's Book of Poems to Remember.* Through the large-print poems and the delightful illustrations, children will hear and read poems clustered around concepts, such as short and sharp, fur and feathers, ghostly and ghastly, and peace and quiet. It is obvious that these poems will tickle kids. Some are old favorites by Robert Louis Stevenson, Edward Lear, and Kate Greenaway. Such poems as "Me" by Kit Wright[14] are perfect for reading aloud.

My Mum is on a diet,
My Dad is on the booze,
My Gran's out playing Bingo
And she was born to lose.

My brother stripped his motorbike
Although it's bound to rain.
My sister's playing Elton John
Over and over again.

What a dim old family!
What a dreary lot!
Sometimes I think that I'm the only
Superstar they've got.

True or not, we have to admit that "unfortunately," many children can picture this image in their minds and can relate to this modern family.

Teachers could use the following books of poetry to help kids develop visual imagery:

1. *Where the Sidewalk Ends* by Shel Silverstein
2. *Light in the Attic* by Shel Silverstein
3. *Falling Up* by Shel Silverstein
4. *It's Raining Pigs and Noodles* by Jack Prelutsky
5. *Virtual Maniac: Silly and Serious Poems for Kids* by Margriet Ruurs
6. *The Feelings and Imagination of a Barefoot Boy Still Inside My Head! Poems and Short Stories for Boys and Girls, Ages 9 to 12* by Richard W. Carlson.

Music in Poetry

The third characteristic of poetry enjoyed by children, according to Ralph Fletcher, is music.[15] In addition to connecting to emotions and providing clear images, poetry must also be music to the ears of children or they are not interested.

Mother Goose and Nursery Rhymes

From their earliest exposure to poetry, children are mesmerized with rhymes, songs, and chants produced by loving caretakers. Nursery and Mother Goose rhymes are the earliest literature of childhood. They are wonderfully compact stories with all the recognized elements of good literature: characters, plot, setting, theme, and point of view. They have the added delight of being rhythmical. Children pick them up easily, partly because they love the way those merry chants feel on their tongues as they form strings of words. Also, the rhymes are easy to learn because they rhyme and the pattern becomes familiar. Furthermore, they provide wonderful opportunities for the little ones to match physical activity to the sounds. They love to fall down with a dramatic flourish at the end of "Ring around the Rosy" and they giggle with delight at Pussy Cat's antics in "Pussy Cat, Pussy Cat, Where Have You Been?" How could that silly cat go to London to visit the Queen and why did he frighten a mouse under the chair? Naughty cat! Many lucky children have played pat-a-cake over and over and learn the first letter of their names when they prick the pancake. We know that nursery rhymes are a wonderful way to help teach phonemic awareness.

The origin of nursery and Mother Goose rhymes is difficult to pin-point. The history of Mother Goose is fascinating and well documented in Iona and Peter Opie's definitive study, *The Oxford Dictionary of Nursery Rhymes*. It is possible that many of the oldest rhymes were told as political commentaries on the times. The theory that Humpty Dumpty was Charles II of England has been bandied about, but the Opies do not give it credence. Instead, they state that linguists believe the rhyme must have been around for thousands of years.[16] Mother Goose rhymes were not originally told for children. They were often bawdy and cruel commentaries on life. However, many have withstood the test of time. Several are at least two hundred years old and the Opies report that one in four of the rhymes was likely to have been known in Shakespeare's time.

The image of the cat and the fiddle, the little dog laughing, and the cow jumping over the moon are vivid and full of joy. Nursery rhymes will continue to be a part of children's lives because they are "music to their ears."

Books of musical poetry, nursery rhymes, and lullabies that children love continue to be published every year. Some recent titles include:

1. *Animal Crackers: A Delectable Collection of Pictures, Poems, and Lullabies for the Very Young* edited by Jane Dyer
2. *The Lucy Cousins Book of Nursery Rhymes* by Lucy Cousins
3. *And the Dish Ran Away With the Spoon* by Janet Stevens and Susan Stevens Crummel
4. *Daisy Says If You're Happy and You Know It* by Jane Simmons

Musical Poetry for the Middle Kids

In Lois Lowry's *Anastasia Krupnik*, Anastasia labors long over a poem for Creative Week. When the day comes to read her poem, she stood up in front of the class and read.

> hush   hush   the sea-soft night is aswim
>   with wrinklesquirm creatures
>
>   listen (!)
>
> to them   move   smooth   in the moistly dark
>   here in the   whisperwarm   wet[17]

Her teacher asked her to read it again. "So Anastasia took a deep breath and read her poem again. She used the same kind of voice that her father did when he read poetry to her, drawing some of the words out as long as licorice sticks, and making some others thumpingly short."[18]

Playing with words, putting together sounds that tease the ear, and even making up new words as Anastasia did with wrinklesquirm and whisperwarm are the creative pleasures that bring children back to poetry. Anastasia's father was a poet and she had been exposed to the sound of poetry all of her life. Most children will not have had such experiences, but you can show them what can be done with the sounds of poetry.

Douglas Florian's *Bing, Bang, Boing* is full of poetry that flows off the tongue and begs kids to come back for more repeated readings. One poem with onomatopoeia (words that are written like they sound) is "Diet Riot":

> Beetles for breakfast,
> Lizards for lunch,
> Dragons for dinner—
> Crunch
> Crunch
> Crunch.[19]

Other poems and collections that appeal to youngsters include:

1. *Come With Me: Poems for a Journey* by Naomi Shihab Nye
2. *Joyful Noise* by Paul Fleishman
3. *Farmers Garden: Rhymes for Two Voices* by David L. Harrison
4. *Delirious: A Collection of Poems for Kids 8-88* by Brian G. Allfrey and Melinda Allfrey
5. *Kids Pick the Funniest Poems* by Bruce Lansky, Steve Carpenter, and Stephen Carpenter
6. *A Bad Case of the Giggles: Kids Pick the Funniest Poems, Book 2* by Bruce Lansky and Stephen Carpenter

Internet Websites for Poetry

Although Internet websites may come and go, it seems reasonable to note that vast resources are available and probably will become more plentiful. At www.poets.org, poetry and biographical sketches of many poets are available. Poets on the website include: Robert Browning, Lewis Carroll, Eugene Field, Rudyard Kipling, Edward Lear, Henry Wadsworth Longfellow, Edgar Allan Poe, James Whitcomb Riley, Robert Louis Stevenson, Ernest Laurence Thayer, Randall Jarrett, Robert Frost, and T. S. Eliott.

Poetry for Later Childhood and Early Adolescence

Stories have been told through poetry since Homer put the stories of Odysseus down in writing around 750 B.C. in ancient Greece. Recently, there has been an increase in adolescent novels written in free verse. Karen Hesse's *Out of the Dust*, Newbery Award winner for 1998 tells the story of a girl during the dust drought of the 1930s and her family's struggles through accidents, death, guilt, and seemingly irreparably damaged relationships. Hope does find its way into this book and readers are so caught up in the story, they actually forget they are reading poetry. A few years later, Ms. Hesse wrote *Witness* in free verse also. In that book, the voices of a dozen folks from a little town in Vermont tell of their soul-searching experiences as the Ku Klux Klan strengthens in their town.

Other books written in free verse and appropriate for middle-level students as well as the older ones are Byrd Baylor's beautiful poems of the American Southwest. *Hawk, I'm Your Brother, Everybody Needs a Rock, The Desert is Theirs,* and *When Clay Sings* are a few of her titles. And we cannot forget Sharon Creech's *Love That Dog,* which offers pure pleasure.

Strategies for Poetry Reading

It doesn't really matter why children choose to read poetry; the important thing is to keep them reading. One way to stop their reading poetry is to ask them to memorize it. Although as adults we probably have a few poems in our memories—some of which were forced upon us—those that we remember most fondly are ones that we memorized through repeated readings with a group of students in choral readings.

Choral Reading

When students read a poetry selection as a group, it is called choral reading. The variation in the sounds of the voices makes such readings pleasing to the ear. By practicing the reading several times to perfect the intonations and expressions, students learn the words quickly.

Poems are meant to be read aloud. We can only find the true rhythm, heart, and voice of the poem upon hearing it. When children read aloud with a group, they are more comfortable exploring the language, the rhythm, and the sound of the words in the poem than when they, alone, read the poem aloud to the class or a group. Poetry is full of emotion and kids are more willing to be expressive when they read in a group. Also, diction must be very precise within the group so articulation and enunciation reaches a high level among the participating chorus members.

Antiphonal Reading

A form of choral reading is antiphonal when groups are assigned various parts of the poem. Sometimes teachers group together the pitches of voices—low voices, high voices, boy voices, and/or girl voices—and will assign sections of the poem to each group. The contrasting sounds as they read are pleasant. Sometimes a variation of this type of reading becomes a line-a-child reading when each line or every two lines are assigned to a different voice.

Simultaneous Reading

Joyful Noise: Poems for Two Voices, 1988 Newbery Award winner by Paul Fleishman, is designed for choral reading. The poems are printed in two columns and each reader or groups of readers follow one column. Sometimes they overlap with either the same words or different words. In "The Moth's Serenade," Reader One says, "Let's clasp" while Reader Two says, "Let's kiss" and the next line is the exact opposite.[20]

Teachers also encourage creative readings by showing children how simultaneous texts may be read with repeated phrases alongside a well-known poem. One elementary teacher introduces her students to this type of reading by having the whole class read Shel Siverstein's "Spaghetti" several times to practice the intonations. Then a small group of students is given the phrase, "oodles and oodles and oodles of noodles," to practice together. When the poem and the phrase are read together, there is a cadence, almost like background music. It is important to allow all children to have an opportunity to be in both groups. Some teachers take this idea a step further and pass out other short poems to groups of students, allowing them to find the right rhythm for an accompanying phrase.

Forms of Poetry

Children start out loving rhyming words and sentences early in their lives. As they proceed through school they discover different forms of poetry. You can easily recognize forms of poetry and, once children learn about them, they will begin looking for them as they read. The earliest form of poetry that children enjoy is rhyming poetry. It makes sense for them to be encouraged to rhyme words and make short poems as they are developing phonemic awareness. The cinquain (pronounced sin-kane) is a familiar type of poetry with a specific pattern and way of forming the lines. Later, as children are in the middle grades of elementary school, they learn the rules of syllabication and can recognize how words are broken into syllables. It is at this time that they are able to write the syllabic poetry such as Haiku and Tanka. Concrete poetry is another form when the poem looks like its topic. The words are often written around and inside the graphic outline of the topic of the poem. Free verse is another form recognized by children and is harder for them to write because it depends on rhythm and its spacing on the printed page. Anastasia, in *Anastasia Krupnik* by Lois Lowry, wrote in free verse about the tidepool.

Rhyming Poetry
Couplet—two-line rhyming verse
Triplet—three-line rhyming verse
Quatrain—four-line rhyming verse with the following possible rhyming combinations: AAAA; AABB; ABAB; or ABBA
Limericks—five lines, one, two, and five rhyme; three and four rhyme and have a distinct meter with fewer words. Look at Arnold Lobel's *Pigericks* as a great guide.

There was a warm pig from Key West.
Of sandcastles, his was the best.
But as soon as he built it,
A wave came to tilt it,
Which dampened that pig from Key West.[21]

Patterned Poetry
Cinquain was originally a five-line, twenty-two syllable poem broken into a syllabic pattern. The first line had two syllables, then four, then six, eight, and ended with two on the fifth line. The form has varied and teachers often use a word pattern instead of a syllable pattern.

1. title (one word)
2. description (two words)
3. verbs ending with ing related to title (three words)
4. emotions regarding title (four words)
5. another word for the title (one word)

There are many forms of the cinquain as well as ideas about it, but the one thing everyone agrees on is that it's five lines!

Wind
Brisk, Cool
Blowing, Puffing, Soothing
I face the wind.
Air

Diamante has seven lines and forms a diamond pattern. It is usually written from top to bottom and bottom to top simultaneously. Look at the pattern and you will see why.

1. one word, subject noun
2. two adjectives
3. three participles (either "ing" or "ed" but not mixture)
4. four nouns (two relate to title subject and two to the opposite of the title subject)
5. three participles related to opposite
6. two adjectives (opposite)
7. one noun opposite subject title

Dog
Gregarious, Playful
Running, Jumping, Barking
Sleek, Black, Soft, White
Slinking, Purring, Curling
Silent, Pensive
Cat

Syllabic Poetry
Haiku is a Japanese form of poetry with seventeen syllables in a five, seven, five pattern in three lines. The theme of a Haiku should relate to nature.

Dusk at riverside

The sun sank behind the trees
Now darkness follows

Senryu is the same form as Haiku but the theme is not restricted to nature.

It's been a long day
Full of hard work, fun, and play
Time to go to sleep

Tanka is another syllabic form of poetry with five lines and thirty-one syllables in the following order: five, seven, five, seven, and seven. Most of these poems are also written about nature.

Running on the beach
The sand and sun are calling
Summer days are here
For making good memories
Let them last awhile longer

Other Ways to Play with Words
Onomatopoeia—words look like they sound, such as buzz, crack, or munch.

Acrostics—word is spelled down the page with each letter beginning a descriptive phrase about the subject.

D—delightful pet
O—on the side of man
G—growls

Similes—comparison of two dissimilar objects using "like" or "as." Examples are "as tall as a house" or "bright like the sun."

Alliteration—similar sounds are used consecutively. An example is "Peter Piper picked a peck of pickled peppers" which uses consonant alliteration, called consonance. When the same vowel sound is used consecutively, it is called assonance. A good example is found in David McCord's poem about the Ladybug. He talks about

her sister, Sadiebug,
her mother, Mrs. Gradybug,
her aunt, that nice oldmaidy bug,
and Baby—she's a fraidybug.[22]

Children Writing Poetry

Jack
Room 105—Miss Stretchberry

September 13
    I don't want to
    because boys
    don't write poetry.
    Girls do.

September 21
    I tried.
    Can't do it.
    Brain's empty.

—Sharon Creech, *Love That Dog*

When it comes to writing poetry, many children feel just like Jack in the above poem. When faced with the task of writing poetry, Jack was intimidated. First, he was sure that only girls write poetry. Then when coaxed into giving it a try, he confessed that his brain could not produce poetry. Through the remainder of this novel, written in free verse, Jack tries his hand at expressing thoughts that represent his world and his life. Reading Jack's responses to his teacher, and reading his attempts at emulating models of poetry, confirms that when children write poetry, they need a great deal of guidance. They also need structure and much encouragement—coupled with the willingness to share the events of their own lives. It is only at the end of this book that the reader realizes how deeply Jack feels about the "blue car" that he writes about in his early attempts, and how events related to that car have impacted his life.

Jack was influenced by every poem that he read. As his teacher gradually introduced him to various styles of poetry, he developed a "theory of poetry in his head." Jack imitated every poetic form and convention that he was introduced to—from concrete poems that visually represent their content to the use of repetitive language. A little worried about how closely he imitated, Jack chose instead to be "inspired" by other poets.

Jack's experience in writing poetry is a classic example of how children can be gently coaxed into using a form of expression such as poetry when many examples are provided, along with support and guidance. Even with Jack's initial reluctance to write poetry, after exposure to it, he began to realize its value and saw reason for writing it himself.

Teaching Strategies for Writing Poetry

Poetry Writers' Workshop

Learning about poetry is a perfect goal for a writers' workshop. In writers' workshops, self-selection of topics for writing is a key to the students' sustained interest. When they can write about a topic of their choice, they will stay focused for a longer period of time and enjoy it more. A suggested structure for Poetry Writers' Workshop includes:

1. teacher reading poetry aloud for three to four minutes;
2. students thinking for about five minutes to allow ideas to begin to flow;
3. teacher checking with each student to determine the status of each in planning;
4. students writing poetry for fifteen minutes;
5. teacher conferencing with some students during the poetry-writing block;
6. students sharing unfinished products and asking for classroom community support with suggestions or comments.

Magazine Lexicon

Each student has a personal lexicon of vocabulary, but when asked to write poetry, many children don't feel they have control over their own language. They have a difficult time finding the right words. So give them a magazine lexicon in this way. Pass out magazines and scissors to teams of two or three students. Ask them to clip as many words as they can within a ten-minute period of time. Make sure they know to find some that rhyme, some of each of the parts of speech, especially verbs, some that describe, and some that are unusual. Remind them to find the words: a, an, the, and as many pronouns as possible. When the time limit has passed, collect magazines and scissors and ask students to set the words aside for a few minutes. Show them how to write two-line couplets that rhyme. Then pass out glue sticks and ask the students in their teams to paste some of their words together into couplets on a sheet of paper. It is amazing how quickly they can create couplets with their magazine words. From the couplets, they may move to triplets and quatrains. They do not feel intimidated by the words they choose because they only have words from their magazine lexicon. If they do not have a good selection of words, they can always blame it on the magazine. Soon the students will begin asking, "May I add a word that I don't have?" When this happens, allow them to do that, and gradually they will start writing more of their own words than the magazine words.

Copycat Published Poetry

Modeling after published poetry is a strategy for guiding students' writing and allowing them an opportunity to be creative without total creation on their part. Once they have seen the pattern of the poem they will mimic, the major work is finding the right words for the desired effect. *Junk Food* is a poem to which most kids will relate. Finding other words to fit into the structure will be easy enough with the same title and other examples of junk food. Changing the title and making listings for other subjects can also be appealing to elementary-age students. Some other areas for topics might include: Big Toys, Veggie Patch, Folktale Characters, or Favorite Cities.

Junk Food

Marshmallow, jelly bean, bubble gum, soup tureen.
Corn dog, pizza pie, onion ring, French fry.
Barbecue, crab-cake, crackerjack, milkshake.
Popcorn, licorice whip, Hershey bar, pickle chip.
Cheeseburger, Jello-jel, Twinkie cake, Taco Bell.
Chocolate malt, Shake n' Bake, Seven-up, STOMACHACHE.[23]

—Anonymous

Let's Really Think: An Expedition

Guiding Questions

1. In what ways should students study poetry to understand it better?
2. What kind of poetry do I really like?
3. Why do I like it?

4. How can reflecting on poetry that I read make me a better writer?
5. Is it all right if I don't like some poetry?
6. Is it all right if I tear up some of my writing that I don't like?
7. Who are some poets whose writing I can imitate? Is that all right to imitate poetry?
8. Could I use technology to help me write or illustrate poetry?
9. Where can I publish my poetry?

Standards

The standards in this expedition are from the language arts standards of the National Council of Teachers of English/International Reading Association.[24]

The students:

1. read a wide range of literature from many periods in many genres to build an understanding of the many dimensions (e.g., philosophical, ethical, aesthetic) of human experience.
2. employ a wide range of strategies as they write and use different writing process elements appropriately to communicate with different audiences for a variety of purposes.
3. use a variety of technological and information resources (e.g., libraries, databases, computer networks, video) to gather and synthesize information and to create and communicate knowledge.

Initial Reading Options for Teacher Read-Aloud, Shared, Guided, and Independent Reading

1. *The Way to Start a Day* by Byrd Baylor
2. *Everybody Needs a Rock* by Byrd Baylor
3. *The Other Way to Listen* by Byrd Baylor
4. *The Desert is Theirs* by Byrd Baylor
5. *I'm in Charge of Celebrations* by Byrd Baylor
6. *Hawk, I'm Your Brother* by Byrd Baylor
7. *Arithme-Tickle: An Even Number of Odd Riddle-Rhymes* by J. Patrick Lewis
8. *Insectlopedia* by Douglas Florian

The following authors have written poetry that students enjoy:

Arnold Adoff
Liz Attenborough
Douglas Florian
Eloise Greenfield
Lee Bennett Hopkins
X. J. Kennedy
Bruce Lansky
Colin McNaughton
Eve Merriam
Lillian Moore
Mary O'Neill
Jack Prelutsky
Shel Silverstein
Eileen Spinelli
Jane Yolen

Fieldwork Options

1. Search Internet sites and libraries for addresses of poets in your city or state to contact and invite them to the Poetry Fest.
2. Interview poets, media specialists, librarians, and high school teachers for information on poetry and poets.

Individual Projects

1. Locate poems that "make one think" and bring them to class for students to decide if they qualify for the bulletin board.
2. Participate in daily writers' workshop to create poetry for the class book.
3. Draft, edit, revise, and publish poetry for the class poetry book.
4. Illustrate poetry using visual media.
5. Read poetry at Poetry Fest.

Class Projects

1. Develop a list of questions to use in interviewing a poet, media specialist, librarian, or teacher about favorite poems and poems that elicit thinking; also ask for suggestions for poets and readers for the Poetry Fest.

2. Prepare a large bulletin board for examples of poems that "make one think."
3. Develop rubric for judging poems that produce questions, imagery, action, reflection, or humor along with other criteria appropriate for poems that "make one think."
4. Plan a Poetry Fest when parents, school district administrators, and community members participate in a weeklong poetry festival of reading and writing poetry.
5. Contact local poets and solicit participation in exchange for naming the Poetry Fest in honor of the poet.
6. Prepare a class book of poetry from writers' workshop productions.
7. Distribute poetry books to an assisted living facility.

Sharing Outlets

1. Class book of poetry. Give a copy to each parent or community member who participates in the Poetry Fest.
2. Individual Poetry book.
3. Publish poetry on children's poetry publishing website:
   a. http://www.geocities.com/EnchantedForest/5165/
   b. http://www.icnet.net/users/eferguso/poetry.htm

Assessment Options

1. Rubric for contributions to class poetry book.
2. Checklist for use of descriptive words in written poems.
3. Self-evaluation on fieldwork assignments.
4. Evaluation of final products from writers' workshop with rubrics and/or analytical scoring.

Notes

1. http://www.elob.org/aboutel/principles.html.

2. Jim Arnosky, *Wild and Swampy* (New York: HarperCollins, 2000).

3. Jean Craighead George, *Everglades*, (New York: HarperCollins, 1995), 24.

4. Sharon Creech, *Fishing in the Air* (New York: Joanne Cotler/HarperCollins, 2000), 27.

5. Judith Langer, *The Process of Understanding Literature* (Albany, N.Y.: Center for the Learning and Teaching of Literature, State University of New York at Albany, 1989).

6. Eloise Greenfield, *Nathaniel Talking* (New York: Black Butterfly Children's Books, 1988), 14.

7. Ralph Fletcher, *Poetry Matters* (New York: HarperCollins, 2002).

8. Ibid., 14.

9. Jim McKenna, 203 Daywood Drive, Baldwinsville, NY 13027, Phone 315-635-5819.

10. Jack Prelutsky, *The Frogs Wore Red Suspenders* (New York: Greenwillow, 2002), 5.

11. *Poetry Matters*, 20–29.

12. Beatrice Schenck de Regniers, Eva Moore, Mary Michaels White, *Poems Children Will Sit Still for: A Selection for the Primary Grades* (New York: Citation Press, 1969), 59.

13. Ibid., 27.

14. Liz Attenborough, *Poetry by Heart: A Child's Book of Poems to Remember* (New York: Chicken House/ Scholastic, 2001), 81.

15. *Poetry Matters*, 30–40.

16. Iona and Peter Opie, *The Oxford Dictionary of Nursery Rhyme* (Oxford, England: Oxford University Press, 1998), 252

17. Lois Lowry, *Anastasia Krupnik* (Boston: Houghton Mifflin, 1979), 11-12.

18. Ibid., 12.

19. Douglas Florian, *Bing, Bang, Boing* (San Diego: Harcourt, 1994), 48.

20. Paul Fleischman, *Joyful Noises: Poems for Two Voices* (New York: Harper, 1988), 19.

21. Arnold Lobel, *Pigericks* (New York: Harper, 1983), 14.

22. *Poems Children Will Sit Still for*, 15.

23 Caroline Feller Bauer, *This Way to Books* (New York: H.W. Wilson, 1983), 72.

24. www.ncte.org

Chapter 12

The Literature Program in the Curriculum

"Do you suppose you could help us attract birds here in our atrium, Eugene?" Mr. Lincoln handed him a book. "And perhaps this would help."

Eugene seemed stunned at first. Then he took the beautiful book on birds in his hands, wrapped it in his arms, and bolted down the hall.

—Patricia Polacco, *Mr. Lincoln's Way*, 2001

Literature is at the heart of the curriculum. And as we have made the point many times in this book, it is also at the heart of life. In the case of Eugene, in Patricia Polacco's *Mr. Lincoln's Way*, "Mean Gene" is a troubled boy. Mr. Lincoln, the principal, recognized that Eugene's behavior was a signal that he needed help and went right to work to find a way to reach him. Eugene's great interest was in birds, so the path to Eugene was clearly through the fifth-grade project of attracting birds to the atrium. Mr. Lincoln gave Eugene a beautiful book on birds. And here is what happened:

> As the days passed, Eugene never seemed to be without the book. His English teacher let Eugene read passages from the book in class. "I'm so pleased to see him reading," Mrs. Dunkle exclaimed. And when he didn't have his nose in that book, he was almost constantly out in the atrium! He and Mr. Lincoln made a list of plants and shrubs to buy, and types of grain and seeds to feed the birds.
> They even built three bird feeders together.[1]

When the need or interest in knowing something matches with trade books and literature on that subject, magic is bound to happen. What is the value of reading without learning something or knowing about a great story? What is the worth of math without having a real-world application? What is the importance of our social studies understandings without knowing that real people lived the histories and created the principles and laws of our society? What is the consequence of knowledge and understanding of scientific and environmental causes without reading about effects? How can the lives of our next generations be as full as possible without the meaningful context of the literature? We need to ask these questions when we contemplate curriculum. Of course, literature cannot do the whole job by itself; there must be interested people with whom learners can talk and listen. Mr. Lincoln knew well the secrets to keeping his students interested and active in the learning process.

> Mr. Lincoln was the coolest principal in the whole world, or so his students thought. He had the coolest clothes, had the coolest smile, and did the coolest things. He had tea parties with Mrs. West's kindergarten every spring. He took Mr. Bliss's sixth-graders on nature walks in the fall. He set up his telescope next to the pond in back of school on special nights and invited kids and their families to come and look at the stars.
> And in the winter he was Santa for the Christmas play, lit the menorah for Chanukah, wore a dashiki for Kwanzaa and a burnoose for Ramadan.
> Mr. Lincoln was just plain cool![2]

When the school leadership gives this kind of attention to curriculum, much learning occurs. Although principals play a role in decisionmaking regarding instruction and content, teachers are on the front line with day-to-day planning. Through this chapter, teachers will find a structure for including literature in their content— and for putting it at the heart of the curriculum!

Values of the Literature Curriculum

Literature plays various roles in the elementary classroom. Consider the values of literature and then define the goals and objectives for your program.

Literature Provides Role Models for Life Issues

Since earliest times, humankind has passed on ideas and ideals from one generation to the next through stories, fables, and principles by which to live. It seems to be a human characteristic to want to share what has been learned and allow others to profit from the mistakes or successes of some.

Very little has changed over the years in this respect, and literature has become more a part of everyday life as it reflects the human condition. Literature allows us to see ourselves in a mirror and to think, "Yes, that is my situation and the way I feel." When students read books that reflect their issues, problems, and questions, they know they are not the first to have such experiences and they learn from characters' trials and errors. Reflective literature is comforting. Judy Blume and Paula Danziger are two authors whose works allow students to reflect on their lives and gather courage for their own battles. Literature may also give us a window through which we can see more clearly than before because we can read about experiences that we have never had, but can empathize with, through the literature. When students read literature from different cultures, from different lifestyles or family compositions, they often carry away insights they could not previously imagine. As Charlotte Huck said many years ago, the "window" books open doors of understanding for readers to vicariously live other lives through the characters.

Life Issues for Students

What issue is greater in the lives of children than learning to read? In the following passage, from Patricia Polacco's *Thank You, Mr. Falker* we feel the intensity.

> She sobbed.
> "But little one, don't you understand, you don't see letters or numbers the way other people do. And you've gotten through school all this time, and fooled many, many good teachers!" He smiled at her. "That took cunning, and smartness, and such, such bravery."
> Then he stood up and finished washing the board. "We're going to change all that, girl. You're going to read—I promise you that."[3]

The reader feels hope after reading or hearing a story of a child with so much emotion and a teacher with such compassion. Children can take this message and know that if there was a teacher like that for Trisha, then surely there must be another one out there for them. Many stories have been mentioned throughout this book about characters who desperately want to learn to read or to teach someone near them to read. Remember these books? Patricia Polacco's *The Bee Tree*, Elizabeth Howard's *Virgie Goes to School with Us Boys*, Denize Lauture's *Running the Road to ABC*, Gary Paulsen's *Nightjohn* and his *Sarny*, Patricia Maclachlan's *Caleb's Story*, and Eve Bunting's *The Wednesday Surprise*.

Of course, learning to read is not the only life issue that young ones experience. Whatever humans experience, children also feel the impact and must face the results of their actions, and sometimes those of their parents or friends. Cynthia Rylant writes of life in a family beleaguered by the father's drinking problem in *A Blue-Eyed Daisy*. For those children who experience the effects of a parent's alcohol abuse, Ellie provides an answer to her own situation that may work for them. Her dog Bullet is there to share her confidences and to let her release some of her anxiety and fear.

Family Issues

The issues that children face include a variety of family situations, such as the one-parent family; custodies that require the child to live in two different houses on a regular basis; divorce and abusive relationships, not to mention the age-old problem of sibling rivalry. Following are some books that deal with these issues: In Paula Danziger's *Amber Brown Wants Extra Credit*, Amber's schoolwork suffers due to her parents' divorce, and in *Totally Uncool* by Janice Levy, a young girl has to adjust to her father's new girlfriend. *Home Is Where We Live: Life at a Shelter Through a Young Girl's Eyes* by Jane Hertensten, editor, and B. L. Groth, photographer, is a firsthand description of what it is like to be homeless and live in a shelter, which is a growing issue.

Health Issues

One of the most difficult life issues facing children is that of family medical problems. When a parent is ill, the child who is often protected from the whole story feels the emotional strain. The child may not know the seriousness of the illness or whether or not to expect the parent to survive. Lack of information can be devastating, so reading about other children who have been through such dilemmas is helpful. A book about an injured butterfly and its recovery, *Elizabeth's Beauty*, by Nancy Markham Alberts shows how far love and care can go in healing. Elizabeth believes that if the butterfly can get well, so can her grandfather. This book could give hope to many children with illness in their families.

Children hear the word "cancer" and are often frightened by their lack of understanding and their fear of who will have cancer next. Some titles that give factual information on this disease are: *What Is Cancer Anyway? Explaining Cancer to Children of All Ages* by Karen L. Carney, *Sammy's Mommy Has Cancer* by Sherry Kohlenberg, and *The Hope Tree: Kids Talk about Breast Cancer* by Laura Joffe Numeroff.

Good Luck, Mrs. K.! by Louise Borden brings the dreaded disease into the classroom. Based on a true story without a happy ending, the third grade class of Mrs. Kempshenski, the most enthusiastic teacher around, learned of her illness when she didn't come to school one day. She was able to visit them after some treatment and the book holds hope of her return to the classroom next year.

A sick child is another disturbing event for children. Reading about other children with similar experiences may relieve some of their fears. When a child is injured or ill for a period of time, it may seem that things will never get back to normal. And maybe they won't, but adaptation will occur and reading about others who have learned to cope may help. A book for young ones who are ill is *How It Feels to Fight for Your Life* by Jill Kremenz.

There are many wonderful books out there to help children in times of trial, but teachers are urged to be cautious when using books dealing with these sensitive topics. Teachers are not trained therapists and do not have the skills to successfully match a child with a book in time of great distress. Knowing the books, however, is an advantage for a teacher, who in conjunction with a counselor and the child's parents may plan for the use of the books. At other times, it is appropriate to have books on the classroom shelf for students to self-select for independent reading. All of the books listed in this section are picture books with easy to midlevels of difficulty, so they can be independent reading for the majority of elementary students.

Social Issues

Many issues of concern are beyond the children's ability to solve. A feeling of helplessness may come over children when faced with such problems. Books that show characters facing obstacles, even those with serious consequences such as drugs, alcohol, and other illegal activities, may help children realize that there are some options available, and there are people in their lives who can help. Claudia Black's *It Will Never Happen to Me* gives a child's perspective on this problem. A professional book that teachers may find helpful in providing support for children going through such problems is Jerry Moe's *Discovery: Finding the Buried Treasure.* This book provides suggestions for activities to help children get through tough times.

Literature Develops Thinking Skills

Critical and creative thinking occurs when children are exposed to varied and diverse positions and are forced to compare what they have previously known or thought to the new information. Literature opens the door for these experiences. Consider the wide range of traits and behaviors found among the characters in children's literature. Consider the situations explored through literature that students also face in their lives. Without the view into someone else's world and that character's attempts at solving the problems, our students would have fewer options for facing their own issues. Consider the way postmodernist writers are exploring realities, giving new—possibly outlandish—ways at looking at ordinary events. These exposures provide breadth and depth to the students' strategies for exploring the world around them.

Mitsumasa Anno's books explore alternative ways of looking at ordinary things and thinking about them. In *Topsy Turvies: More Pictures to Stretch the Imagination*, a wordless picture book, Anno takes little elflike characters through manipulations of the physical world, perspectives on size and shape, and leads one to wonder about impossibilities. Anno asks, "Impossible? No, that's a word used only by 'grownups.' Nothing is impossible to the young, not until we become caught in the problems of living and forget to make-believe. Perhaps these pictures of mine will keep all of us young a little longer, will stretch our imaginations enough to help keep us magically human. I hope so, I believe so—for nothing is impossible."[4]

Dr. Anno's imaginary wonders include *Anno's Counting Book*, *Anno's Journey*, *Anno's Mysterious Multiplying Jar*, and *Anno's USA*.

Wordplay is another avenue for creating sharp-minded thinking in our students. The epitome of wordplay is Lewis Carroll's works with his "Jabberwocky" poem and *Through the Looking Glass with Alice in Wonderland*. A recent book that will stretch vocabulary meanings and pronunciations is *Miss Alaneus: A Vocabulary Disaster* by Debra Frasier. Hearing a word list over the phone led to interpreting the word "miscellaneous" as Miss Alaneus. The focus on vocabulary then becomes comical, while at the same time young readers can identify with mismatches in vocabulary.

When children read, they confirm knowledge and attitudes; they also recognize new pieces of information and perspectives that are different from their own. Sometimes the incoming information is just added to their existing frameworks of understanding, often called "schemas," but other times, there are conflicts between the new information and what the child knows or feels. In these cases, there is a disequilibrium that must be satisfied. The learner must reconcile the differences, either by thinking them through and accepting the new information or totally rejecting the new thoughts and determining why they are not believed. This cognitive process, described by Jean Piaget as equilibration, leads to higher-level thinking.[5]

The books listed and discussed here stand out as ones that deliberately stretch the mind and the imagination. Books from every genre also accomplish this purpose, often in more subtle ways. Every book that a child reads leaves an imprint of some kind.

Literature is Text for Reading

Our professional stances on reading have shifted over the last few decades with more or less emphasis on the mechanical or the aesthetic focuses on reading. We have gone from the teaching of phonics in isolation to the exclusion of phonics altogether; we have used basal texts, have thrown them out in some parts of the country, and reinstated them with fulltext literature as their basis. As a profession, we have run a full gamut of strategies and approaches and many of us, these authors included, believe that there is no one answer to reading success for all children. The answers lie in using a variety of strategies that include good literature, motivation for reading, and direct instruction as needed for understanding the language components necessary for reading and comprehension.

The phonological system consists of the sounds of the language and the hearing and production of the phonemes in the language. Recognizing the graphic symbols for the phonemes and putting the sounds together into comprehensible meaning then becomes part of the task of reading. Once children recognize the pleasures and values of making sense of the printed word, they may need specific and direct instruction in strategies for determining how words are pronounced, so detection of meaning becomes easier for them.

Books are the medium for students to learn such strategies. When the motivation is already present for understanding the content of the story or information, students welcome the direct instruction that will show them ways to understand the phonological aspects of decoding while they are expanding their comprehension.

The morphological-semantical system in language refers to the meanings of the utterances that we make. Utterances, also called morphemes, are the smallest units of meaning in our language. We have core words that have meaning and then by adding endings, affixes (prefixes and suffixes), by changing a regular verb to an irregular one, or by showing possession, we change the meaning of the word. When children read—or listen to a reader—they expand their vocabulary. Great strides are often made when children hear books read to them that are above their reading level but on the appropriate listening level. Through hearing vocabulary within a piece of written work, and then participating in the discussion of why a certain word was used or how it was used, children's personal lexicon of language usage is extended. Again, it is clear that when instruction in the language system is coupled with interesting, age-appropriate literature, the reading instructional objectives are met.

The syntactical system in language refers to the grammatical aspects, and most children come to school with a strong understanding of the grammar of the language. As they learn to speak, they internalize the rules of the grammar system. They know where to put a noun or a verb in their spoken language. They cannot tell you the name of the parts of speech, but they know how they are used. As children read or hear dialogue, their understandings of how the language is arranged will be confirmed. When listening to dialogue of speakers of non-Standard English, they may be curious about the discrepancies between this language and what they are being taught.

We have to be realistic and realize that although Standard English is the language of the business and education worlds, it is not necessarily the language of children coming into your classrooms. There will be English Language learners who have internalized a previous language. There may be students who have internalized colloquial language or grammar that is not standard. In the reading program, students may encounter stories of characters who also have learned a different grammar system. In those cases, it is good for children to discuss the differences and to be aware of variations among speakers. The Standard English model is the language that students need to know for interaction in the education world, so we must give direct instruction, along with constant modeling and reasons for the students to want to use this standard. Literature opens the door for these discussions while providing the best models possible for the multilingual children of today.

The pragmatic system in the language is one that may also be explored in literature. When language learners understand appropriate language and know how to speak in different circumstances, they have learned the pragmatics of language. We see an example of lack of pragmatic knowledge when Soup, in Robert Newton Peck's *Soup*, asks his teacher if she has had a bowel movement today! The teacher had asked Soup that question and he thought it was fine to reply in kind.

Not a pragmatic response, and needless to say, he was in trouble. By reading the dialogue of characters, students can emulate or learn how to avoid fiascos with the language.

The most important aspect of looking at literature for reading instruction is to realize that through the use of actual literature, instead of isolated workbook pages or contrived text created solely to teach a skill, students experience the joy of reading while learning the support skills to enhance the meaning. Literature needs to be the base of the reading program, including read-aloud books, shared reading, guided reading, and independent reading.

Literature Provides the Base for Curriculum Content

As the school day becomes crowded with requirements and accountability for standards, it is evermore important for the teacher to be efficient. Integration of curriculum is one of the smartest ways teachers can be more efficient. When instructional objectives can be merged to incorporate multiple skills and strategies, learning is reinforced because it has more connections to other areas and time is saved. Rather than spending an hour on social studies and then an hour on language arts, why not spend two hours on a combination of the two as they complement each other?

While middle level students are learning about the events of the Civil War and the effects on the people on both sides, they can read Seymour Riet's *Behind Rebel Lines: The Incredible Story of Emma Edmonds, Civil War Spy*. This book was recreated from historical documents, including the characters' memoirs. Both human elements and historical information are present in the book. It will meet the goals and objectives of both social studies and language arts curricula. The reader sees things from the perspectives of slaves, military personnel, and civilians living during the mid-1800s. Just think of the language study possibilities from this excerpt: "Cuff nodded and scuffed his shoes. 'Mawnin',' he said. 'Mah name Cuff. Ah'm lost.'"[6]

Social studies and science trade books, as well as fiction, provide quality literature along with opportunities for reading and strengthening the language arts skills. Following is a list of authors whose work is excellent and whose books will provide many opportunities for integrating social studies and science with language arts and reading:

Caroline Arnold
Vicki Cobb
Joanna Cole
Christopher Collier
James Lincoln Collier
Margery Facklam
Russell Freedman
Jean Fritz
Gail Gibbons
Patricia MacLachlan
Sandra Markle
Scott O'Dell
Katherine Paterson
Laurence Pringle
Seymour Simon
Elizabeth George Speare
Mildred Taylor

Literature is a Reward

Children are easily "hooked" on a good story when it is appropriate and presented well to them. Knowing how much they can become involved in a story, it is with knowledge of reality—as well as considerable guilt—that we suggest using literature as a management technique. Children deserve regular read-aloud or silent sustained reading periods of time. The teacher can let the students know that the reading periods may be expanded, depending on the students' work habits during a given time. For example early Tuesday morning, the teacher can tell the class that an extra read-aloud period is possible if all work is completed with good work habits and quality performances by a given time. Children will work hard for a reward that they consider a reward. Extra time for reading is rewarding for children who have learned the value of the experience.

Also, if students know that the teacher will begin reading from an ongoing chapter book immediately upon returning to the classroom from a special activity, they will return to their seats as quickly as possible. They will get organized much more quickly and quietly than if there is no motivation to do so. An idea is to use books without pictures or deliberately not show the pictures while using this strategy. If class members are struggling to see pictures, they may become distracted, but if they know they must make the pictures in their minds, they will do so and do it quietly.

Keep in mind that reading a good story to your students is also a reward for you!

Literature Inspires Aesthetic Growth

Children love illustrations in picture books. They count and point and laugh and look, because those are the actions solicited by much of the literature for young ones. They learn about the beauty in the world and know where they can look to see it for themselves. Books are where aesthetic appreciation begins, and when they develop it, children's lives will be richer.

The good feelings perpetuated by the artwork in books for early childhood set the stage for children to view literature from an aesthetic perspective. Many of the newer picture books offer art to the reader— not just illustrations. One book that presents not only beautiful artwork, but text that causes the reader to revel in the union of creative thoughts with paintings is *Rough Sketch Beginning* written by James Berry with original art by Robert Florczak. It folds the descriptions into paintings of our environment. The beginning text is "I came to sketch my ideas for my picture."[7]

Many children experience their first genuine introduction to art when they are looking at picture books. Teachers can provide those experiences in the classroom with books such as Thomas Locker's *Mountain Dance* and *Water Dance*. Locker also did the paintings for Candace Christensen's *Sky Tree: Seeing Science through Art.*

Strategies for Using Literature in the Curriculum

Throughout this book, we have noted teaching strategies such as interactive concrete activities for very young children, shared and guided reading and writing, character sets, character webs, literature treasure hunts, biography cubes, clusters and chains, Venn diagrams, criteria charts, nature walks, reflective logs, poetry writers' workshop, and copycat publishing. These are variations for your curriculum that keep the students motivated and bring more excitement and interest into the classroom.

Core Strategies

There are also strategies that are so much a part of the curriculum that you will use them weekly—if not daily. These are the strategies that become the core of your curriculum.

Read Aloud
There is little that can compare to reading aloud for establishing motivation for reading. So many wonderful books are on bookstore, library, and teachers' shelves, but without the teacher's opening the door to those books, children will miss some of the best. Often books that spark a student's interest are far too difficult for that child to read. If the books aren't read aloud, the child will never experience them.

Literature Discussion Groups
When groups of students read a common book (or in the case of an author study they may read from the same author, and then come together to discuss what they have read to compare ideas from the books and to hear other perspectives on the stories) we have the supreme opportunity for children to solidify their comprehension of what they have read. These groups, sometimes called "literature circles," are highly motivating for students. They simply enjoy talking about what they have read—assuming the books are selected appropriately. Giving students some voice in selecting the book they will read for these group discussions is a sound practice. Some teachers give book talks on four or five books and allow students to negotiate the selections. Sometimes teachers must control the groups, but when children can be given a voice in the books to be read, they will have the interest that will be beneficial in the long run

In these groups, students are given roles or certain activities and are held accountable. Harvey Daniels's *Literature Circles: Voice and Choice in Book Clubs and Reading Groups* is an excellent guide for getting started with materials and the routine for these groups. Several teachers have websites with directions for how they have used these circles. A quick search will give you many ideas for getting started.

Literacy Workshops
Reading and writing workshops are strategies that you will use daily in your curriculum. With these literacy workshops, you will provide students with opportunities for ongoing literacy processes. The workshop approach usually has these components and is carried out daily for one to two hours:

1. Read aloud or teacher modeling writing.
2. Mini lesson composed of direct instruction on a strategy or skill.
3. Working block of time for reading, writing, or both
4. Teacher conferencing or teaching small groups for short sessions on specific needs
5. Sharing time for letting others know what is being accomplished and for asking for help from the classroom community.

With this strategy, literature becomes an integral part of the base for instruction and for modeling.

Cooperative Book Sharing (CBS)
Sometimes there are books that need to be read and discussed in one classroom session. The CBS strategy permits the reading of a novel in a short period of time. With this strategy, a book is actually torn apart into the number of groups that will be reading the story. Sometimes the grouping may be by chapters, or it may be by number of pages. With a class of thirty students, you may want to team the students into pairs and give each pair a section of the book with instructions to read it together, talk about what they have read, and be prepared to tell their part back to the class in a predetermined time period. Depending on the book, you might want to give them fifteen to thirty minutes for this preparation. Then with the class in a setting that is conducive to storytelling, maybe in a circle on the floor, the team that had the beginning pages will start by telling about their section. If you break the book by chapters, they will keep up with which chapter comes next. They should be listening, however, and be able to tell that they have the section that follows. As the story unfolds, there will be "ahas" as students learn the roles of characters, the motivations for actions, and the results of some events. The story retelling holds the students' interests and they often have many questions at the end that show the kind of comprehension and reasoning going on in their minds.

A book that we have used very successfully with this strategy is Natalie Babbitt's *Tuck Everlasting*. The teacher may read the prologue for some background before the students read their sections. After the discussion, the students will be excited for the teacher to read the epilogue aloud, and the ending will be satisfying. Other books that have worked well with this strategy include John Christopher's *The White Mountains* and Lois Lowry's *Number the Stars*.

Young Authors' Conference (YAC)

An annual event that you will certainly want in your curriculum is a Young Authors' Conference. These conferences celebrate young writers by holding a special event when children bring their completed books for sharing with other children, and often professional writers and storytellers are invited to speak to the group. Some YACs are held district or schoolwide, but they may be planned for one classroom also. They usually include grouping the students for writing or illustrating workshops, sharing sessions, and participating with guests or speakers. Many children's authors and illustrators are available for such events with honoraria ranging from a few hundred dollars to several thousand. Authors are usually contacted through their publishers, but many have websites giving information on their speaking schedules and requirements. Often local storytellers are pleased to come to such events with nominal or no fees. The local libraries are the best sources for locating these resources.

Assessment

The strategies in a curriculum provide opportunities for students to meet the standards, goals, and objectives of the program. Students are then held accountable for meeting those benchmarks. From the values discussed, it is clear that goals for the literature program expect students to:

1. read about role models for life issues;
2. read to develop cognitive skills;
3. read to learn to read;
4. read to learn curriculum content;
5. read for pleasure;
6. read for aesthetic appreciation.

Student Assessment

The assessment of students' performances on these goals and objectives then becomes the measure by which the program may be deemed successful or not. Options for assessment of individual students include the following:

Profile Charts are simply charts, often carried on clipboards by the teacher, that have each student's name down the side and criteria for evaluation across the top. Columns for each criterion allow the teacher to check off or insert information on each child's progress. Accomplishment of strategies or skills may be listed for charting, or benchmarks from state standards may be checked off. These are ongoing records that give the teacher detailed information on children's progress.

Checklists are detailed sequences for the accomplishment of specific tasks. The teacher may have a checklist for each student and by the end of a given unit of study or expedition, the student will be expected to have completed all parts of the checklist. For example, checklists are useful in monitoring students' participation or completion of fieldwork in expeditions. If children have an assignment to interview grandparents for their remembrances of learning to read, a checklist may be sufficient to record the completion of this assignment.

Goal Statements are written by students as they decide on their literacy goals for the next grading period or the following expedition. Time must be set aside for students to reflect on what they have accomplished in a previous period and what their next steps are in their learning process. Children may set goals for themselves to read from an unknown genre, to read a certain number of books, to write more in depth in their logs, or to keep a personal word bank of new vocabulary encountered in their reading. These are reasonable goals for elementary students and when they set them, they are likely to accomplish them.

Self-evaluation precedes and follows the creation of goal statements. Students can judge their needs with guidance from the teacher, and they are adept at determining how well they have met their goals. Opportunities to reflect and write about their accomplishments or challenges to their attempts are critical in this part of the assessment process.

Rubrics have become a popular and worthwhile assessment tool for students and teachers. Rubrics simply identify the criteria on which assignments or accomplishments of objectives are based. The best rubrics are those that are developed by the students with the guidance of the teacher and are available to the students as they begin their work toward their goals. Simply stated, when students know what is expected and how they are judged, they will meet the standard.

Portfolio Assessment allows insight into growth over time. Some teachers expect specified numbers of products to be placed in portfolios every grading period. At the end of the school year, the products may be compared for improvement in specific areas. These are valuable when students have a voice in which artifacts become a part of the portfolio and when they are required to write documentation on the meaning of each artifact and how it shows some accomplishment or attainment of a goal. Students' insights on their own growth in portfolios are valuable sources for assessment.

These selected assessment indicators may be used along with traditional assessment instruments to give a clear picture of how individual students are progressing toward accomplishment of the goals and objectives of the total curriculum.

Program Assessment

Assessing students is one way to determine the validity of a literature program within the curriculum. It is also imperative that the program itself is examined. In *The Integration of Language Arts through Literature*,[8] Carolyn Spillman asks these fifty questions of our language arts/literature programs:

1. Is there excitement in the classroom that invites students to read and write, speak and listen?
2. Are there comfortable reading areas with at least five books per child on the reading shelves?
3. Are the books from all genres and different levels of reading?
4. Are there books related to the unit or theme study on the shelves?
5. Does the schedule provide for daily reading and writing?
6. Does the plan for the day include teacher reading aloud to the students?
7. Is there a silent sustained reading period when everyone in the classroom reads?
8. Is there a silent sustained writing period when everyone in the classroom writes?
9. Are there materials available for children to use for writing, such as unlined paper, lined paper (by second grade), colored paper, markers, pencils, crayons?
10. Is there a daily talk and listen time when children have a chance to talk to a buddy?
11. Is there evidence in the room of writing and reading for real purposes?
12. Are mechanical support skills directly and indirectly taught to children with developmentally appropriate strategies at the relevant time for each child?
13. Are students involved in developing their own literacy goals?

14. When writing, do children draft first and then worry about mechanics?
15. Do they read for meaning first and then after a second reading, participate in activities to promote support skills?
16. Does the curriculum show real-life reasons for learning the mechanics of literacy?
17. Are the students bound to their spelling vocabularies for their writing or are they able to reach into listening and reading vocabularies for their writing?
18. Are young children encouraged to spell words as they sound?
19. Are older children encouraged to spell words as they sound while they draft with a suggestion that editing will come later, after the thoughts are on paper?
20. Are experience charts being written by teachers who take dictation from students in kindergarten through fifth grade?
21. Are experience charts hung on walls for frequent choral readings?
22. Are students encouraged to write a copycat story with a few changes to give them confidence that they can use the language?
23. Does spelling instruction begin only after children have started using short vowels and have phonemic awareness of basic sounds?
24. Are there games and activities for trying out stage appropriate spelling generalizations?
25. Do all children who write keep a spelling notebook of words they can spell or a word bank?
26. Do children have opportunities to hear a variety of literary genres?
27. Do they have opportunities to respond personally to the literature they hear and read?
28. Are there many opportunities for books to be reread?
29. Do they write group copycat stories to imitate different genres?
30. Do they have genre studies and compare stories within a genre?
31. Are students aware of literary conventions that authors and illustrators use as they write and illustrate?
32. Do they have author and illustrator studies and focus on models of excellence in children's literature?
33. Are children aware of books that have won awards?

34. Do students keep reading records of how much and what they are reading?
35. Are there opportunities for students to excel in writing with various text structures (narrative, expository, poetry)?
36. Do students know the names of well-known authors who write in expository or narrative texts?
37. Are they familiar with more than two or three poets?
38. Are theme studies conducted that lead to discussions of values that promote better human relationships?
39. Are the worth of humans, animal life, and the earth on which we live valued through literary discussions?
40. Are possibilities of conflict resolutions clearer to students because of literary discussions and experiences?
41. Through this program are students able to think for themselves and accept the responsibility of making decisions?
42. Are subjects related as much as possible without being artificially connected?
43. Are there always books and stories related to themes and units?
44. Are there large blocks of time with several integrated objectives met through each activity?
45. Do students enjoy reading during class and on their own?
46. Do they read at home?
47. Do they have library cards and visit the library often?
48. Do they sometimes spontaneously mention storybook characters?
49. When asked, "If you could select anyone in the world, whom would you like for a friend?" do they ever mention a character from a story?
50. Do students ever indicate they would like to be authors or illustrators of books someday?

If each question is answered with a "yes," you can be sure that the program is of high quality and the literature goals are being met.

Planning for a Literature Program

"Must Have" Components for Your Program

Much of this chapter has focused on the objectives of a literature program, the strategies used, and how you assess the students' performance and the program as a whole. After the goals, strategies, and assessment tools have been considered, it is time to develop a framework for your literature program within your curriculum. There will be some components that you "must have" in your program.

Themes for Integrating Across the Curriculum

Think about your program in terms of the time blocks that you have in a school year. You will have 180 days, thirty-six weeks, nine months, or four nine-week grading periods. As you begin planning for meeting the goals and objectives of your program, you will want to determine the broad themes into which you will integrate much of your curriculum and the time frame for these themes. Many early childhood teachers focus their studies around topics that will hold the interest of the children for a week or two. In the middle elementary grades, momentum for an expedition or a unit may last for more than a month—sometimes a whole grading period of nine weeks. It is advisable to consider themes that are broad enough to include all of your subject matter and that can be explored in many different ways.

Suggested Themes for Primary Grades Include:

1. *My Family and Other Families.* This study could include traditional and nontraditional families, families from this country and other countries, human and animal families, word families, and family needs all over the world.
2. *Jobs for All.* In this study, young children can become aware of career opportunities in the business world, the health world, the entertainment industry, service professions and an endless number of connections to all areas of the curriculum.

Suggested Themes for Middle Elementary Grades Might Include:

1. *Where in the World Are We?* This study could expand to all parts of the world with objectives from geography, history, civics, science, health, and of course would be supported with literature and literacy.
2. *What was happening in our state or country 300-500 years ago? (16th–18th centuries).* In this study, students will examine the exploration of our country, the physical features of our

land and oceans, the structures of ships and modes of transportation in those days, food supplies, and other needs.

3. *What was happening in our state or country 200 years ago? (19th century).* This study lends itself to the struggle for freedom and the Civil War, the agriculture versus industrial needs, the personalities involved in the struggles, and corresponding health and environmental issues.

4. *What was happening in our state or country 100 years ago? (20th century).* This theme could complete the four grading periods of the academic year and could include the Great Depression, the World Wars, the geography and economic factors through these years, along with science that might investigate matter and molecules or technology and tools.

Read-Aloud Books

A component of your literature plan must include a list of books that you will use to read aloud to your students. As you read more and more children's books, you will see connections from one book to another. A collection of these books will make an excellent text set for reading aloud and for having in the classroom for independent reading.

An example of a text set that could accompany a theme on Animals of the World of which "dog stories" could be a part follows:

1. *Love That Dog* by Sharon Creech (free verse chapter book)
2. *Shiloh* by Phyllis Naylor (chapter book)
3. *Because of Winn-Dixie* by Kate DiCamillo (chapter book)
4. *Winterdance: The Fine Madness of Running the Iditarod* by Gary Paulsen (chapter book)
5. *The Miracle of Island Girl* by Stephen Gage (picture book)
6. *Remember Rafferty: A Book about the Death of a Pet for Children of All Ages* by Joy Johnson (picture book)

Writing Models

One of the most beneficial facets of the literature program is that the literature itself becomes a model for students to emulate, to imitate, and to incorporate into their own standards.

Narrative writing is a requirement in the schools today as students are expected to create "stories" with a middle, beginning, and ending. The stories will be replete with characters, plot, attempts to solve a problem, and a resolution. Authors usually employ dialogue as a way to help tell the story. Jim LaMarche uses dialogue in the first line of *The Raft*.

> "There's nobody to play with," I complained. "She doesn't even have a TV."
> Dad grinned, "Well, she's not your normal kind of grandma, I guess," he said. "Calls herself a river rat." He chuckled. "But I promise, she'll find plenty for you to do. And you know I can't take you with me this summer, Nicky. There'll be no kids there, and I'll be spending all my time at the plant."[9]

Notwithstanding the identification that many children will have with the situation, many of them will be able to understand how this conversation could take place and what it might mean for the rest of the story. It is a model that hooks kids immediately and gives them a sound example.

Other literacy devices that children model in their writing include these:

1. First-person narrative: *Nathaniel Talking* by Eloise Greenfield
2. Third-person narrative: *The Real McCoy* by Wendy Towle
3. Voices of characters alternate in chapters: *Words of Stone* by Kevin Henkes
4. Diaries: *The Journey* by Sarah Stewart
5. Flashbacks: *Mrs. Frisby and the Rats of NIMH* by Robert O'Brien
6. Circular story: *Rosie's Walk* by Pat Hutchins
7. "I have a problem" story: *Are You My Mother?* by P. D. Eastman

Expository writing is writing that gives information. Models of such writing are found primarily in nonfiction and biographical writings. Students can see a model of expository writing in Seymour Simon's *They Walk the Earth*. "Lemmings—small rodents about the size of a fist—also go on journeys each year. But once every thirty years or so, huge numbers of Norwegian lemmings pour down from their homes in the mountains toward a distant sea, where they plunge in and drown by the thousands."[10] Simon describes the lemming and in the same paragraph sets the stage for the reader to ask, "why?" This cause and effect writing is another characteristic of expository writing and one that young writers can use as a model. The writings of Jean Craighead George, James Cross Giblin, and Vicki Cobb, along with the books of Seymour Simon are good sources for teachers to use with direct instruction in guided reading and writing.

Poetry Every Day

Reading and writing poetry has been discussed in chapter eleven with numerous resources provided. Poetry should be shared with students every day. Poetry week or poetry month will give a short, concentrated focus on poetry, but for students to learn to love it, it must be a regular part of each day. Starting the day with the reading of a poem usually sets a positive mood. Reading poetry as students return from lunch settles them and provides a transition back into the curriculum. The teacher doesn't always have to be the one doing the reading. A different student could be assigned to be the poetry finder and reader for each day of the week. Through the school year, students would have numerous occasions to share some favorite poems. Several collections or anthologies should be placed in a prominent place in the classroom for students to use.

Author Studies

Planning a curriculum should include regular author studies during which the books of a certain author are celebrated while the life and works of the author are researched and studied and shared. As you begin planning for the themes of your curriculum, notice certain authors whose works begin to emerge in that theme. Judith Viorst, who wrote books such as *Alexander and the Terrible, Horrible, No Good, Very Bad Day*, could be highlighted as an author when children are studying families. For the theme about events in this country during the twentieth century, Karen Hesse would be an excellent candidate for an author study. Many of her books are set in the first half of the century and would give contemporary readers a glimpse into the historical fiction of that day. Good examples would be *Witness, Out of the Dust*, and *Letters from Rifka*.

Final Thoughts on Literature in the Curriculum

As you move through your journey of shaping the minds and spirits of young students, we hope that you will read to them and show them by example how literacy opens unbelievable doors. We hope that you will be a model of the design principles for your students and that your own discoveries will keep the passion for reading burning within you.

Notes

1. Patricia Polacco, *Mr. Lincoln's Way* (New York: Philomel, 2001), 14.

2 Ibid., 1.

3. Patricia Polacco, *Thank You, Mr. Falker* (New York: Philomel, 1998), 32.

4. Mitsumasa Anno, *Topsy Turvies* (New York: Philomel, 1989), 28.

5. Teresa M. McDevitt and Jeanne Ellis Ormrod, *Child Development and Education* (Upper Saddle River, N.J.: Merrill Prentice Hall, 2002), 113.

6. Seymour Reit, *Behind Rebel Lines* (San Diego: Gulliver, 2001), 45.

7. James Berry and Robert Florczak, *Rough Sketch Beginning* (San Diego: Harcourt, 1996.)

8. Carolyn Spillman, *The Integration of Language Arts through Literature* (Phoenix, Ariz.: Oryx Press, 1996).

9. Jim LaMarche, *The Raft* (New York: HarperCollins, 2000).

10. Seymour Simon, *They Walk the Earth* (San Diego: Harcourt, 2000), 3.

Appendix

Children's Book Awards

John Newbery Medal

The John Newbery medal is presented to the author of the book considered the most distinguished contribution to American literature for children published during the preceding year. The author must be an American citizen or a permanent resident of the United States. Honor books may also be chosen.

The award is determined by a committee of fifteen members and sponsored by the American Library Association.

2003 Medal Winner:
Crispin: The Cross of Lead by Avi (Hyperion)
Honor Books:
The House of the Scorpion by Nancy Farmer (Atheneum)
Picture of Hollis Woods by Patricia Reilly Giff (Wendy Lamb/Random House)
Hoot by Carl Hiaasen (Knopf)
A Corner of the Universe by Ann M. Martin (Scholastic)
Surviving the Applewhites by Stephanie S. Tolan (HarperCollins)
2002 Medal Winner:
A Single Shard by Linda Sue Park (Clarion/Houghton Mifflin)
Honor Books:
Everything on a Waffle by Polly Horvath (Farrar, Straus & Giroux)
Carver: A Life In Poems by Marilyn Nelson (Front Street)
2001 Medal Winner:
A Year Down Yonder by Richard Peck (Dial)
Honor Books:
Hope Was Here by Joan Bauer (Putnam)
Because of Winn-Dixie by Kate DiCamillo (Candlewick Press)
Joey Pigza Loses Control by Jack Gantos (Farrar, Straus & Giroux)
The Wanderer by Sharon Creech (Joanna Cotler/HarperCollins)
2000 Medal Winner:
Bud, Not Buddy by Christopher Paul Curtis (Delacorte)
Honor Books:
Getting Near to Baby Audrey Columbus (Putnam)

Our Only May Amelia by Jennifer L. Holm (HarperCollins)
26 Fairmount Avenue by Tomie dePaola (Putnam)
1999 Medal Winner:
Holes by Louis Sachar (Frances Foster)
Honor Book:
A Long Way from Chicago by Richard Peck (Dial)
1998 Medal Winner:
Out of the Dust by Karen Hesse (Scholastic)
Honor Books:
Ella Enchanted by Gail Carson Levine (HarperCollins)
Lily's Crossing by Patricia Reilly Giff (Delacorte)
Wringer by Jerry Spinelli (HarperCollins)
1997 Medal Winner:
The View from Saturday by E. L. Konigsburg (Jean
Karl/Atheneum)
Honor Books:
A Girl Named Disaster by Nancy Farmer (Richard
Jackson/Orchard Books)
Moorchild by Eloise McGraw (Margaret McElderry/Simon &
Schuster)
The Thief by Megan Whalen Turner (Greenwillow/Morrow)
Belle Prater's Boy by Ruth White (Farrar, Straus & Giroux)
1996 Medal Winner:
The Midwife's Apprentice by Karen Cushman (Clarion)
Honor Books:
What Jamie Saw by Carolyn Coman (Front Street)
The Watsons Go to Birmingham: 1963 by Christopher Paul Curtis
(Delacorte)
Yolonda's Genius by Carol Fenner (Margaret K. McElderry/Simon
& Schuster)
The Great Fire by Jim Murphy (Scholastic)
1995 Medal Winner:
Walk Two Moons by Sharon Creech (HarperCollins)
Honor Books:
Catherine, Called Birdy by Karen Cushman (Clarion)
The Ear, the Eye and the Arm by Nancy Farmer (Richard
Jackson/Orchard)
1994 Medal Winner:
The Giver by Lois Lowry (Houghton Mifflin)
Honor Books:
Crazy Lady by Jane Leslie Conly (HarperCollins)
Dragon's Gate by Laurence Yep (HarperCollins)

Eleanor Roosevelt: A Life of Discovery by Russell Freedman (Clarion)

1993 Medal Winner:

Missing May by Cynthia Rylant (Richard Jackson/Orchard)

Honor Books:

What Hearts by Bruce Brooks (Laura Geringer/HarperCollins)

The Dark-thirty: Southern Tales of the Supernatural by Patricia McKissack (Knopf)

Somewhere in the Darkness by Walter Dean Myers (Scholastic)

1992 Medal Winner:

Shiloh by Phyllis Reynolds Naylor (Atheneum)

Honor Books:

Nothing But The Truth: A Documentary Novel by Avi (Richard Jackson/Orchard)

The Wright Brothers: How They Invented the Airplane by Russell Freedman (Holiday House)

1991 Medal Winner:

Maniac Magee by Jerry Spinelli (Little, Brown)

Honor Book:

The True Confessions of Charlotte Doyle by Avi (Richard Jackson/Orchard)

1990 Medal Winner:

Number the Stars by Lois Lowry (Houghton Mifflin)

Honor Books:

Afternoon of the Elves by Janet Taylor Lisle (Richard Jackson/Orchard)

Shabanu, Daughter of the Wind by Suzanne Fisher Staples (Knopf)

The Winter Room by Gary Paulsen (Richard Jackson/Orchard)

1989 Medal Winner:

Joyful Noise: Poems for Two Voices by Paul Fleischman (HarperCollins)

Honor Books:

In the Beginning: Creation Stories from Around the World by Virginia Hamilton (Harcourt)

Scorpions by Walter Dean Myers (Harper)

1988 Medal Winner:

Lincoln: A Photobiography by Russell Freedman (Clarion)

Honor Books:

After The Rain by Norma Fox Mazer (Morrow)

Hatchet by Gary Paulsen (Bradbury)

1987 Medal Winner:

The Whipping Boy by Sid Fleischman (Greenwillow)

Honor Books:
A Fine White Dust by Cynthia Rylant (Bradbury)
On My Honor by Marion Dane Bauer (Clarion)
Volcano: The Eruption and Healing of Mount St. Helens by Patricia Lauber (Bradbury)

1986 Medal Winner:
Sarah, Plain and Tall by Patricia MacLachlan (Harper)
Honor Books:
Commodore Perry in the Land of the Shogun by Rhoda Blumberg (Lothrop)
Dogsong by Gary Paulsen (Bradbury)

1985 Medal Winner:
The Hero and the Crown by Robin McKinley (Greenwillow)
Honor Books:
Like Jake and Me by Mavis Jukes (Knopf)
The Moves Make the Man by Bruce Brooks (Harper)
One-Eyed Cat by Paula Fox (Bradbury)

1984 Medal Winner:
Dear Mr. Henshaw by Beverly Cleary (Morrow)
Honor Books:
The Sign of the Beaver by Elizabeth George Speare (Houghton Mifflin)
A Solitary Blue by Cynthia Voigt (Atheneum)
Sugaring Time by Kathryn Lasky (Macmillan)
The Wish Giver: Three Tales of Coven Tree by Bill Brittain (Harper)

1983 Medal Winner:
Dicey's Song by Cynthia Voigt (Atheneum)
Honor Books:
The Blue Sword by Robin McKinley (Greenwillow)
Doctor DeSoto by William Steig (Farrar, Straus & Giroux)
Graven Images by Paul Fleischman (Harper)
Homesick: My Own Story by Jean Fritz (Putnam)
Sweet Whispers, Brother Rush by Virginia Hamilton (Philomel)

1982 Medal Winner:
A Visit to William Blake's Inn: Poems for Innocent and Experienced Travelers by Nancy Willard (Harcourt)
Honor Books:
Ramona Quimby, Age 8 by Beverly Cleary (Morrow)
Upon the Head of the Goat: A Childhood in Hungary 1939–1944 by Aranka Siegal (Farrar, Straus & Giroux)

1981 Medal Winner:
Jacob Have I Loved by Katherine Paterson (Crowell)
 Honor Books:
The Fledgling by Jane Langton (Harper)
A Ring of Endless Light by Madeleine L'Engle (Farrar, Straus & Giroux)
1980 Medal Winner:
A Gathering of Days: A New England Girl's Journal, 1830–1832 by Joan W. Blos (Scribner)
 Honor Book:
The Road from Home: The Story of an Armenian Girl by David Kherdian (Greenwillow)
1979 Medal Winner:
The Westing Game by Ellen Raskin (Dutton)
 Honor Book:
The Great Gilly Hopkins by Katherine Paterson (Crowell)
1978 Medal Winner:
Bridge to Terabithia by Katherine Paterson (Crowell)
 Honor Books:
Ramona and Her Father by Beverly Cleary (Morrow)
Anpao: An American Indian Odyssey by Jamake Highwater (Lippincott)
1977 Medal Winner:
Roll of Thunder, Hear My Cry by Mildred D. Taylor (Dial)
 Honor Books:
Abel's Island by William Steig (Farrar, Straus & Giroux)
A String in the Harp by Nancy Bond (Atheneum)
1976 Medal Winner:
The Grey King by Susan Cooper (McElderry/Atheneum)
 Honor Books:
The Hundred Penny Box by Sharon Bell Mathis (Viking)
Dragonwings by Laurence Yep (Harper)
1975 Medal Winner:
M. C. Higgins, the Great by Virginia Hamilton (Macmillan)
 Honor Books:
Figgs and Phantoms by Ellen Raskin (Dutton)
My Brother Sam is Dead by James Lincoln Collier and Christopher Collier (Four Winds)
The Perilous Gard by Elizabeth Marie Pope (Houghton Mifflin)
Philip Hall Likes Me, I Reckon Maybe by Bette Greene (Dial)
1974 Medal Winner:
The Slave Dancer by Paula Fox (Bradbury)

Honor Book:
The Dark is Rising by Susan Cooper (McElderry/Atheneum)

1973 Medal Winner:
Julie of the Wolves by Jean Craighead George (Harper)
  Honor Books:
Frog and Toad Together by Arnold Lobel (Harper)
The Upstairs Room by Johanna Reiss (Crowell)
The Witches of Worm by Zilpha Keatley Snyder (Atheneum)

1972 Medal Winner:
Mrs. Frisby and the Rats of NIMH by Robert C. O'Brien (Atheneum)
  Honor Books:
Incident at Hawk's Hill by Allan W. Eckert (Little, Brown)
The Planet of Junior Brown by Virginia Hamilton (Macmillan)
The Tombs of Atuan by Ursula K. LeGuin (Atheneum)
Annie and the Old One by Miska Miles (Little, Brown)
The Headless Cupid by Zilpha Keatley Snyder (Atheneum)

1971 Medal Winner:
Summer of the Swans by Betsy Byars (Viking)
  Honor Books:
Knee Knock Rise by Natalie Babbitt (Farrar, Straus & Giroux)
Enchantress From the Stars by Sylvia Louise Engdahl (Atheneum)
Sing Down the Moon by Scott O'Dell (Houghton Mifflin)

1970 Medal Winner:
Sounder by William H. Armstrong (HarperCollins)
  Honor Books:
Our Eddie by Sulamith Ish-Kishor (Pantheon)
The Many Ways of Seeing: An Introduction to the Pleasures of Art by Janet Gaylord Moore (World)
Journey Outside by Mary Q. Steele (Viking)

1969 Medal Winner:
The High King by Lloyd Alexander (Holt)
  Honor Books:
To Be a Slave by Julius Lester (Dial)
When Shlemiel Went to Warsaw and Other Stories by Isaac Bashevis Singer (Farrar, Straus & Giroux)

1968 Medal Winner:
From the Mixed-Up Files of Mrs. Basil E. Frankweiler by E. L. Konigsburg (Atheneum)

Honor Books:
Jennifer, Hecate, Macbeth, William McKinley, and Me, Elizabeth
by E. L. Konigsburg (Atheneum)
The Black Pearl by Scott O'Dell (Houghton Mifflin)
The Fearsome Inn by Isaac Bashevis Singer (Scribner)
The Egypt Game by Zilpha Keatley Snyder (Atheneum)

1967 Medal Winner:
Up a Road Slowly by Irene Hunt (Follett)
Honor Books:
The King's Fifth by Scott O'Dell (Houghton Mifflin)
Zlateh the Goat and Other Stories by Isaac Bashevis Singer
(HarperCollins)
The Jazz Man by Mary Hays Weik (Atheneum)

1966 Medal Winner:
I, Juan de Pareja by Elizabeth Borton de Trevino (Farrar, Straus &
Giroux)
Honor Books:
The Black Cauldron by Lloyd Alexander (Holt)
The Animal Family by Randall Jarrell (Pantheon)
The Noonday Friends by Mary Stolz (Harper)

1965 Medal Winner:
Shadow of a Bull by Maia Wojciechowska (Atheneum)
Honor Book:
Across Five Aprils by Irene Hunt (Follett)

1964 Medal Winner:
It's Like This, Cat by Emily Neville (Harper)
Honor Books:
Rascal: A Memoir of a Better Era by Sterling North (Dutton)
The Loner by Ester Wier (McKay)

1963 Medal Winner:
A Wrinkle in Time by Madeleine L'Engle (Farrar, Straus &
Giroux)
Honor Books:
Thistle and Thyme: Tales and Legends from Scotland by Sorche
Nic Leodhas, pseud. (Leclaire Alger) (Holt)
Men of Athens by Olivia Coolidge (Houghton Mifflin)

1962 Medal Winner:
The Bronze Bow by Elizabeth George Speare (Houghton Mifflin)
Honor Books:
Frontier Living by Edwin Tunis (World)
The Golden Goblet by Eloise Jarvis McGraw (Coward)
Belling the Tiger by Mary Stolz (Harper)

1961 Medal Winner:
   Island of the Blue Dolphins by Scott O'Dell (Houghton Mifflin)
   Honor Books:
   America Moves Forward: A History for Peter by Gerald W.
   Johnson (Morrow)
   Old Ramon by Jack Schaefer (Houghton Mifflin)
   The Cricket in Times Square by George Selden, pseud. (George
   Thompson) (Farrar, Straus & Giroux)

1960 Medal Winner:
   Onion John by Joseph Krumgold (Crowell)
   Honor Books:
   My Side of the Mountain by Jean Craighead George (Dutton)
   America Is Born: A History for Peter by Gerald W. Johnson
   (Morrow)
   The Gammage Cup by Carol Kendall (Harcourt)

1959 Medal Winner:
   The Witch of Blackbird Pond by Elizabeth George Speare
   (Houghton Mifflin)
   Honor Books:
   The Family Under the Bridge by Natalie Savage Carlson (Harper)
   Along Came a Dog by Meindert Dejong (Harper)
   Chucaro: Wild Pony of the Pampa by Francis Kalnay (Harcourt)
   The Perilous Road by William O. Steele (Harcourt)

1958 Medal Winner:
   Rifles for Watie by Harold Keith (Crowell)
   Honor Books:
   The Horsecatcher by Mari Sandoz (Westminster)
   Gone-Away Lake by Elizabeth Enright (Harcourt)
   The Great Wheel by Robert Lawson (Viking)
   Tom Paine, Freedom's Apostle by Leo Gurko (Crowell)

1957 Medal Winner:
   Miracles on Maple Hill by Virginia Sorenson (Harcourt)
   Honor Books:
   Old Yeller by Fred Gipson (Harper)
   The House of Sixty Fathers by Meindert DeJong (Harper)
   Mr. Justice Holmes by Clara Ingram Judson (Follett)
   The Corn Grows Ripe by Dorothy Rhoads (Viking)
   Black Fox of Lorne by Marguerite de Angeli (Doubleday)

1956 Medal Winner:
   Carry On, Mr. Bowditch by Jean Lee Latham (Houghton Mifflin)
   Honor Books:
   The Secret River by Marjorie Kinnan Rawlings (Scribner)
   The Golden Name Day by Jennie Lindquist (Harper)

Men, Microscopes, and Living Things by Katherine Shippen (Viking)

1955 Medal Winner:

The Wheel on the School by Meindert DeJong (Harper)

Honor Books:

Courage of Sarah Noble by Alice Dalgliesh (Scribner)

Banner in the Sky by James Ullman (Lippincott)

1954 Medal Winner:

. . .And Now Miguel by Joseph Krumgold (Crowell)

Honor Books:

All Alone by Claire Huchet Bishop (Viking)

Shadrach by Meindert Dejong (Harper)

Hurry Home, Candy by Meindert Dejong (Harper)

Theodore Roosevelt, Fighting Patriot by Clara Ingram Judson (Follett)

Magic Maize by Mary and Conrad Buff (Houghton Mifflin)

1953 Medal Winner:

Secret of the Andes by Ann Nolan Clark (Viking)

Honor Books:

Charlotte's Web by E. B. White (Harper)

Moccasin Trail by Eloise Jarvis McGraw (Coward)

Red Sails to Capri by Ann Weil (Viking)

The Bears on Hemlock Mountain by Alice Dalgliesh (Scribner)

Birthdays of Freedom, Vol. 1 by Genevieve Foster (Scribner)

1952 Medal Winner:

Ginger Pye by Eleanor Estes (Harcourt)

Honor Books:

Americans Before Columbus by Elizabeth Baity (Viking)

Minn of the Mississippi by Holling C. Holling (Houghton Mifflin)

The Defender by Nicholas Kalashnikoff (Scribner)

The Light at Tern Rock by Julia Sauer (Viking)

The Apple and the Arrow by Mary and Conrad Buff (Houghton Mifflin)

1951 Medal Winner:

Amos Fortune, Free Man by Elizabeth Yates (Dutton)

Honor Books:

Better Known as Johnny Appleseed by Mabel Leigh Hunt (Lippincott)

Gandhi, Fighter Without a Sword by Jeanette Eaton (Morrow)

Abraham Lincoln, Friend of the People by Clara Ingram Judson (Follett)

The Story of Appleby Capple by Anne Parrish (Harper)

1950 Medal Winner:
> *The Door in the Wall* by Marguerite de Angeli (Doubleday)
> **Honor Books:**
> *Tree of Freedom* by Rebecca Caudill (Viking)
> *The Blue Cat of Castle Town* by Catherine Coblentz (Longmans)
> *Kildee House* by Rutherford Montgomery (Doubleday)
> *George Washington* by Genevieve Foster (Scribner)
> *Song of the Pines: A Story of Norwegian Lumbering in Wisconsin* by Walter and Marion Havighurst (Winston)

1949 Medal Winner:
> *King of the Wind* by Marguerite Henry (Rand McNally)
> **Honor Books:**
> *Seabird* by Holling C. Holling (Houghton Mifflin)
> *Daughter of the Mountain* by Louise Rankin (Viking)
> *My Father's Dragon* by Ruth S. Gannett (Random House)
> *Story of the Negro* by Arna Bontemps (Knopf)

1948 Medal Winner:
> *The Twenty-One Balloons* by William Pène du Bois (Viking)
> **Honor Books:**
> *Pancakes-Paris* by Claire Huchet Bishop (Viking)
> *Li Lun, Lad of Courage* by Carolyn Treffinger (Abingdon)
> *The Quaint and Curious Quest of Johnny Longfoot* by Catherine Besterman (Bobbs-Merrill)
> *The Cow-Tail Switch, and Other West African Stories* by Harold Courlander (Holt)
> *Misty of Chincoteague* by Marguerite Henry (Rand McNally)

1947 Medal Winner:
> *Miss Hickory* by Carolyn Sherwin Bailey (Viking)
> **Honor Books:**
> *Wonderful Year* by Nancy Barnes (Messner)
> *Big Tree* by Mary and Conrad Buff (Viking)
> *The Heavenly Tenants* by William Maxwell (Harper)
> *The Avion My Uncle Flew* by Cyrus Fisher, pseud. (Darwin L. Teilhet) (Appleton)
> *The Hidden Treasure of Glaston* by Eleanor Jewett (Viking)

1946 Medal Winner:
> *Strawberry Girl* by Lois Lenski (Lippincott)
> **Honor Books:**
> *Justin Morgan Had a Horse* by Marguerite Henry (Rand McNally)
> *The Moved-Outers* by Florence Crannell Means (Houghton Mifflin)
> *Bhimsa, the Dancing Bear* by Christine Weston (Scribner)
> *New Found World* by Katherine Shippen (Viking)

1945 Medal Winner:
   Rabbit Hill by Robert Lawson (Viking)
   Honor Books:
   The Hundred Dresses by Eleanor Estes (Harcourt)
   The Silver Pencil by Alice Dalgliesh (Scribner)
   Abraham Lincoln's World by Genevieve Foster (Scribner)
   Lone Journey: The Life of Roger Williams by Jeanette Eaton
   (Harcourt)
1944 Medal Winner:
   Johnny Tremain by Esther Forbes (Houghton Mifflin)
   Honor Books:
   These Happy Golden Years by Laura Ingalls Wilder (Harper)
   Fog Magic by Julia Sauer (Viking)
   Rufus M. by Eleanor Estes (Harcourt)
   Mountain Born by Elizabeth Yates (Coward)
1943 Medal Winner:
   Adam of the Road by Elizabeth Janet Gray (Viking)
   Honor Books:
   The Middle Moffat by Eleanor Estes (Harcourt)
   Have You Seen Tom Thumb? by Mabel Leigh Hunt (Lippincott)
1942 Medal Winner:
   The Matchlock Gun by Walter Edmonds (Dodd)
   Honor Books:
   Little Town on the Prairie by Laura Ingalls Wilder (Harper)
   George Washington's World by Genevieve Foster (Scribner)
   Indian Captive: The Story of Mary Jemison by Lois Lenski
   (Lippincott)
   Down Ryton Water by Eva Roe Gaggin (Viking)
1941 Medal Winner:
   Call It Courage by Armstrong Sperry (Macmillan)
   Honor Books:
   Blue Willow by Doris Gates (Viking)
   Young Mac of Fort Vancouver by Mary Jane Carr (Crowell)
   The Long Winter by Laura Ingalls Wilder (Harper)
   Nansen by Anna Gertrude Hall (Viking)
1940 Medal Winner:
   Daniel Boone by James Daugherty (Viking)
   Honor Books:
   The Singing Tree by Kate Seredy (Viking)
   Runner of the Mountain Tops: The Life of Louis Agassiz by Mabel
   Robinson (Random House)
   By the Shores of Silver Lake by Laura Ingalls Wilder (Harper)
   Boy with a Pack by Stephen W. Meader (Harcourt)

1939 Medal Winner:
> *Thimble Summer* by Elizabeth Enright (Rinehart)
> **Honor Books:**
> *Nino* by Valenti Angelo (Viking)
> *Mr. Popper's Penguins* by Richard and Florence Atwater (Little, Brown)
> *Hello the Boat!* by Phyllis Crawford (Holt)
> *Leader By Destiny: George Washington, Man and Patriot* by Jeanette Eaton (Harcourt)
> *Penn* by Elizabeth Janet Gray (Viking)

1938 Medal Winner:
> *The White Stag* by Kate Seredy (Viking)
> **Honor Books:**
> *Pecos Bill* by James Cloyd Bowman (Little, Brown)
> *Bright Island* by Mabel Robinson (Random House)
> *On the Banks of Plum Creek* by Laura Ingalls Wilder (Harper)

1937 Medal Winner:
> *Roller Skates* by Ruth Sawyer (Viking)
> **Honor Books:**
> *Phoebe Fairchild: Her Book* by Lois Lenski (Stokes)
> *Whistler's Van* by Idwal Jones (Viking)
> *The Golden Basket* by Ludwig Bemelmans (Viking)
> *Winterbound* by Margery Bianco (Viking)
> *The Codfish Musket* by Agnes Hewes (Doubleday)
> *Audubon* by Constance Rourke (Harcourt)

1936 Medal Winner:
> *Caddie Woodlawn* by Carol Ryrie Brink (Macmillan)
> **Honor Books:**
> *Honk, the Moose* by Phil Stong (Dodd)
> *The Good Master* by Kate Seredy (Viking)
> *Young Walter Scott* by Elizabeth Janet Gray (Viking)
> *All Sail Set: A Romance of the Flying Cloud* by Armstrong Sperry (Winston)

1935 Medal Winner:
> *Dobry* by Monica Shannon (Viking)
> **Honor Books:**
> *Pageant of Chinese History* by Elizabeth Seeger (Longmans)
> *Davy Crockett* by Constance Rourke (Harcourt)
> *Day On Skates: The Story of a Dutch Picnic* by Hilda Von Stockum (Harper)

1934 Medal Winner:
Invincible Louisa: The Story of the Author of Little Women by Cornelia Meigs (Little, Brown)
 Honor Books:
The Forgotten Daughter by Caroline Snedeker (Doubleday)
Swords of Steel by Elsie Singmaster (Houghton Mifflin)
ABC Bunny by Wanda Gág (Coward)
Winged Girl of Knossos by Erik Berry, pseud. (Allena Best) (Appleton)
New Land by Sarah Schmidt (McBride)
Big Tree of Bunlahy: Stories of My Own Countryside by Padraic Colum (Macmillan)
Glory of the Seas by Agnes Hewes (Knopf)
Apprentice of Florence by Ann Kyle (Houghton Mifflin)

1933 Medal Winner:
Young Fu of the Upper Yangtze by Elizabeth Lewis (Winston)
 Honor Books:
Swift Rivers by Cornelia Meigs (Little, Brown)
The Railroad To Freedom: A Story of the Civil War by Hildegarde Swift (Harcourt)
Children of the Soil: A Story of Scandinavia by Nora Burglon (Doubleday)

1932 Medal Winner:
Waterless Mountain by Laura Adams Armer (Longmans)
 Honor Books:
The Fairy Circus by Dorothy P. Lathrop (Macmillan)
Calico Bush by Rachel Field (Macmillan)
Boy of the South Seas by Eunice Tietjens (Coward-McCann)
Out of the Flame by Eloise Lownsbery (Longmans)
Jane's Island by Marjorie Allee (Houghton Mifflin)
Truce of the Wolf and Other Tales of Old Italy by Mary Gould Davis (Harcourt)

1931 Medal Winner:
The Cat Who Went to Heaven by Elizabeth Coatsworth (Macmillan)
 Honor Books:
Floating Island by Anne Parrish (Harper)
The Dark Star of Itza: The Story of A Pagan Princess by Alida Malkus (Harcourt)
Queer Person by Ralph Hubbard (Doubleday)
Mountains are Free by Julie Davis Adams (Dutton)
Spice and the Devil's Cave by Agnes Hewes (Knopf)
Meggy MacIntosh by Elizabeth Janet Gray (Doubleday)

Garram the Hunter: A Boy of the Hill Tribes by Herbert Best
(Doubleday)

Ood-Le-Uk the Wanderer by Alice Lide and Margaret Johansen
(Little, Brown)

1930 Medal Winner:

Hitty, Her First Hundred Years by Rachel Field (Macmillan)

  Honor Books:

A Daughter of the Seine: The Life of Madame Roland by Jeanette
Eaton (Harper)

Pran of Albania by Elizabeth Miller (Doubleday)

Jumping-Off Place by Marion Hurd McNeely (Longmans)

The Tangle-Coated Horse and Other Tales by Ella Young
(Longmans)

Vaino by Julia Davis Adams (Dutton)

Little Blacknose by Hildegarde Swift (Harcourt Brace)

1929 Medal Winner:

The Trumpeter of Krakow by Eric P. Kelly (Macmillan)

  Honor Books:

Pigtail of Ah Lee Ben Loo by John Bennett (Longmans)

Millions of Cats by Wanda Gág (Coward-McCann)

The Boy Who Was by Grace Hallock (Dutton)

Clearing Weather by Cornelia Meigs (Little, Brown)

Runaway Papoose by Grace Moon (Doubleday)

Tod of the Fens by Elinor Whitney (Macmillan)

1928 Medal Winner:

Gay Neck, the Story of a Pigeon by Dhan Gopal Mukerji (Dutton)

  Honor Books:

The Wonder Smith and His Son by Ella Young (Longmans)

Downright Dencey by Caroline Snedeker (Doubleday)

1927 Medal Winner:

Smoky, the Cowhorse by Will James (Scribner)

  Honor Books:

[None recorded]

1926 Medal Winner:

Shen of the Sea by Arthur Bowie Chrisman (Dutton)

  Honor Book:

The Voyagers: Being Legends and Romances of Atlantic Discovery
by Padraic Colum (Macmillan)

1925 Medal Winner:

Tales from Silver Lands by Charles Finger (Doubleday)

  Honor Books:

Nicholas: A Manhattan Christmas Story by Annie Carroll Moore
(Putnam)

The Dream Coach by Anne Parrish (Macmillan)

1924 Medal Winner:

The Dark Frigate by Charles Hawes (Little, Brown)

  Honor Books:

[None recorded]

1923 Medal Winner:

The Voyages of Doctor Dolittle by Hugh Lofting (Lippincott)

  Honor Books:

[None recorded]

1922 Medal Winner:

The Story of Mankind by Hendrik Willem van Loon (Liveright)

  Honor Books:

The Great Quest by Charles Hawes (Little, Brown)

Cedric the Forester by Bernard Marshall (Appleton)

The Old Tobacco Shop: A True Account of What Befell a Little Boy in Search of Adventure by William Bowen (Macmillan)

The Golden Fleece and the Heroes Who Lived Before Achilles by Padraic Colum (Macmillan)

The Windy Hill by Cornelia Meigs (Macmillan)

Randolph Caldecott Medal

The Randolph Caldecott Medal is presented to the illustrator of the book considered the most distinguished picture book for children published during the preceding year. The author must be an American citizen or a permanent resident of the United States. Honor books may also be chosen.

The award is determined by a committee of fifteen members and sponsored by the American Library Association.

2003 Medal Winner:

My Friend Rabbit by Eric Rohmann (Roaring Brook Press/Millbrook Press)

  Honor Books:

The Spider and the Fly illustrated by Tony DiTerlizzi, Text: Mary Howitt (Simon & Schuster)

Hondo & Fabian by Peter McCarty (Holt)

Noah's Ark by Jerry Pinkney (SeaStar/North-South)

2002 Medal Winner:

The Three Pigs by David Wiesner (Clarion/Houghton Mifflin)

  Honor Books:

The Dinosaurs of Waterhouse Hawkins illustrated by Brian Selznick; Text: Barbara Kerley (Scholastic)

Martin's Big Words: The Life of Dr. Martin Luther King, Jr. illustrated by Bryan Collier; Text: Doreen Rappaport (Jump at the Sun/Hyperion)

The Stray Dog by Marc Simont (HarperCollins)

2001 Medal Winner:

So You Want to be President? illustrated by David Small; Text: Judith St. George (Philomel)

Honor Books:

Casey at the Bat: A Ballad of the Republic Sung in the Year 1888 illustrated by Christopher Bing; Text: Ernest Lawrence Thayer (Handprint Books)

Click, Clack, Moo: Cows that Type illustrated by Betsy Lewin; Text: Doreen Cronin (Simon & Schuster)

Olivia by Ian Falconer (Simon & Schuster/Atheneum)

2000 Medal Winner:

Joseph Had a Little Overcoat by Simms Taback (Viking)

Honor Books:

A Child's Calendar illustrated by Trina Schart Hyman; Text: John Updike (Holiday House)

Sector 7 by David Wiesner (Clarion)

When Sophie Gets Angry—Really, Really Angry by Molly Bang (Scholastic)

The Ugly Duckling illustrated by Jerry Pinkney; Text: Hans Christian Andersen, adapted by Jerry Pinkney (Morrow)

1999 Medal Winner:

Snowflake Bentley illustrated by Mary Azarian; Text: Jacqueline Briggs Martin (Houghton Mifflin)

Honor Books:

Duke Ellington: The Piano Prince and the Orchestra illustrated by Brian Pinkney; Text: Andrea Davis Pinkney (Hyperion)

No, David! by David Shannon (Scholastic)

Snow by Uri Shulevitz (Farrar, Straus & Giroux)

Tibet Through the Red Box by Peter Sis (Frances Foster)

1998 Medal Winner:

Rapunzel by Paul O. Zelinsky (Dutton)

Honor Books:

The Gardener illustrated by David Small; Text: Sarah Stewart (Farrar, Straus & Giroux)

Harlem illustrated by Christopher Myers; Text: Walter Dean Myers (Scholastic)

There Was an Old Lady Who Swallowed a Fly by Simms Taback (Viking)

1997 Medal Winner:

Golem by David Wisniewski (Clarion)

  Honor Books:

Hush! A Thai Lullaby illustrated by Holly Meade; Text: Minfong Ho (Melanie Kroupa/Orchard Books)

The Graphic Alphabet by David Pelletier (Orchard Books)

The Paperboy by Dav Pilkey (Richard Jackson/Orchard)

Starry Messenger by Peter Sís (Frances Foster Books/Farrar, Straus & Giroux)

1996 Medal Winner:

Officer Buckle and Gloria by Peggy Rathmann (Putnam)

  Honor Books:

Alphabet City by Stephen T. Johnson (Viking)

Zin! Zin! Zin! a Violin illustrated by Marjorie Priceman; Text: Lloyd Moss (Simon & Schuster)

The Faithful Friend illustrated by Brian Pinkney; Text: Robert D. San Souci (Simon & Schuster)

Tops and Bottoms adapted and illustrated by Janet Stevens (Harcourt)

1995 Medal Winner:

Smoky Night illustrated by David Diaz; Text: Eve Bunting (Harcourt)

  Honor Books:

John Henry illustrated by Jerry Pinkney; Text: Julius Lester (Dial)

Swamp Angel illustrated by Paul O. Zelinsky; Text: Anne Issacs (Dutton)

Time Flies by Eric Rohmann (Crown)

1994 Medal Winner:

Grandfather's Journey by Allen Say; Text: edited by Walter Lorraine (Houghton Mifflin)

  Honor Books:

Peppe the Lamplighter illustrated by Ted Lewin; Text: Elisa Bartone (Lothrop)

In the Small, Small Pond by Denise Fleming (Holt)

Raven: A Trickster Tale from the Pacific Northwest by Gerald McDermott (Harcourt)

Owen by Kevin Henkes (Greenwillow)

Yo! Yes? illustrated by Chris Raschka; Text: edited by Richard Jackson (Orchard)

1993 Medal Winner:
> *Mirette on the High Wire* by Emily Arnold McCully (Putnam)
> **Honor Books:**
> *The Stinky Cheese Man and Other Fairly Stupid Tales* illustrated
> by Lane Smith; Text: Jon Scieszka (Viking)
> *Seven Blind Mice* by Ed Young (Philomel Books)
> *Working Cotton* illustrated by Carole Byard; Text: Sherley Anne
> Williams (Harcourt)

1992 Medal Winner:
> *Tuesday* by David Wiesner (Clarion)
> **Honor Book:**
> *Tar Beach* by Faith Ringgold (Crown/Random House)

1991 Medal Winner:
> *Black and White* by David Macaulay (Houghton Mifflin)
> **Honor Books:**
> *Puss in Boots* illustrated by Fred Marcellino; Text: Charles
> Perrault, trans. by Malcolm Arthur (Di Capua/Farrar, Straus &
> Giroux)
> *"More More More," Said the Baby: Three Love Stories* by Vera B.
> Williams (Greenwillow)

1990 Medal Winner:
> *Lon Po Po: A Red-Riding Hood Story from China* by Ed Young
> (Philomel)
> **Honor Books:**
> *Bill Peet: An Autobiography* by Bill Peet (Houghton Mifflin)
> *Color Zoo* by Lois Ehlert (Lippincott)
> *The Talking Eggs: A Folktale from the American South* illustrated
> by Jerry Pinkney; Text: Robert D. San Souci (Dial)
> *Hershel and the Hanukkah Goblins* illustrated by Trina Schart
> Hyman; Text: Eric Kimmel (Holiday House)

1989 Medal Winner:
> *Song and Dance Man* illustrated by Stephen Gammell; Text: Karen
> Ackerman (Knopf)
> **Honor Books:**
> *The Boy of the Three-Year Nap* illustrated by Allen Say; Text:
> Diane Snyder (Houghton Mifflin)
> *Free Fall* by David Wiesner (Lothrop)
> *Goldilocks and the Three Bears* by James Marshall (Dial)
> *Mirandy and Brother Wind* illustrated by Jerry Pinkney; Text:
> Patricia C. McKissack (Knopf)

1988 Medal Winner:
> *Owl Moon* illustrated by John Schoenherr; Text: Jane Yolen
> (Philomel)

Honor Book:

Mufaro's Beautiful Daughters: An African Tale by John Steptoe (Lothrop)

1987 Medal Winner:

Hey, Al illustrated by Richard Egielski; Text: Arthur Yorinks (Farrar, Straus & Giroux)

Honor Books:

The Village of Round and Square Houses by Ann Grifalconi (Little, Brown)

Alphabatics by Suse MacDonald (Bradbury)

Rumpelstiltskin by Paul O. Zelinsky (Dutton)

1986 Medal Winner:

The Polar Express by Chris Van Allsburg (Houghton Mifflin)

Honor Books:

The Relatives Came illustrated by Stephen Gammell; Text: Cynthia Rylant (Bradbury)

King Bidgood's in the Bathtub illustrated by Don Wood; Text: Audrey Wood (Harcourt)

1985 Medal Winner:

Saint George and the Dragon illustrated by Trina Schart Hyman; Text: retold by Margaret Hodges (Little, Brown)

Honor Books:

Hansel and Gretel illustrated by Paul O. Zelinsky; Text: retold by Rika Lesser (Dodd)

Have You Seen My Duckling? by Nancy Tafuri (Greenwillow)

The Story of Jumping Mouse: A Native American Legend, retold and illustrated by John Steptoe (Lothrop)

1984 Medal Winner:

The Glorious Flight: Across the Channel with Louis Bleriot by Alice and Martin Provensen (Viking)

Honor Books:

Little Red Riding Hood, retold and illustrated by Trina Schart Hyman (Holiday)

Ten, Nine, Eight by Molly Bang (Greenwillow)

1983 Medal Winner:

Shadow, translated and illustrated by Marcia Brown; original text in French by Blaise Cendrars (Scribner)

Honor Books:

A Chair for My Mother by Vera B. Williams (Greenwillow)

When I Was Young in the Mountains illustrated by Diane Goode; Text: Cynthia Rylant (Dutton)

1982 Medal Winner:

Jumanji by Chris Van Allsburg (Houghton Mifflin)

Honor Books:
Where the Buffaloes Begin illustrated by Stephen Gammell; Text: Olaf Baker (Warne)
On Market Street illustrated by Anita Lobel; Text: Arnold Lobel (Greenwillow)
Outside Over There by Maurice Sendak (Harper)
A Visit to William Blake's Inn: Poems for Innocent and Experienced Travelers illustrated by Alice and Martin Provensen; Text: Nancy Willard (Harcourt)

1981 Medal Winner:
Fables by Arnold Lobel (Harper)
  Honor Books:
The Bremen-Town Musicians, retold and illustrated by Ilse Plume (Doubleday)
The Grey Lady and the Strawberry Snatcher by Molly Bang (Four Winds)
Mice Twice by Joseph Low (McElderry/Atheneum)
Truck by Donald Crews (Greenwillow)

1980 Medal Winner:
Ox-Cart Man illustrated by Barbara Cooney; Text: Donald Hall (Viking)
  Honor Books:
Ben's Trumpet by Rachel Isadora (Greenwillow)
The Garden Of Abdul Gasazi by Chris Van Allsburg (Houghton Mifflin)
The Treasure by Uri Shulevitz (Farrar, Straus & Giroux)

1979 Medal Winner:
The Girl Who Loved Wild Horses by Paul Goble (Bradbury)
  Honor Books:
Freight Train by Donald Crews (Greenwillow)
The Way to Start a Day illustrated by Peter Parnall; Text: Byrd Baylor (Scribner)

1978 Medal Winner:
Noah's Ark by Peter Spier (Doubleday)
  Honor Books:
Castle by David Macaulay (Houghton Mifflin)
It Could Always Be Worse retold and illustrated by Margot Zemach (Farrar, Straus & Giroux)

1977 Medal Winner:
Ashanti to Zulu: African Traditions illustrated by Leo and Diane Dillon; Text: Margaret Musgrove (Dial)
  Honor Books:
The Amazing Bone by William Steig (Farrar, Straus & Giroux)

The Contest retold and illustrated by Nonny Hogrogian (Greenwillow)

Fish for Supper by M. B. Goffstein (Dial)

The Golem: A Jewish Legend by Beverly Brodsky McDermott (Lippincott)

Hawk, I'm Your Brother illustrated by Peter Parnall; Text: Byrd Baylor (Scribner)

1976 Medal Winner:

Why Mosquitoes Buzz in People's Ears illustrated by Leo and Diane Dillon; Text: retold by Verna Aardema (Dial)

Honor Books:

The Desert is Theirs illustrated by Peter Parnall; Text: Byrd Baylor (Scribner)

Strega Nona by Tomie de Paola (Prentice-Hall)

1975 Medal Winner:

Arrow to the Sun by Gerald McDermott (Viking)

Honor Books:

Jambo Means Hello: A Swahili Alphabet Book illustrated by Tom Feelings; Text: Muriel Feelings (Dial)

1974 Medal Winner:

Duffy and the Devil illustrated by Margot Zemach; Text: retold by Harve Zemach (Farrar, Straus & Giroux)

Honor Books:

Three Jovial Huntsmen by Susan Jeffers (Bradbury)

Cathedral by David Macaulay (Houghton Mifflin)

1973 Medal Winner:

The Funny Little Woman illustrated by Blair Lent; Text: retold by Arlene Mosel (Dutton)

Honor Books:

Anansi the Spider: A Tale from the Ashanti adapted and illustrated by Gerald McDermott (Holt)

Hosie's Alphabet illustrated by Leonard Baskin; Text: Hosea, Tobias and Lisa Baskin (Viking)

Snow-White and the Seven Dwarfs illustrated by Nancy Ekholm Burkert; Text: translated by Randall Jarrell, retold from the Brothers Grimm (Farrar, Straus & Giroux)

When Clay Sings illustrated by Tom Bahti; Text: Byrd Baylor (Scribner)

1972 Medal Winner:

One Fine Day retold and illustrated by Nonny Hogrogian (Macmillan)

Honor Books:

Hildilid's Night illustrated by Arnold Lobel; Text: Cheli Durán Ryan (Macmillan)
If All the Seas Were One Sea by Janina Domanska (Macmillan)
Moja Means One: Swahili Counting Book illustrated by Tom Feelings; Text: Muriel Feelings (Dial)

1971 Medal Winner:
A Story A Story retold and illustrated by Gail E. Haley (Atheneum)
Honor Books:
The Angry Moon illustrated by Blair Lent; Text: retold by William Sleator (Atlantic)
Frog and Toad are Friends by Arnold Lobel (Harper)
In the Night Kitchen by Maurice Sendak (Harper)

1970 Medal Winner:
Sylvester and the Magic Pebble by William Steig (Windmill Books)
Honor Books:
Goggles! by Ezra Jack Keats (Macmillan)
Alexander and the Wind-Up Mouse by Leo Lionni (Pantheon)
Pop Corn and Ma Goodness illustrated by Robert Andrew Parker; Text: Edna Mitchell Preston (Viking)
Thy Friend, Obadiah by Brinton Turkle (Viking)
The Judge: An Untrue Tale illustrated by Margot Zemach; Text: Harve Zemach (Farrar, Straus & Giroux)

1969 Medal Winner:
The Fool of the World and the Flying Ship illustrated by Uri Shulevitz; Text: retold by Arthur Ransome (Farrar, Straus & Giroux)
Honor Books:
Why the Sun and the Moon Live in the Sky illustrated by Blair Lent; Text: Elphinstone Dayrell (Houghton Mifflin)

1968 Medal Winner:
Drummer Hoff illustrated by Ed Emberley; Text: adapted by Barbara Emberley (Prentice-Hall)
Honor Books:
Frederick by Leo Lionni (Pantheon)
Seashore Story by Taro Yashima (Viking)
The Emperor and the Kite illustrated by Ed Young; Text: Jane Yolen (World)

1967 Medal Winner:
Sam, Bangs and Moonshine by Evaline Ness (Holt)
Honor Book:
One Wide River to Cross illustrated by Ed Emberley; Text: adapted by Barbara Emberley (Prentice-Hall)

1966 Medal Winner:
Always Room for One More illustrated by Nonny Hogrogian; Text: Sorche Nic Leodhas, pseud. (Leclair Alger) (Holt)
 Honor Books:
Hide and Seek Fog illustrated by Roger Duvoisin; Text: Alvin Tresselt (Lothrop)
Just Me by Marie Hall Ets (Viking)
Tom Tit Tot retold and illustrated by Evaline Ness (Scribner)

1965 Medal Winner:
May I Bring a Friend? illustrated by Beni Montresor; Text: Beatrice Schenk de Regniers (Atheneum)
 Honor Books:
Rain Makes Applesauce illustrated by Marvin Bileck; Text: Julian Scheer (Holiday)
The Wave illustrated by Blair Lent; Text: Margaret Hodges (Houghton Mifflin)
A Pocketful of Cricket illustrated by Evaline Ness; Text: Rebecca Caudill (Holt)

1964 Medal Winner:
Where the Wild Things Are by Maurice Sendak (Harper)
 Honor Books:
Swimmy by Leo Lionni (Pantheon)
All in the Morning Early illustrated by Evaline Ness; Text: Sorche Nic Leodhas, pseud. (Leclaire Alger) (Holt)
Mother Goose and Nursery Rhymes illustrated by Philip Reed (Atheneum)

1963 Medal Winner:
The Snowy Day by Ezra Jack Keats (Viking)
 Honor Books:
The Sun is a Golden Earring illustrated by Bernarda Bryson; Text: Natalia M. Belting (Holt)
Mr. Rabbit and the Lovely Present illustrated by Maurice Sendak; Text: Charlotte Zolotow (Harper)

1962 Medal Winner:
Once a Mouse retold and illustrated by Marcia Brown (Scribner)
 Honor Books:
Fox Went out on a Chilly Night: An Old Song by Peter Spier (Doubleday)
Little Bear's Visit illustrated by Maurice Sendak; Text: Else H. Minarik (Harper)
The Day We Saw the Sun Come Up illustrated by Adrienne Adams; Text: Alice E. Goudey (Scribner)

1961 Medal Winner:
Baboushka and the Three Kings illustrated by Nicolas Sidjakov;
Text: Ruth Robbins (Parnassus)
  Honor Book:
Inch by Inch by Leo Lionni (Obolensky)
1960 Medal Winner:
Nine Days to Christmas illustrated by Marie Hall Ets; Text: Marie
Hall Ets and Aurora Labastida (Viking)
  Honor Books:
Houses from the Sea illustrated by Adrienne Adams; Text: Alice E.
Goudey (Scribner)
The Moon Jumpers illustrated by Maurice Sendak; Text: Janice
May Udry (Harper)
1959 Medal Winner:
Chanticleer and the Fox illustrated by Barbara Cooney; Text:
adapted from Chaucer's Canterbury Tales by Barbara Cooney
(Crowell)
Honor Books:
The House that Jack Built: La Maison Que Jacques A Batie by
Antonio Frasconi (Harcourt)
What Do You Say, Dear? illustrated by Maurice Sendak; Text:
Sesyle Joslin (W. R. Scott)
Umbrella by Taro Yashima (Viking)
1958 Medal Winner:
Time of Wonder by Robert McCloskey (Viking)
  Honor Books:
Fly High, Fly Low by Don Freeman (Viking)
Anatole and the Cat illustrated by Paul Galdone; Text: Eve Titus
(McGraw-Hill)
1957 Medal Winner:
A Tree is Nice illustrated by Marc Simont; Text: Janice Udry
(Harper)
  Honor Books:
Mr. Penny's Race Horse by Marie Hall Ets (Viking)
1 is One by Tasha Tudor (Walck)
Anatole illustrated by Paul Galdone; Text: Eve Titus (McGraw-
Hill)
Gillespie and the Guards illustrated by James Daugherty; Text:
Benjamin Elkin (Viking)
Lion by William Pène du Bois (Viking)
1956 Medal Winner:
Frog Went A-Courtin' illustrated by Feodor Rojankovsky; Text: retold
by John Langstaff (Harcourt)

Honor Books:
Play With Me by Marie Hall Ets (Viking)
Crow Boy by Taro Yashima (Viking)

1955 Medal Winner:
Cinderella, or the Little Glass Slipper illustrated by Marcia Brown; Text: translated from Charles Perrault by Marcia Brown (Scribner)
 Honor Books:
Book of Nursery and Mother Goose Rhymes illustrated by Marguerite de Angeli (Doubleday)
Wheel on the Chimney illustrated by Tibor Gergely; Text: Margaret Wise Brown (Lippincott)
The Thanksgiving Story illustrated by Helen Sewell; Text: Alice Dalgliesh (Scribner)

1954 Medal Winner:
Madeline's Rescue by Ludwig Bemelmans (Viking)
 Honor Books:
Journey Cake, Ho! illustrated by Robert McCloskey; Text: Ruth Sawyer (Viking)
When Will the World Be Mine? illustrated by Jean Charlot; Text: Miriam Schlein (W. R. Scott)
The Steadfast Tin Soldier illustrated by Marcia Brown; Text: Hans Christian Andersen, translated by M. R. James (Scribner)
A Very Special House illustrated by Maurice Sendak; Text: Ruth Krauss (Harper)
Green Eyes by A. Birnbaum (Capitol)

1953 Medal Winner:
The Biggest Bear by Lynd Ward (Houghton Mifflin)
 Honor Books:
Puss in Boots illustrated by Marcia Brown; Text: translated from Charles Perrault by Marcia Brown (Scribner)
One Morning in Maine by Robert McCloskey (Viking)
Ape in a Cape: An Alphabet of Odd Animals by Fritz Eichenberg (Harcourt)
The Storm Book illustrated by Margaret Bloy Graham; Text: Charlotte Zolotow (Harper)
Five Little Monkeys by Juliet Kepes (Houghton Mifflin)

1952 Medal Winner:
Finders Keepers illustrated by Nicolas, pseud. (Nicholas Mordvinoff); Text: Will, pseud. (William Lipkind) (Harcourt)
 Honor Books:
Mr. T. W. Anthony Woo by Marie Hall Ets (Viking)
Skipper John's Cook by Marcia Brown (Scribner)

All Falling Down illustrated by Margaret Bloy Graham; Text: Gene Zion (Harper)

Bear Party by William Pène du Bois (Viking)

Feather Mountain by Elizabeth Olds (Houghton Mifflin)

1951 Medal Winner:

The Egg Tree by Katherine Milhous (Scribner)

 Honor Books:

Dick Whittington and his Cat by Marcia Brown (Scribner)

The Two Reds illustrated by Nicolas, pseud. (Nicholas Mordvinoff); Text: Will, pseud. (William Lipkind) (Harcourt)

If I Ran the Zoo by Dr. Seuss, pseud. (Theodor Seuss Geisel) (Random House)

The Most Wonderful Doll in the World illustrated by Helen Stone; Text: Phyllis McGinley (Lippincott)

T-Bone, the Baby Sitter by Clare Turlay Newbery (Harper)

1950 Medal Winner:

Song of the Swallows by Leo Politi (Scribner)

 Honor Books:

America's Ethan Allen illustrated by Lynd Ward; Text: Stewart Holbrook (Houghton Mifflin)

The Wild Birthday Cake illustrated by Hildegard Woodward; Text: Lavinia R. Davis (Doubleday)

The Happy Day illustrated by Marc Simont; Text: Ruth Krauss (Harper)

Bartholomew and the Oobleck by Dr. Seuss, pseud. (Theodor Seuss Geisel) (Random House)

Henry Fisherman by Marcia Brown (Atheneum)

1949 Medal Winner:

The Big Snow by Berta and Elmer Hader (Macmillan)

 Honor Books:

Blueberries for Sal by Robert McCloskey (Viking)

All Around the Town illustrated by Helen Stone; Text: Phyllis McGinley (Lippincott)

Juanita by Leo Politi (Scribner)

Fish in the Air by Kurt Wiese (Viking)

1948 Medal Winner:

White Snow, Bright Snow illustrated by Roger Duvoisin; Text: Alvin Tresselt (Lothrop)

 Honor Books:

Stone Soup by Marcia Brown (Scribner)

McElligot's Pool by Dr. Seuss, pseud. (Theodor Seuss Geisel) (Random House)

Bambino the Clown by Georges Schreiber (Viking)

Roger and the Fox illustrated by Hildegard Woodward; Text:
Lavinia R. Davis (Doubleday)
Song of Robin Hood illustrated by Virginia Lee Burton; Text:
edited by Anne Malcolmson (Houghton Mifflin)
1947 Medal Winner:
The Little Island illustrated by Leonard Weisgard; Text: Golden
MacDonald, pseud. (Margaret Wise Brown) (Doubleday)
  Honor Books:
Rain Drop Splash illustrated by Leonard Weisgard; Text: Alvin
Tresselt (Lothrop)
Boats on the River illustrated by Jay Hyde Barnum; Text: Marjorie
Flack (Viking)
Timothy Turtle illustrated by Tony Palazzo; Text: Al Graham
(Welch)
Pedro, the Angel of Olvera Street by Leo Politi (Scribner)
Sing in Praise: A Collection of the Best Loved Hymns illustrated by
Marjorie Torrey; Text: selected by Opal Wheeler (Dutton)
1946 Medal Winner:
The Rooster Crows by Maude and Miska Petersham (Macmillan)
  Honor Books:
Little Lost Lamb illustrated by Leonard Weisgard; Text: Golden
MacDonald, pseud. (Margaret Wise Brown) (Doubleday)
Sing Mother Goose illustrated by Marjorie Torrey; Music: Opal
Wheeler (Dutton)
My Mother is the Most Beautiful Woman in the World illustrated
by Ruth Gannett; Text: Becky Reyher (Lothrop)
You Can Write Chinese by Kurt Wiese (Viking)
1945 Medal Winner:
Prayer for a Child illustrated by Elizabeth Orton Jones; Text:
Rachel Field (Macmillan)
  Honor Books:
Mother Goose illustrated by Tasha Tudor (Oxford University
Press)
In the Forest by Marie Hall Ets (Viking)
Yonie Wondernose by Marguerite de Angeli (Doubleday)
The Christmas Anna Angel illustrated by Kate Seredy; Text: Ruth
Sawyer (Viking)
1944 Medal Winner:
Many Moons illustrated by Louis Slobodkin; Text: James Thurber
(Harcourt)
  Honor Books:
Small Rain: Verses from the Bible illustrated by Elizabeth Orton
Jones; Text: selected by Jessie Orton Jones (Viking)

Pierre Pigeon illustrated by Arnold E. Bare; Text: Lee Kingman (Houghton Mifflin)
The Mighty Hunter by Berta and Elmer Hader (Macmillan)
A Child's Good Night Book illustrated by Jean Charlot; Text: Margaret Wise Brown (W. R. Scott)
Good-Luck Horse illustrated by Plato Chan; Text: Chih-Yi Chan (Whittlesey)

1943 Medal Winner:
The Little House by Virginia Lee Burton (Houghton Mifflin)
Honor Books:
Dash and Dart by Mary and Conrad Buff (Viking)
Marshmallow by Clare Turlay Newbery (Harper)

1942 Medal Winner:
Make Way for Ducklings by Robert McCloskey (Viking)
Honor Books:
An American ABC by Maud and Miska Petersham (Macmillan)
In My Mother's House illustrated by Velino Herrera; Text: Ann Nolan Clark (Viking)
Paddle-To-The-Sea by Holling C. Holling (Houghton Mifflin)
Nothing At All by Wanda Gág (Coward-McCann)

1941 Medal Winner:
They Were Strong and Good by Robert Lawson (Viking)
Honor Book:
April's Kittens by Clare Turlay Newbery (Harper)

1940 Medal Winner:
Abraham Lincoln by Ingri and Edgar Parin d'Aulaire (Doubleday)
Honor Books:
Cock-a-Doodle Doo by Berta and Elmer Hader (Macmillan)
Madeline by Ludwig Bemelmans (Viking)
The Ageless Story by Lauren Ford (Dodd)

1939 Medal Winner:
Mei Li by Thomas Handforth (Doubleday)
Honor Books:
Andy and the Lion by James Daugherty (Viking)
Barkis by Clare Turlay Newbery (Harper)
The Forest Pool by Laura Adams Armer (Longmans)
Snow White and the Seven Dwarfs by Wanda Gág (Coward-McCann)
Wee Gillis illustrated by Robert Lawson; Text: Munro Leaf (Viking)

1938 Medal Winner:
Animals of the Bible, A Picture Book illustrated by Dorothy P. Lathrop, selected by Helen Dean Fish (Lippincott)

Honor Books:
Four and Twenty Blackbirds illustrated by Robert Lawson,
compiled by Helen Dean Fish (Stokes)
Seven Simeons: A Russian Tale, retold and illustrated by Boris
Artzybasheff (Viking)

The Coretta Scott King Award

This award is presented annually to authors and illustrators of African
descent whose distinguished books promote an understanding and
appreciation of the dream held by Dr. Martin Luther King, Jr. The
medal also commemorates the ongoing work of Dr. King's widow in
promoting peace and world brotherhood.

A seven-member committee chooses the Coretta Scott King Award
books.

2003 Author Award Winner:
Bronx Masquerade by Nikki Grimes (Dial)
Honor Books:
The Red Rose Box by Brenda Woods (Putnam)
Talkin' About Bessie: the Story of Aviator Elizabeth Coleman by
Nikki Grimes (Orchard Books/Scholastic)
2003 Illustrator Award Winner:
Talkin' About Bessie: The Story of Aviator Elizabeth Coleman
illustrated by E. B. Lewis; Text: Nikki Grimes
(Orchard/Scholastic)
Honor Books:
Rap A Tap Tap: Here's Bojangles-Think of That by Leo and Diane
Dillion (Blue Sky/Scholastic)
Visiting Langston by Bryan Collier (Holt)
2002 Author Award Winner:
The Land by Mildred Taylor (Phyllis Fogelman/Penguin Putnam)
Honor Books:
Money-Hungry by Sharon G. Flake (Jump at the Sun/Hyperion)
Carver: A Life in Poems by Marilyn Nelson (Front Street)
2002 Illustrator Award Winner:
Goin' Someplace Special illustrated by Jerry Pinkney; Text:
Patricia McKissack (Anne Schwartz/Atheneum)
Honor Books:
Martin's Big Words illustrated by Bryan Collier; Text: Doreen
Rappoport (Jump at the Sun/Hyperion)

2001 Author Award Winner:
Miracle's Boys by Jacqueline Woodson (Putnam)
  Honor Books:
Let It Shine! Stories of Black Women Freedom Fighters by Andrea
Davis Pinkney illustrated by Stephen Alcorn (Gulliver/Harcourt)
2001 Illustrator Award Winner:
Uptown by Bryan Collier (Holt)
  Honor Books:
Freedom River by Bryan Collier (Jump at the Sun/Hyperion)
Only Passing Through: The Story of Sojourner Truth illustrated by
R. Gregory Christie; Text: Anne Rockwell (Random House)
Virgie Goes to School with Us Boys illustrated by E.B. Lewis;
Text: Elizabeth Fitzgerald Howard (Simon & Schuster)
2000 Author Award Winner:
Bud, Not Buddy by Christopher Paul Curtis (Delacorte)
  Honor Books:
Francie by Karen English (Farrar, Straus & Giroux)
Black Hands, White Sails: The Story of African-American Whalers
by Patricia C. and Frederick L. McKissack (Scholastic)
Monster by Walter Dean Myers (Harper)
2000 Illustrator Award Winner:
In the Time of the Drums illustrated by Brian Pinkney; Text: Kim
L. Siegelson (Jump at the Sun/Hyperion)
Honor Books:
My Rows and Piles of Coins illustrated by E. B. Lewis; Text:
Tololwa M. Mollel (Clarion)
Black Cat by Christopher Myers (Scholastic)
1999 Author Award Winner:
Heaven by Angela Johnson (Simon & Schuster)
  Honor Books:
Jazmin's Notebook by Nikki Grimes (Dial Books)
*Breaking Ground, Breaking Silence: The Story of New York's
African Burial Ground* by Joyce Hansen and Gary McGowan
(Holt)
The Other Side: Shorter Poems by Angela Johnson (Orchard)
1999 Illustrator Award Winner:
i see the rhythm illustrated by Michele Wood; Text: Toyomi Igus
(Children's Book Press)
  Honor Books:
I Have Heard of a Land illustrated by Floyd Cooper; Text: Joyce
Carol Thomas (Joanna Cotler/HarperCollins)
The Bat Boy and His Violin illustrated by E.B. Lewis; Text: Gavin
Curtis (Simon & Schuster)

Duke Ellington: The Piano Prince and His Orchestra illustrated by Brian Pinkney; Text: Andrea Davis Pinkney (Hyperion)

1998 Author Award Winner:

Forged by Fire by Sharon M. Draper (Atheneum)

   Honor Books:

Bayard Rustin: Behind the Scenes of the Civil Rights Movement by James Haskins (Hyperion)

I Thought My Soul Would Rise and Fly: The Diary of Patsy, a Freed Girl by Joyce Hansen (Scholastic)

1998 Illustrator Award Winner:

In Daddy's Arms I am Tall: African Americans Celebrating Fathers illustrated by Javaka Steptoe; Text: Alan Schroeder (Lee and Low)

   Honor Books:

Ashley Bryan's ABC of African American Poetry by Ashley Bryan (Jean Karl/Atheneum)

Harlem illustrated by Christopher Myers; Text: Walter Dean Myers (Scholastic)

The Hunterman and the Crocodile by Baba Wagué Diakité (Scholastic)

1997 Author Award Winner:

Slam by Walter Dean Myers (Scholastic)

   Honor Books:

Rebels Against Slavery: American Slave Revolts by Patricia C. and Frederick L. McKissack (Scholastic)

1997 Illustrator Award Winner:

Minty: A Story of Young Harriet Tubman illustrated by Jerry Pinkney; Text: Alan Schroeder (Dial)

   Honor Books:

The Palm of My Heart: Poetry by African American Children illustrated by Gregorie Christie; edited by Davida Adedjouma (Lee and Low)

Running the Road To ABC illustrated by Reynold Ruffins; Text: Denize Lauture (Simon & Schuster)

Neeny Coming, Neeny Goin illustrated by Synthia Saint James; Text: Karen English (BridgeWater Books)

1996 Author Award Winner:

Her Stories by Virginia Hamilton (Blue Sky/Scholastic)

   Honor Books:

The Watsons Go to Birmingham—1963 by Christopher Paul Curtis (Delacorte)

Like Sisters on the Homefront by Rita Williams-Garcia (Delacorte)

From the Notebooks of Melanin Sun by Jacqueline Woodson (Blue Sky/Scholastic)

1996 Illustrator Award Winner:

The Middle Passage: White Ships Black Cargo by Tom Feelings (Dial)

 Honor Books:

Her Stories illustrated by Leo and Diane Dillon; Text: Virginia Hamilton (Blue Sky/Scholastic)

The Faithful Friend illustrated by Brian Pinkney; Text: Robert San Souci (Simon & Schuster))

1995 Author Award Winner:

Christmas in the Big House, Christmas in the Quarters by Patricia C. and Frederick L. McKissack (Scholastic)

 Honor Books:

The Captive by Joyce Hansen (Scholastic)

I Hadn't Meant to Tell You This by Jacqueline Woodson (Delacorte)

Black Diamond: Story of the Negro Baseball League by Patricia C. and Frederick L. McKissack (Scholastic)

1995 Illustrator Award Winner:

The Creation illustrated by James Ransome; Text: James Weldon Johnson (Holiday House)

Honor Books:

The Singing Man illustrated by Terea Shaffer; Text: Angela Shelf Medearis (Holiday House)

Meet Danitra Brown illustrated by Floyd Cooper; Text: Nikki Grimes (Lothrop, Lee and Shepard)

1994 Author Award Winner:

Toning the Sweep by Angela Johnson (Orchard)

 Honor Books:

Brown Honey in Broom Wheat Tea by Joyce Carol Thomas; illustrated by Floyd Cooper (Harper)

Malcolm X: By Any Means Necessary by Walter Dean Myers (Scholastic)

1994 Illustrator Award Winner:

Soul Looks Back in Wonder illustrated by Tom Feelings; Text: edited by Phyllis Fogelman (Dial)

 Honor Books:

Brown Honey in Broom Wheat Tea illustrated by Floyd Cooper; Text: Joyce Carol Thomas (Harper)

Uncle Jed's Barbershop illustrated by James Ransome; Text: Margaree King Mitchell (Simon & Schuster)

1993 Author Award Winner:
Dark Thirty: Southern Tales of the Supernatural by Patricia A. McKissack (Knopf)
 Honor Books:
Mississippi Challenge by Mildred Pitts Walter (Bradbury)
Sojourner Truth: Ain't I a Woman? by Patricia C. and Frederick L. McKissack (Scholastic)
Somewhere in the Darkness by Walter Dean Myers (Scholastic)
1993 Illustrator Award Winner:
The Origin of Life on Earth: an African Creation Myth illustrated by Kathleen Atkins Wilson; retold by David A. Anderson/SANKOFA (Sights)
 Honor Books:
Little Eight John illustrated by Wil Clay; Text: Jan Wahl (Lodestar)
Sukey and the Mermaid illustrated by Brian Pinkney; Text: Robert San Souci (Four Winds)
Working Cotton illustrated by Carole Byard; Text: Sherley Anne Williams (Harcourt)
1992 Author Award Winner:
Now is Your Time: The African American Struggle for Freedom by Walter Dean Myers (Harper)
Honor Books:
Night on Neighborhood Street by Eloise Greenfield illustrated by Jan Spivey Gilchrist (Dial)
1992 Illustrator Award Winner:
Tar Beach by Faith Ringgold (Crown)
 Honor Books:
All Night, All Day: A Child's First Book of African American Spirituals illustrated and selected by Ashley Bryan (Atheneum)
 Night on Neighborhood Street illustrated by Jan Spivey Gilchrist; Text: Eloise Greenfield (Dial)
1991 Author Award Winner:
The Road to Memphis by Mildred D. Taylor (Dial)
 Honor Books:
Black Dance in America by James Haskins (Crowell)
When I Am Old With You by Angela Johnson (Orchard)
1991 Illustrator Award Winner:
Aida illustrated by Leo and Diane Dillon; Text: Leontyne Price (Harcourt)
1990 Author Award Winner:
A Long Hard Journey: The Story of the Pullman Porter by Patricia C. and Frederick L. McKissack (Walker)

Honor Books:
Nathaniel Talking by Eloise Greenfield illustrated by Jan Spivey Gilchrist (Black Butterfly)
The Bells of Christmas by Virginia Hamilton (Harcourt)
Martin Luther King, Jr., and the Freedom Movement by Lillie Patterson (Facts on File)
1990 Illustrator Award Winner:
Nathaniel Talking illustrated by Jan Spivey Gilchrist; Text: Eloise Greenfield (Black Butterfly)
  Honor Books:
The Talking Eggs illustrated by Jerry Pinkney; Text: Robert San Souci (Dial)
1989 Author Award Winner:
Fallen Angels by Walter Dean Myers (Scholastic)
  Honor Books:
A Thief in the Village and Other Stories by James Berry (Orchard)
Anthony Burns: The Defeat and Triumph of a Fugitive Slave by Virginia Hamilton (Knopf)
1989 Illustrator Award Winner:
Mirandy and Brother Wind illustrated by Jerry Pinkney; Text: Patricia McKissack (Knopf)
  Honor Books:
Under the Sunday Tree illustrated by Amos Ferguson; Text: Eloise Greenfield (Harper)
Storm in the Night illustrated by Pat Cummings; Text: Mary Stolz (Harper)
1988 Author Award Winner:
The Friendship by Mildred L. Taylor (Dial)
  Honor Books:
An Enchanted Hair Tale by Alexis De Veaux (HarperCollins)
The Tales of Uncle Remus: The Adventures of Brer Rabbit by Julius Lester (Dial)
1988 Illustrator Award Winner:
Mufaro's Beautiful Daughters: An African Tale by John Steptoe (Lothrop)
  Honor Books:
What a Morning! The Christmas Story in Black Spirituals illustrated by Ashley Bryan; selected by John Langstaff (Macmillan)
The Invisible Hunters: A Legend from the Miskito Indians of Nicaragua illustrated by Joe Sam; compiled by Harriet Rohmer, et al. (Children's Press)

1987 Author Award Winner:
Justin and the Best Biscuits in the World by Mildred Pitts Walter (Lothrop)
 Honor Books:
Lion and the Ostrich Chicks and Other African Folk Tales by Ashley Bryan (Atheneum)
Which Way Freedom by Joyce Hansen (Walker)
1987 Illustrator Award Winner:
Half a Moon and One Whole Star illustrated by Jerry Pinkney; Text: Crescent Dragonwagon (Macmillan)
 Honor Books:
Lion and the Ostrich Chicks and Other African Folk Tales by Ashley Bryan (Atheneum)
C.L.O.U.D.S. by Pat Cummings (Lothrop)
1986 Author Award Winner:
The People Could Fly: American Black Folktales by Virginia Hamilton; illustrated by Leo and Diane Dillon (Knopf)
 Honor Books:
Junius Over Far by Virginia Hamilton (Harper)
Trouble's Child by Mildred Pitts Walter (Lothrop)
1986 Illustrator Award Winner:
The Patchwork Quilt illustrated by Jerry Pinkney; Text: Valerie Flournoy (Dial)
 Honor Books:
The People Could Fly: American Black Folktales illustrated by Leo and Diane Dillon; Text: Virginia Hamilton (Knopf)
1985 Author Award Winner:
Motown and Didi by Walter Dean Myers (Viking)
 Honor Books:
Circle of Gold by Candy Dawson Boyd (Apple/Scholastic)
A Little Love by Virginia Hamilton (Philomel)
1985 Illustrator Award Winner:
[No award]
1984 Author Award Winner:
Everett Anderson's Good-bye by Lucille Clifton (Holt)
Special Citation: *The Words of Martin Luther King, Jr.* Coretta Scott King, compiler (Newmarket Press)
 Honor Books:
The Magical Adventures of Pretty Pearl by Virginia Hamilton (Harper)
Lena Horne by James Haskins (Coward-McCann)
Bright Shadow by Joyce Carol Thomas (Avon)
Because We Are by Mildred Pitts Walter (Morrow)

1984 Illustrator Award Winner:
My Mama Needs Me illustrated by Pat Cummings; Text: Mildred Pitts Walter (Lothrop)

1983 Author Award Winner:
Sweet Whispers, Brother Rush by Virginia Hamilton (Philomel)
Honor Books:
This Strange New Feeling by Julius Lester (Dial)

1983 Illustrator Award Winner:
Black Child by Peter Mugabane (Knopf)
Honor Books:
All the Colors of the Race illustrated by John Steptoe; Text: Arnold Adoff (Lothrop)
I'm Going to Sing: Black American Spirituals illustrated by Ashley Bryan (Atheneum)
Just Us Women illustrated by Pat Cummings; Text: Jeanette Caines (Harper)

1982 Author Award Winner:
Let the Circle Be Unbroken by Mildred D. Taylor (Dial)
Honor Books:
Rainbow Jordan by Alice Childress (Coward-McCann)
Lou in the Limelight by Kristin Hunter (Scribner)
Mary: An Autobiography by Mary E. Mebane (Viking)

1982 Illustrator Award Winner:
Mother Crocodile; An Uncle Amadou Tale from Sengal illustrated by John Steptoe; Text: Rosa Guy (Delacorte)
Honor Books:
Daydreamers illustrated by Tom Feelings; Text: Eloise Greenfield (Dial)

1981 Author Award Winner:
This Life by Sidney Poitier (Knopf)
Honor Books:
Don't Explain: A Song of Billie Holiday by Alexis De Veaux (Harper)

1981 Illustrator Award Winner:
Beat the Story Drum, Pum-Pum by Ashley Bryan (Atheneum)
Honor Books:
Grandmama's Joy illustrated by Carole Byard; Text: Eloise Greenfield (Harper)
Count on Your Fingers African Style illustrated by Jerry Pinkney; Text: Claudia Zaslavsky (Crowell)

1980 Author Award Winner:
The Young Landlords by Walter Dean Myers (Viking)

Honor Books:
Movin' Up by Berry Gordy (HarperCollins)
Childtimes: A Three-Generation Memoir by Eloise Greenfield and
Lessie Jones Little (Harper)
Andrew Young: Young Man With a Mission by James Haskins
(Lothrop)
James Van Der Zee: The Picture Takin' Man by James Haskins
(Dodd)
1980 Illustrator Award Winner:
Cornrows illustrated by Carole Byard; Text: Camille Yarborough
(Coward-McCann)
1979 Author Award Winner:
Escape to Freedom by Ossie Davis (Viking)
Honor Books:
Benjamin Banneker by Lillie Patterson (Abingdon)
I Have a Sister, My Sister is Deaf by Jeanne W. Peterson (Harper)
Justice and Her Brothers by Virginia Hamilton (Greenwillow)
Skates of Uncle Richard by Carol Fenner (Random House)
1978 Illustrator Award Winner:
Something on My Mind illustrated by Tom Feelings; Text: Nikki
Grimes (Dial)
1978 Author Award Winner:
Africa Dream by Eloise Greenfield; illustrated by Carole Bayard
(Crowell)
Honor Books:
*The Days When the Animals Talked: Black Folk Tales and How
They Came to Be* by William J. Faulkner (Follett)
Marvin and Tige by Frankcina Glass (St. Martin's)
Mary McCleod Bethune by Eloise Greenfield (Crowell)
Barbara Jordan by James Haskins (Dial)
Coretta Scott King by Lillie Patterson (Garrard)
*Portia: The Life of Portia Washington Pittman, the Daughter of
Booker T. Washington* by Ruth Ann Stewart (Doubleday)
1978 Illustrator Award Winner:
Africa Dream illustrated by Carole Bayard; Text: Eloise Greenfield
(Crowell)
1977Author Award Winner:
The Story of Stevie Wonder by James Haskins (Lothrop)
1977 Illustrator Award Winner:
[No award]
1976 Author Award Winner:
Duey's Tale by Pearl Bailey (Harcourt)

1976 Illustrator Award Winner:
[No award]
1975 Author Award Winner:
The Legend of Agricana by Dorothy Robinson (Johnson Publishing)
1975 Illustrator Award Winner:
[No award]
1974 Author Award Winner:
Ray Charles by Sharon Bell Mathis; illustrated by George Ford (Crowell)
1974 Illustrator Award Winner:
Ray Charles illustrated by George Ford; Text: Sharon Bell Mathis (Crowell)
(**Note***:* Before 1974, the CSK Award was given to authors only)
1973 Award Winner:
I Never Had It Made: the Autobiography of Jackie Robinson, as told to Alfred Duckett (Putnam)
1972 Award Winner:
17 Black Artists by Elton C. Fax (Dodd)
1971 Award Winner:
Black Troubador: Langston Hughes by Charlemae Rollins (Rand McNally)
1970 Award Winner:
Martin Luther King, Jr.: Man of Peace by Lillie Patterson (Garrard)

The John Steptoe Award

The Coretta Scott King committee also chooses the winners of the John Steptoe Award for new talent. These books affirm new talent and offer visibility to excellence in writing or illustration at the beginning of a career as a published book creator.

2003 Award Winner:
Author: Janet McDonald for **Chill Wind** (Frances Foster/Farrar, Straus and Giroux)
Illustrator: Randy DuBruke for **The Moon Ring** (Chronicle Books)
2002 Award Winner:
Illustrator: Jerome Lagarrigue for *Freedom Summer*; Text*:* Deborah Wiles (Atheneum)

2001 Award Winner:
[No award]
2000 Award Winner:
[No award]
1999 Award Winner:
Illustrator: Eric Velasquez for *The Piano Man*; Text: Debbie
Chocolate (Walker)
Author: Sharon Flake for *The Skin I'm In* (Jump at the
Sun/Hyperion)
1998 Award Winner:
[No award]
1997 Award Winner:
Author: Martha Southgate for *Another Way to Dance* (Delacorte)
1996 Award Winner:
[No award]

Pura Belpré Award

The Pura Belpré awards are given every two years by the Association
for Library Service to Children and the National Association to
Promote Library Services to the Spanish Speaking.

The awards are given for books written and illustrated by
Latino/Latina authors and illustrators that celebrate the Latino culture.
Pura Belpré was a librarian in New York City who enriched the lives of
many Puerto Rican children through the preservation of Latino
literature.

2002 Medal Winners:
For Narrative:
Medal Winner:
Esperanza Rising by Pam Munoz Ryan (Scholastic)
Honor Books:
Francisco Jiménez. *Breaking Through* (Houghton Mifflin)
Iguanas in the Snow illustrated by Maya Christina Gonzalez; Text:
Francisco X. Alarcón (Children's Book Press)
For Illustration:
Medal Winner:
Chato and the Party Animals illustrated by Susan Guevara; Text:
Gary Soto (Putnam)
Honor Book:
Juan Bobo Goes to Work illustrated by Joe Cepeda; Retold by
Marisa Montes (HarperCollins)

2000 Medal Winners:
For Narrative:
  Medal Winner:
  Under the Royal Palms A Childhood in Cuba by Alma Flor Ada
  (Atheneum)
  Honor Books:
  From the Bellybutton of the Moon and Other Summer Poems/Del
  Ombligo de la Luna y Otro Poemas de Veran illustrated by Maya
  Christina Gonzalez; Text: Francisco X. Alarcón (Children's Book
  Press)
  Laughing out Loud, I Fly: Poems in English and Spanish
  illustrated by Karen Barbour; Text: Juan Felipe Herrera.
  (HarperCollins)
For Illustration:
  Medal Winner:
  Magic Window by Carmen Lomas Garza (Children's Book Press)
  Honor Books:
  Barrio: José's Neighborhood by George Ancona (Harcourt Brace)
  The Secret Stars illustrated by Felipe Dávalos; Text: Joseph Slate
  (Marshall Cavendish).
  Mama and Papa Have a Store by Amelia Lau Carling (Dial)
1998 Medal Winners:
For Narrative:
  Parrot in the Oven: mi vida by Victor Martinez (Joanna
  Cotler/HarperCollins)
For Illustration:
  Snapshots from the Wedding illustrated by Stephanie Garcia; Text:
  Gary Soto (Putnam)
1998 Honor Books:
For Narrative:
  Laughing Tomatoes and Other Spring Poems/Jitomates Risueños y
  otros poemas de primavera illustrated by Maya Christina
  Gonzalez; Text: Alarcón, Francisco (Children's Book Press)
  Spirits of the High Mesa by Floyd Martinez (Arte Público Press)
For Illustration:
  In My Family / En mi familia by Carmen Lomas Garza (Children's
  Book Press)
  The Golden Flower: A Taino Myth from Puerto Rico illustrated by
  Enrique O. Sánchez; Text: Nina Jaffe (Simon & Schuster)
  Gathering the Sun: An Alphabet in Spanish and English illustrated
  by Simón Silva; Text: Alma Flor Ada; English translation by Rosa
  Zubizarreta (Lothrop)

1996 Medal Winners:
For Narrative:
An Island Like You: Stories of the Barrio by Judith Ortiz Cofer
(Melanie Kroupa / Orchard Books)
For Illustration:
Chato's Kitchen illustrated by Susan Guevara; Text: Gary Soto
(Putnam)
1996 Honor Books:
For Narrative:
The Bossy Gallito/El Gallo de Bodas: A Traditional Cuban Folktale illustrated by Lulu Delacre; Text: Lucía González
(Scholastic)
Baseball in April, and Other Stories by Gary Soto (Harcourt)
For Illustration:
Pablo Remembers: The Fiesta of the Day of the Dead by George Ancona (Lothrop). Also published in a Spanish language edition:
Pablo Recuerda: La Fiesta de Día de los Muertos (Lothrop)
The Bossy Gallito / El Gallo de Bodas: A Traditional Cuban Folktale illustrated by Lulu Delacre; retold by Lucía González
(Scholastic)
Family Pictures / Cuadros de Familia by Carment Lomas Garza; Spanish language; Text: Rosalma Zubizaretta (Children's Book Press)

Laura Ingalls Wilder Award

The Laura Ingalls Wilder award is sponsored by the American Library Association and presented to the author or illustrator whose books are published in the United States and who has made a substantial and lasting contribution to children over the years. The award was established in 1954 and was given every five years from 1960 through 1980. Since then it has been given every three years.

1954 Laura Ingalls Wilder
1960 Clara Ingram Judson
1965 Ruth Sawyer
1970 E. B. White
1975 Beverly Cleary
1980 Dr. Seuss (Theodore Seuss Geisel)
1983 Maurice B. Sendak
1986 Jean Fritz
1989 Elizabeth George Speare

1992 Marcia Brown
1995 Virginia Hamilton
1998 Russell Freedman
2001 Milton Meltzer

The Mildred L. Batchelder Award

The Mildred L. Batchelder award was established in honor of a former executive director of the Association for Library Service to Children whose life's work was "to eliminate barriers to understanding between people of different cultures, races, nations, and languages." The award, established in her honor in 1966, is a citation awarded to an American publisher for a children's book considered to be the most outstanding of those books originally published in a foreign language in a foreign country, and subsequently translated into English and published in the United States.

2001 Medal Winner:
Arthur A. Levine/Scholastic for *Samir and Yonatan* by Daniella Carmi. Translated from the Hebrew by Yael Lotan.
Honor:
David R. Godine for *Ultimate Game* by Christian Lehmann. Translated from the French by William Rodarmor.
2000 Medal Winner:
Walker for *The Baboon King* by Anton Quintana. Translated from the Dutch by John Nieuwenhuizen.
Honors:
Farrar, Straus & Giroux for *Collector of Moments* by Quint Buchholz. Translated from the German by Peter F. Neumeyer.
Rands Books for *Vendela in Venice* illustrated by Inga-Karin Eriksson; Text: by Christina Björk. Translated from the Swedish by Patricia Crampton.
Front Street, for *Asphalt Angels* by Ineke Holtwijk. Translated from the Dutch by Wanda Boeke.
1999 Medal Winner:
Dial for *Thanks to My Mother* by Schoschana Rabinovici, 1998. Translated from the German by James Skofield.
Honor:
Viking for *Secret Letters from 0 to 10* by Susie Morgenstern. Translated from the French by Gill Rosner.
1998 Medal Winner:
Holt for *The Robber and Me* by Josef Holub, 1996.

Edited by Mark Aronson and translated from the German by
Elizabeth D. Crawford.

Honors:

Scholastic for *Hostage to War: a True Story* by Tatjana
Wassiljewa. Translated from German by Anna Trenter.

Viking Publishing for *Nero Corleone: a Cat's Story* by Elke
Heidenrich. Translated from German by Doris Orgel.

1997 Medal Winner:

Farrar, Straus & Giroux for *The Friends* by Kazumi Yumoto,
1996. Translated from Japanese by Cathy Hirano.

1996 Medal Winner:

Houghton Mifflin for *The Lady with the Hat* by Uri Orlev, 1995.
Translated from Hebrew by Hillel Halkin.

Honors:

Holt for *Damned Strong Love: The True Story of Willi G. And
Stephan K.* by Lutz Van Dijk, 1995. Translated from German by
Elizabeth D. Crawford.

Walker for *Star of Fear, Star of Hope* by Jo Hoestlandt, 1995.
Translated from French by Mark Polizzotti.

1995 Medal Winner:

Dutton for *The Boys from St. Petri* by Bjarne Reuter, 1994.
Translated from Danish by Anthea Bell.

Honor:

Lothrop, Lee and Shepard for *Sister Shako and Kolo the Goat:
Memories of My Childhood in Turkey* by Vedat Dalokay, 1994.
Translated from Turkish by Güner Ener.

1994 Medal Winner:

Farrar, Straus & Giroux for *The Apprentice* by Pilar Molina
Llorente, 1993. Translated from Spanish by Robin Longshaw.

Honors:

Farrar, Straus & Giroux for *The Princess in the Kitchen Garden* by
Annemie and: Margriet Heymans, 1993. Translated from Dutch by
Johanna H. Prins and Johanna W. Prins.

Viking for *Anne Frank Beyond the Diary: A Photographic
Remembrance* by Ruud van der Rol and Rian Verhoeven, in
association with the Anne Frank House, 1993. Translated from
Dutch by Tony Langham and Plym Peters.

1993 Medal Winner:

[No award]

1992 Medal Winner:

Houghton Mifflin Company for *The Man from the Other Side* by
Uri Orlev, 1991. Translated from Hebrew by Hillel Halkin.

1991 Medal Winner:
Dutton for *A Hand Full of Stars* by Rafik Schami, 1990. Translated from German by Rika Lesser.

1990 Medal :
Dutton for *Buster's World* by Bjarne Reuter, 1989. Translated from Danish by Anthea Bell.

1989 Medal Winner:
Lothrop, Lee and Shepard for *Crutches* by Peter Härtling, 1988. Translated from German by Elizabeth D. Crawford.

1988 Medal Winner:
McElderry for *If You Didn't Have Me* by Ulf Nilsson, 1987. Translated from Swedish by Lone Thygesen Clecher and George Blecher.

1987 Medal Winner:
Lothrop, Lee and Shepard for *No Hero for the Kaiser* by Rudolph Frank, 1986. Translated from German by Patricia Crampton.

1986 Medal Winner:
Creative Education for *Rose Blanche* by Christophe Gallaz and Robert Innocenti, 1985. Translated from Italian by Martha Coventry and Richard Craglia.

1985 Medal Winner:
Houghton Mifflin for *The Island on Bird Street* by Uri Orlev. 1984. Translated from Hebrew by Hillel Halkin.

1984 Medal Winner:
Viking Press for *Ronia, the Robber's Daughter* by Astrid Lindgren, 1983. Translated from Swedish by Patricia Crampton.

1983 Medal Winner:
Lothrop, Lee and Shepard for *Hiroshima No Pika* by Toshi Maruki, 1982. Translated from Japanese through Kurita-Bando Literary Agency.

1982 Medal Winner:
Bradbury for *The Battle Horse* by Harry Kullman, 1981. Translated from Swedish by George Blecher and Lone Thygesen Blecher.

1981 Medal Winner:
Morrow for *The Winter When Time Was Frozen* by Els Pelgrom, 1980. Translated from Dutch by Maryka and Raphael Rudnik.

1980 Medal Winner:
Dutton for *The Sound of the Dragon's Feet* by Aliki Zei, 1979. Translated from Greek by Edward Fenton.

1979 Medal Winner:
Two awards given:

Harcourt Brace Jovanovich for *Rabbit Island* by Jörg Steiner, 1978. Translated from German by Ann Conrad Lammers.
Franklin Watts for *Konrad* by Christine Nöstlinger, 1977. Translated from German by Anthea Bell.

1978 Medal Winner:
[No award]

1977 Medal Winner:
Atheneum for *The Leopard* by Cecil Bødker, 1975. Translated from Danish by Gunnar Poulsen.

1976 Medal Winner:
Henry Z. Walck for *The Cat and Mouse Who Shared a House* by Ruth Hürlimann, 1973. Translated from German by Anthea Bell.

1975 Medal Winner:
Crown for *An Old Tale Carved Out of Stone* by A. Linevskii,1973. Translated from Russian by Maria Polushkin.

1974 Medal Winner:
Dutton for *Petros' War* by Aliki Zei, 1972.
Translated from Greek by Edward Fenton.

1973 Medal Winner:
Morrow for *Pulga* by S. R. Van Iterson, 1971.
Translated from Dutch by Alexander and Alison Gode.

1972 Medal Winner:
Holt, Rinehart and Winston for *Friedrich* by Hans Peter Richter, 1970. Translated from German by Edite Kroll.

1971 Medal Winner:
Pantheon for *In the Land of Ur, the Discovery of Ancient Mesopotamia* by Hans Baumann, 1969. Translated from German by Stella Humphries.

1970 Medal Winner:
Holt, Rinehart and Winston for *Wildcat Under Glass* by Aliki Zei. Translated from Greek by Edward Fenton.

1969 Medal Winner:
Scribner's for *Don't Take Teddy* by Babbis Friis-Baastad, 1967. Translated from Norwegian by Lise Sømme McKinnon.

1968 Medal Winner:
Knopf for *The Little Man* by Erich Kästner, 1966. Translated from German by James Kirkup.

Bibliography

PreK Level

Brown, Margaret Wise. *Goodnight Moon*. New York: HarperFestival, 1991.

Burningham, John. *Come Away from the Water, Shirley*. New York: Random House, 1992.

Carle, Eric. *Let's Paint a Rainbow: A Play-And-Read Book*. New York: Cartwheel Books, 1998.

Christelow, E. and J. Giblin, eds. *Five Little Monkeys Sitting in a Tree*. New York: Clarion Books, 1991.

Cousins, Lucy. *Country Animals*. Cambridge, Mass.: Candlewick Press, 1999.

———. *Kite in the Park*. Cambridge, Mass.: Candlewick Press, 1992.

———. *Farm Animals*. Cambridge, Mass.: Candlewick Press, 1999.

———. *Flower in the Garden*. Cambridge, Mass.: Candlewick Press, 1992.

———. *Garden Animals*. Cambridge, Mass.: Candlewick Press, 1999.

———. *The Lucy Cousins Book of Nursery Rhymes*. New York: Puffin/Penguin, 1999.

———. *Pet Animals*. Cambridge, Mass.: Candlewick Press, 1999.

Cowley, Rich. *Bang, Bang, Toot, Toot*. Buffalo, N.Y.: Firefly Books, 1996.

Dyer, Jane, ed. *Animal Crackers: A Delectable Collection of Pictures, Poems, and Lullabies for the Very Young*. Boston, Mass.: Little, Brown, 1996.

Ehlert, Lois. *Red Leaf, Yellow Leaf.* San Diego: Harcourt, 1991.

———. *Color Farm*. New York: HarperCollins, 1997.

Eisen, Armand, ed. *The Classic Mother Goose*. New York: Courage Books, 1997.

Elgar, Rebecca. *Jack: It's Bedtime*. New York: Larousse Kingfisher Chambers, 1998.

Emberley, Ed. *Drummer Hoff*. New York: Simon & Schuster, 1988.

Fleming, Denise. *In a Small, Small Pond*. New York: Holt, 1993.

———. *Count*. New York: Holt, 1997.

Fox, Mem. *Sleepy Bears*. San Diego: Harcourt Brace, 1999.

Gage, Stephen. *The Miracle of Island Girl*. Irving, Tex.: Authorlink Press, 2000.

Hannant, Judith Stuller. *The Doorknob Collection of Nursery Rhymes*. Boston, Mass.: Little, Brown, 1991.

Henkes, Kevin. *The Biggest Boy*. New York: Greenwillow, 1995.

Henley, Claire. *ABC One Two Three: A First Lift-the-Flap Book*. New York: Silver Dolphin, 1994.

Hill, Eric. *Where's Spot?* New York: Putnam, 1990.

Ho, Minfong. *Hush! A Thai Lullaby*. New York: Orchard, 1996.

Hoban, Tana. *Count and See*. New York: Simon & Schuster, 1972.

———.*1,2,3*. New York: Morrow, 1985.

———. *Is it Red? Is it Yellow? Is it Blue?* New York: Morrow, 1987.

———. *26 Letters and 99 Cents*. New York: Greenwillow, 1987.

———. *Colors Everywhere*. New York: Greenwillow, 1995.

———. *So Many Circles, So Many Squares*. New York: Greenwillow, 1998.

———. *Let's Count*. New York: Greenwillow, 1999.

Hutchins, Pat. *Rosie's Walk*. New York: Scholastic, 1987.

Kunhardt, Dorothy. *Pat the Bunny*. New York: Golden Books, 1990.

Lamut, Sonja. *Peek-A-Boo*. New York: Grossett & Dunlap, 1997

Mayer, Mercer. *I Smell Christmas*. New York: Inchworm Press, 1997.

Miranda, Anne. *To Market, To Market*. San Diego: Harcourt, 1997.

Ochiltree, Dianne. *Ten Monkey Jamboree*. New York: Margaret McElderry, 2001.

Patrick, Denise Lewis. *What Does Baby See?* New York: Grossett & Dunlap, 1990.

Peek, Merle. *Roll Over*. Boston, Mass.: Houghton Mifflin, 1981.

Pienkowski, Jan. *Fun*. New York: Little Simon, 1996.

———. *Play*. New York: Little Simon, 1996.

———. *Farm Animals*. New York: Piggy Toes Press, 1998.

Potter, Beatrix. *Appley Dappley Nursery Rhymes*. London: Frederick Warne, 1987.

———. *Cecily Parsley's Nursery Rhymes*. London: Frederick Warne, 1987.

Prater, John. *Number One, Tickle Your Tum*. Hauppauge, N.Y.: Barrons Juvenile, 1999.

Ross, Anna. *Knock, Knock, Who's There?* New York: Random House, 1994.

Tafuri, Nancy. *Have You Seen My Duckling?* New York: Greenwillow, 1984.

Tong, Willabel L. *Farm Faces*. New York: Piggy Toes Press, 2000.

———. *Zoo Faces*. New York: Piggy Toes Press, 2000.

Tucker, Sian. *1,2,3 Count With Me*. New York: Little Simon, 1996.

Wellington, Monica. *Baby in a Buggy*. New York: Dutton, 1995.

———. *Baby in a Car*. New York: Dutton, 1995.

Wells, Rosemary. *Max's Toys*. New York: Dial, 1998.

Westling, A. *Choo Choo*. New York: Grossett & Dunlap, 1999.

Wildsmith, Brian. *The Apple Bird*. London: Oxford, 1997.

Zimmerman, Andrea. *Trashy Town*. New York: HarperCollins, 1999.

Primary Level

Aardema, Verna. *Borreguita and the Coyote: A Tale from Ayutla, Mexico*. New York: Knopf, 1991.

———. *How the Ostrich Got its Long Neck*. New York: Scholastic, 1995.

Ackerman, Karen. *Song and Dance Man*. New York: Knopf, 1988.

Adler, David. *A Picture Book of Sitting Bull*. New York: Holiday House, 1993.

———. *Lou Gehrig: The Luckiest Man*. San Diego: Harcourt, 1997.

Adoff, Arnold. *All the Colors of the Race*. New York: Beech Tree Books, 1992.

———. *Daring Dog and Captain Cat*. New York: Simon & Schuster, 2001.

Alberts, Nancy Markham. *Elizabeth's Beauty*. Harrisburg, Pa.: Morehouse, 1996.

Andersen, Hans Christian. *The Ugly Duckling*. New York: Morrow, 1999.

Anzaldua, Gloria. *Friends from the Other Side/Amigos del Otro Lado*. San Francisco: Children's Book Press, 1993.

Archambault, John. *Chicka Chicka Boom Boom*. New York: Scholastic, 1989.

Attenborough, Liz. *Poetry by Heart: A Child's Book of Poems to Remember*. New York: The Chicken House, Scholastic, 2001.

Aylesworth, Jim. *The Burger and the Hot Dog*. New York: Atheneum, 2001.

Babbitt, Natalie. *Ouch!* New York: HarperCollins, 1998.

Bacmeister, Rhoda. "Galoshes." In *Poems Children Will Sit Still for: A Selection for the Primary Grades* by Beatrice Schenk De Regniers, Eva Moore, and Mary Michaels White. New York: Citation, 1969.

Baker, Olaf. *Where the Buffalos Begin*. London: Frederick Warne, 1984.

Bang, Molly. *The Grey Lady and the Strawberry Snatcher*. New York: Simon & Schuster, 1980.

———. *When Sophie Gets Angry—Really, Really Angry*. New York: Scholastic, 1999.

Bannerman, Helen. *Little Black Sambo*. New York: Harper, 1923.

Bercaw, Edna Coe. *Halmoni's Day*. New York: Dial, 2000.

Berenstein, Stan and Jan. *The Berenstein Bears Don't Pollute (Anymore)*. New York: Random House, 1991.

Borden, Louise. *Good-bye Charles Lindbergh*. New York: Aladdin Paperbacks, 1998.

Bradby, Marie. *More Than Anything Else*. New York: Orchard, 1995.

Brett, Jan. *The Mitten*. New York: Putnam, 1989.

Brown, Don. *Alice Ramsey's Grand Adventure*. Boston: Houghton Mifflin, 1993.

———. *Ruth Law Thrills a Nation*. New York: Ticknor & Fields, 1993.

———. *Rare Treasures: Mary Anning and Her Remarkable Discoveries*. Boston: Houghton Mifflin, 1999.

Brown, Margaret Wise. *The Runaway Bunny*. New York: Harper, 1942.

Bunting, Eve. *Smoky Night*. San Diego: Harcourt, 1994.

———. *Peepers*. San Diego: Harcourt, 2001.

Burleigh, Robert. *Flight*. New York: Putnam & Grosset, 1991.

———. *Lookin' for Bird in the Big City*. San Diego: Harcourt, 2001.

Bynum, Jane. *Altoona Up North*. San Diego: Harcourt, 2001.

Carney, Karen. *What Is Cancer Anyway? Explaining Cancer to Children of All Ages*. New York: Dragonfly, 1998.

Cherry, Lynne. *The Great Kapok Tree*. San Diego: Harcourt, 1990.

Chute, Marchette. "Dogs." In *Poems Children Will Sit Still For: A Selection for the Primary Grades* by Beatrice Schenk De Regniers, Eva Moore, and Mary Michaels White, New York: Citation, 1969.

Cohen, Barbara. *Molly's Pilgrim*. New York: Bantam, 1983.

Cole, Henry. *I Took a Walk*. New York: Greenwillow, 1998.

Coleman, Evelyn. *White Socks Only*. Morton Grove, Ill.: Whitman, 1996.

Cooney, Barbara. *Miss Rumphius*. New York: Puffin Books, 1982.

Cottle, Joan. *Miles Away from Home*. San Diego: Harcourt, 2001.

Creech, Sharon. *Fishing in the Air*. New York: Joanna Cotler/HarperCollins, 2000.

Cronin, Doreen. *Click, Clack, Moo: Cows That Type*. New York: Simon & Schuster, 2000.

Curtis, Jamie Lee. *Tell Me Again About the Night I was Born*. New York: HarperCollins, 1996.

Davol, Marguerite. *Black, White, Just Right!* Morton Grove, Ill.: Whitman, 1993.

Day, Alexandra. *Good Dog, Carl*. New York: Little Simon, 1996.

Day, Trevor. *Youch! Real Live Monsters Up Close*. New York: Simon & Schuster, 2000.

De Regniers, Beatrice Schenk, Eva Moore, and Mary Michaels White. *Poems Children Will Sit Still For: A Selection for the Primary Grades.* New York: Citation, 1969.

Degen, Bruce. *Jamberry.* New York: HarperFestival 1995.

dePaola, Tomie. *Charlie Needs a Cloak.* New York: Prentice-Hall, 1974.

———. *The Lady of Guadalupe.* New York: Holiday House, 1988.

Dooley, Norah. *Everybody Cooks Rice.* New York: Scholastic, 1992.

Duncan, Pamela. *Dinorella: A Prehistoric Fairytale.* New York: Hyperion, 1997.

Eastman, P. D. *Are You My Mother?* New York: Random House, 1988.

Everitt, Betsy. *Mean Soup.* San Diego: Harcourt, 1992.

———. *TV Dinner.* San Diego: Harcourt, 1994.

Falconer, Ian. *Olivia.* New York: Atheneum, 2000.

———. *Olivia Saves the Circus.* New York: Atheneum, 2001.

Falwell, Cathryn. *Turtle Splash! Countdown at the Pond.* New York: Greenwillow, 2001.

Flor Ada, Alma. *Gathering the Sun: An Alphabet in Spanish and English.* New York: Lothrop, Lee & Shepard, 1997.

———. *With Love, Little Red Hen.* New York: Atheneum, 2001.

Gág, Wanda. *Millions of Cats.* New York: Coward-McCann, 1989.

George, Jean Craighead. *The Everglades.* New York: HarperCollins, 1995.

Gibbons, Gail. *Soaring with the Wind: The Bald Eagle.* New York: Morrow, 1998.

Glaser, Linda. *The Borrowed Hanukkah Latkes.* Morton Grove, Ill.: Whitman, 1997.

Greenfield, Eloise. *Nathaniel Talking.* New York: Black Butterfly, 1993.

Hall, Donald. *Ox-Cart Man.* New York: Penguin Putnam, 1979.

———. *Lucy's Summer.* San Diego: Voyager Picture Books, 1998.

Hamilton, Virginia. *The Girl Who Spun Gold.* New York: Scholastic, 2000.

Harper, Dan. *Sit, Truman.* San Diego: Harcourt, 2001.

Harrison, David L. *Farmer's Garden: Rhymes for Two Voices.* Littleton, Colo.: Wordsong, 2000.

Heine, Helme. *Pig's Wedding.* New York: Atheneum, 1986.

Henkes, Kevin. *Sheila Rae, the Brave.* New York: Greenwillow, 1987

———. *Chrysanthemum.* New York: Greenwillow, 1991.

———. *Owen.* New York: Greenwillow, 1993.

———. *Lilly's Purple Plastic Purse.* New York: Greenwillow, 1996.

———. *Wemberly Worried.* New York: Greenwillow, 2000.

Herron, Carolivia. *Nappy Hair*. New York: Knopf, 1997.

Hines, Anna Grossnickle. *Whose Shoes?* San Diego: Harcourt, 2001.

Hopkinson, Deborah. *Sweet Clara and the Freedom Quilt*. New York: Random House, 1995.

———. *Fannie in the Kitchen*. New York: Atheneum, 2001.

Horenstein, Henry. *A is for. . . ? A Photographer's Alphabet of Animals*. San Diego: Harcourt Brace, 1999.

Hurst, Margaret N. *Grannie and the Jumbie*. New York: Laura Geringer, 2001.

Hutchins, Pat. *Happy Birthday*. New York: Greenwillow, 1978.

Isaacs, Anne. *Swamp Angel*. New York: Penguin, 1994.

Jackson, Ellen. *Cinder Edna*. New York: Lothrop, Lee & Shepard, 1994.

James, Simon. *Leon and Bob*. Cambridge, Mass.: Candlewick, 2001.

Johnson, Stephen T. *Alphabet City*. New York: Puffin, 1999.

Johnston, Tony. *The Wagon*. New York: Morrow, 1996.

Keats, Ezra Jack. *Peter's Chair*. New York: Viking, 1962.

———. *Jennie's Hat*. New York: HarperCollins, 1979.

———. *The Snowy Day*. New York: Viking, 1998.

Kimmel, Eric. *The Adventures of Hershel of Ostopol*. New York: Holiday House, 1998.

Kroll, Virginia. *Sweet Magnolia*. Watertown, Mass.: Charlesbridge, 1995.

Lasky, Kathryn. *Vision of Beauty: The Story of Sarah Breedlove Walker*. Cambridge, Mass.: Candlewick Press, 2000.

Lauture, Denise. *Running the Road to ABC*. New York: Simon & Schuster, 1996.

Lawson, Robert. *The Story of Ferdinand*. New York: Viking, 1997.

Lehn, Barbara. *What Is A Scientist?* Brookfield, Conn.: Millbrook, 1998.

LeMarche, Jim. *The Raft*. New York: HarperCollins, 2000.

Leodhas, Sorche Nic. *Always Room for One More*. New York: Holt, 1982.

Lester, Julius. *John Henry*. New York: Dial, 1994.

———. *Sam and the Tigers*. New York: Dial, 1996.

Lionni, Leo. *Swimmy*. New York: Knopf, 1991.

Lobel, Arnold. *Fables*. New York: HarperTrophy, 1983.

Lorbiecki, Marybeth. *Sister Anne's Hands*. New York: Dial, 1998.

Lowell, Susan. *The Tortoise and the Jackrabbit*. Flagstaff, Ariz.: Rising Moon, 1994.

MacDonald, Suse. *Alphabetics*. New York: Aladdin Paperbacks, 1992.

Mak, Kam. *My Chinatown: One Year in Poems*. New York: Harper-Collins, 2002.

Manushkin, Fran. *Miriam's Cup: A Passover Story*. New York: Scholastic, 1998.

Martin, Bill, Jr. *Polar Bear, Polar Bear, What Do You Hear?* New York: Holt, 1991.

Martin, Jacqueline. *Snowflake Bentley*. Boston: Houghton Mifflin, 1998.

McCloskey, Robert. *Blueberries for Sal*. New York: Viking, 1987.

———. *Make Way for Ducklings*. New York: Viking, 1941.

McCord, David. "Ladybug." In *Poems Children Will Sit Still for: A Selection for the Primary Grades* by Beatrice Schenk De Regniers, Eva Moore, and Mary Michaels White. New York: Citation, 1969.

McCully, Emily Arnold. *Mirette on the High Wire*. New York: Putnam & Grosset, 1992.

McDermott, Gerald. *Arrow to the Sun*. New York: Viking, 1997.

———. *Jabuti the Tortoise*. New York: Harcourt, 2001.

McNulty, Faith. *Endangered Animal*. New York: Scholastic, 1996.

Meddaugh, Susan. *Cinderella's Rat*. Boston: Houghton Mifflin, 1997.

Minters, Frances. *Cinder Elly*. New York: Puffin, 1997.

Mollel, Tolowa M. *Subira, Subira*. New York: Houghton Mifflin, 2000.

Montresor, Beni. *Hansel and Gretel*. New York: Atheneum, 2001.

Mosel, Arlene. *The Funny Little Woman*. New York: Dutton, 1977.

Munsterberg, Peggy. *Beastly Banquet: Tasty Treats for Animal Appetites*. New York: Dial, 1997.

Musgrove, Margaret. *From Ashanti to Zulu*. New York: Dial, 1992.

Napoli, Donna Jo and Richard Chen. *How Hungry Are You?* New York: Atheneum, 2001.

Nourse, Deborah. *Cinderhazel, the Cinderella of Halloween*. New York: Scholastic, 1997.

Palatini, Margie. *Tub-Boo-Boo*. New York: Simon & Schuster, 2001.

Perez, Amada Irma. *My Very Own Room/Mi Propio Cuartito*. San Francisco: Children's Book Press, 2000.

Pinkney, Brian. *The Faithful Friend*. New York: Simon & Schuster, 1995.

———. *Min's Christmas Jam*. San Diego: Harcourt, 2001.

Polacco, Patricia. *The Keeping Quilt*. New York: Simon & Schuster, 1988.

———. *Thunder Cake*. New York: Putnam & Grosset, 1990.

———. *My Rotten Redheaded Older Brother*. New York: Simon & Schuster, 1994.

———. *Mr. Lincoln's Way.* New York: Philomel, 2001.

Opie, Iona and Peter Opie, eds. *The Oxford Dictionary of Nursery Rhymes.* Oxford, England: Oxford University Press, 1998.

Potter, Beatrix. *The Tale of Peter Rabbit.* London: Warne, 1987.

Prelutsky, Jack. *Random House Book of Poetry for Children.* New York: Random House, 1983.

———. *The Frog Wore Red Suspenders.* New York: Greenwillow, 2002.

Priceman, Margorie. *Zin! Zin! Zin! A Violin.* New York: Simon & Schuster, 1995.

Raschka, Chris. *Yo! Yes?* New York: Scholastic, 1993.

Rathmann, Peggy. *Officer Buckle and Gloria.* New York: Putnam 1995.

Ringgold, Faith. *Tar Beach.* New York: Scholastic, 1991.

Rockwell, Anne. *Morgan Plays Soccer.* New York: HarperCollins, 2001.

Rosen, Michael. *We're Going on a Bear Hunt.* New York: Margaret McElderry, 1989.

Ryder, Joanne. *Each Living Thing.* San Diego: Harcourt, 2000.

Rylant, Cynthia. *In November.* San Diego: Harcourt, 2000.

Sandburg, Carl. *From Daybreak to Good Night: Poems for Children.* Toronto: Annick Press, 2001.

Schroeder, Alan. *Minty: A Story of Young Harriet Tubman.* New York: Dial, 1996.

———. *Smoky Mountain Rose.* New York: Dial, 1997.

Scieszka, Jon. *Stinky Cheese Man and Other Fairly Stupid Tales.* New York: Viking, 1993.

———. *The True Story of the Three Little Pigs.* New York: Viking, 1989.

Seuss, Dr. (Theodore Seuss Geisel). *And to Think that I Saw it on Mulberry Street.* New York: Random House, 1989.

Sierra, Judy. *The Gift of the Crocodile.* San Diego: Simon & Schuster, 2000.

———. *Monster Goose.* San Diego: Harcourt, 2001.

Simmons, Jane. *Daisy Says If You're Happy and You Know It.* Boston: Little, Brown, 2002.

Spier, Peter. *Rain.* Garden City, N.Y.: Doubleday, 1982.

Steig, William. *Sylvester and the Magic Pebble.* New York: Simon & Schuster, 1969.

———. *The Amazing Bone.* New York: Farrar Straus and Giroux, 1984.

Steptoe, John. *Mufaro's Beautiful Daughters: An African Tale.* New York: Lothrop, Lee & Shepard 1987.

Stevens, Janet and Susan Stevens Crummel. *And the Dish Ran Away with the Spoon.* San Diego: Harcourt, 2001.

Stewart, Sarah. *The Library.* New York: Farrar, Straus & Giroux, 1995.

———. *The Gardener.* New York: Farrar, Straus & Giroux1997.

———. *The Journey.* New York: Farrar, Straus & Giroux, 2001.

Taback, Simms, ret. *There Was an Old Woman Who Swallowed a Fly.* New York: Viking, 1997.

———. *Joseph Had a Little Overcoat.* New York: Viking, 1999.

Tapahonso, Luci and Eleanor Schick. *Navajo ABC: A Dinè Alphabet Book.* New York: Macmillan, 1995.

Tresselt, Alvin. *The Gift of the Tree.* New York: Lothrop, Lee & Shepard, 1992.

Trivizas, Eugene. *The Three Little Wolves and the Big Bad Pig.* New York: Margaret McElderry, 1993.

Udry, Janice. *A Tree is Nice.* New York: Harper, 1956.

Van Laan, Nancy. *Teeny Tiny Tingly Tales.* New York: Atheneum, 2001.

Viorst, Judith. *Alexander and the Terrible, Horrible, No Good, Very Bad Day.* New York: Atheneum, 1972.

Wallace, Karen. *Gentle Giant Octopus.* Cambridge, Mass.: Candlewick Press, 1998.

Ward, Leila. *I Am Eye—Ni Macho.* New York: Scholastic, 1978.

Ward, Lynd. *The Biggest Bear.* Boston: Houghton Mifflin, 1952.

Weatherford, Carol Boston. *The Sound That Jazz Makes.* New York: Walker, 2000.

Weiss, Nicki. *Where Does the Brown Bear Go?* New York: Greenwillow, 1989.

Willey, Margaret. *Clever Beatrice.* New York: Atheneum, 2001.

Williams, Margery. *The Velveteen Rabbit.* New York: Doubleday, 1988.

Williams, Vera B. *A Chair for My Mother.* New York: Greenwillow, 1983.

Winter, Jeanette. *My Name is Georgia: A Portrait.* New York: Silver Whistle, 1998.

Wood, Audrey. *The Red Racer.* New York: Simon & Schuster, 1996.

Wright, Kit. "Me." In *Poetry By Heart: A Child's Book of Poems to Remember* ed. by Liz Attenborough. New York: Chicken House/ Scholastic, 2001

Wyeth, Sharon Dennis. *Something Beautiful.* New York: Doubleday, 1998.

Yolen, Jane. *Owl Moon.* New York: Scholastic, 1987.
——. *Street Rhymes from Around the World.* Boyds Mills, Pa.: Boyds Mills, 2000.
——. *Welcome to the Ice House.* New York: Putnam, 1998.
Young, Ed, ret. *Lon Po Po.* New York: Philomel, 1989.
Zagwyn, Deborah Turney. *Turtle Spring.* Berkeley, Calif.: Tricycle Press, 1998.
Zelinsky, Paul O. *Rumpelstiltskin.* New York: Dutton, 1987.
——. *Rapunzel.* New York: Dutton, 1997.
Zolotow, Charlotte. *Mr. Rabbit and His Lovely Present.* New York: Harper, 1962.
——. *When the Wind Stops.* New York: HarperCollins, 1995.

Middle Elementary Level

Aamundsen, Nina. *Two Shorts and One Long.* Boston: Houghton Mifflin, 1990.
Adedjouma, Davida. *The Palm of My Heart: Poetry By African American Children.* New York: Lee & Low, 1996.
Allfrey, Brian and Melinda Allfrey. *Delirious: A Collection of Poems for Kids 8–88.* Fishers, Ind.: Delirous Publications, 1999.
Altman, Linda Jacobs. *Amelia's Road.* New York: Lee & Low, 1993.
Ancona, George. *Barrio: Jose's Neighborhood.* San Diego: Harcourt Brace, 1998.
Andersen, Hans Christian. *Fairy Tales of Hans Christian Andersen.* New York: Viking, 1995.
Anno, Masaichiro and Mitsumasa Anno. *Anno's Mysterious Multiplying Jar.* New York: PaperStar, 1999.
Anno, Mitsumasa. *Anno's USA.* New York: Philomel, 1983.
——.*Anno's Counting Book.* New York: Harper, 1986.
——. *Anno's Journey.* New York: Philomel, 1992.
Anonymous. "Junk Food." In *This Way to Books* ed. By Caroline Feller Bauer. New York: H. W. Wilson, 1983.
Arnold, Caroline. *Australian Animals.* New York: HarperCollins, 2000.
Ash, Russell. *Incredible Comparisons.* Toronto: Viking, 1996.
Atwater, Richard and Florence. *Mr. Popper's Penguins.* Boston: Little, Brown, 1988.
Babbitt, Natalie. *Tuck Everlasting.* New York: Farrar, Straus & Giroux, 1975.
Bahr, Mary. *The Memory Box: Gathering the Keepsakes of the Heart.* Morton Grove, Ill.: Whitman, 1992.

Baylor, Byrd. *When Clay Sings.* New York: Holiday House, 1972.

———. *The Desert is Theirs.* New York: Scribner's, 1976.

———. *Hawk, I'm Your Brother.* New York: Scribner's, 1976.

———. *Everybody Needs a Rock.* New York: Atheneum, 1978.

———. *The Other Way to Listen.* New York: Scribner's, 1978.

———. *The Way to Start a Day.* New York: Macmillan, 1978.

———. *I'm In Charge of Celebrations.* New York: Scribner's, 1986.

Berry, James. *Rough Sketch Beginning.* San Diego: Harcourt, 1996.

Blume, Judy. *Tales of A Fourth Grade Nothing.* New York: Dutton, 1972.

Booth, David. *The Dust Bowl.* Toronto: Kids Can Press, 1996.

Bouchard, David. *The Dragon New Year: A Chinese Legend.* Atlanta: Peachtree, 1999.

Bradby, Marie. *Momma, Where Are You From?* New York: Orchard, 2000,.

Bridges, Ruby and Margo Lundell,. *Through My Eyes: The Autobiography of Ruby Bridges.* New York: Scholastic, 1999.

Brown, Don. *One Giant Leap: The Story of Neil Armstrong.* Boston: Houghton Mifflin, 1998.

———. *Uncommon Traveler: Mary Kingsley in Africa.* Boston: Houghton Mifflin, 2000.

———. *Across a Dark and Wild Sea.* Brookfield, Conn.: Roaring Brook/Millbrook, 2002.

Bruchac, Joseph and Jonathan London. *Thirteen Moons on Turtle's Back: A Native America.* New York: Philomel, 1992.

———. *A Boy Called Slow: The True story of Sitting Bull.* New York: Philomel, 1994.

Bunting, Eve. *Dreaming of America: An Ellis Island Story.* Mahwah, N.J.: Bridge Water, 2000.

———. *The Wednesday Surprise.* New York: Clarion, 1989.

Burnett, Frances Hodgson. *The Secret Garden.* New York: Dell, 1911.

Burton, Virginia Lee. *The Little House.* Boston: Houghton Mifflin, 1942.

Carroll, Lewis. *Alice's Adventures in Wonderland.* New York: HarperCollins, 2001

Chase, Richard. *Jack Tales.* Boston: Houghton Mifflin, 1943.

———. *Grandfather's Tales.* Boston: Houghton Mifflin, 1973.

Cherry, Lynne. *The River Ran Wild.* San Diego: Harcourt, 1992.

———. *The Shaman's Apprentice.* San Diego: Harcourt, 1998.

Chorlton, Windsor. *Woolly Mammoth: Life, Death, and Rediscovery.* New York: Scholastic, 2001.

Christensen, Candace with Thomas Locker. *Sky Tree: Seeing Science through Art*. New York: HarperCollins, 1995.

Cleary, Beverly. *Ramona Quimby, Age 8*. New York: Yearling, 1993.

Clements, Andrew. *Frindle*. New York: Simon & Schuster, 1996.

———. *The School Story*. New York: Simon & Schuster, 2001.

Climo, Shirley. *The Egyptian Cinderella*. New York: Crowell, 1989.

Cowley, Joy. *Gracias, The Thanksgiving Turkey*. New York: Scholastic, 1996.

Creech, Sharon. *Love That Dog*. New York: HarperCollins, 2001.

Curlee, Lynn. *Brooklyn Bridge*. New York: Atheneum, 2001.

D'Aulaire, Ingri and Edgar Parin D'Aulaire. *Book of Greek Myths*. New York: Doubleday, 1962.

Dahl, Roald. *Charlie and the Chocolate Factory*. New York: Knopf, 1964.

Danziger, Paula. *Amber Brown Wants Extra Credit*. New York: Putnam, 1996.

De Paola, Tomie. *Helga's Dowry*. New York: Harcourt Brace Jovanovich, 1977.

———. *26 Fairmount Avenue*. New York: Putnam, 1999.

DiCamillo, Kate. *Because of Winn-Dixie*. Cambridge, Mass.: Candlewick, 2000.

Duggleby, John. *Story Painter: The Life of Jacob Lawrence*. San Francisco: Chronicle Books, 1998.

Esbensen, Barbara. *Echoes for the Eye: Poems to Celebrate Patterns in Nature*. New York: HarperCollins, 1996.

Filapovic, Zlata. *Zlata's Diary: A Childhood in Sarajevo*. New York: Scholastic, 1994.

Fleischman, Paul. *Joyful Noise: Poems for Two Voices*. New York: Harper & Row, 1988.

Flor Ada, Alma. *Under the Royal Palms: A Childhood in Cuba*. New York: Atheneum, 1998.

Florian, Douglas. *Bing, Bang, Boing*. San Diego: Harcourt, 1994.

———. *Insectlopedia*. San Diego: Harcourt, 1998.

Frasier, Debra. *Miss Alaneus: A Vocabulary Disaster*. San Diego: Harcourt, 2000.

Fritz, Jean. *And Then What Happened, Paul Revere?* New York: Coward-McCann, 1973.

———. *Why Don't You Get a Horse, Sam Adams?* New York: Coward-McCann, 1974.

———. *Where Was Patrick Henry on the 29th of May?* New York: Scholastic, 1975.

————. *What's the Big Idea, Ben Franklin?* New York: Coward-McCann, 1976.

————. *Can't You Make Them Behave, King George?* New York: Coward-McCann, 1977.

————. *You Want to Vote, Lizzie Stanton?* New York: Putnam, 1995.

Frost, Robert. *You Come, Too: Favorite Poems for All Ages.* New York: Holt, 1967.

Gantos, Jack. *Joey Pigza Swallowed the Key.* New York: Farrar, Straus & Giroux, 1998.

Garland, Sherry. *The Summer Sands.* San Diego: Harcourt, 1995.

George, Jean Craighead. *My Side of the Mountain.* New York: Dutton, 1959.

————. *The Talking Earth.* New York: Harper, 1987.

Gilbert, Thomas W. *Roberto Clemente.* New York: Chelsea House, 1995.

Goble, Paul. *Iktomi and the Boulder: A Plains Indian Story.* New York: Orchard, 1988.

Grahame, Kenneth. *Wind in the Willows.* New York: Scribner's's, 1940.

Greenfield, Eloise. *Nathaniel Talking.* New York: Black Butterfly Children's Books, 1988.

Guback, Georgia. *Luka's Quilt.* New York: Greenwillow, 1994.

Gündisch, Karin. *How I Became An American.* New York: Cricket, 2001.

Hamilton, Virginia. *Second Cousins.* New York: Blue Sky/Scholastic, 1998.

————. *Bluish: A Novel.* New York: Blue Sky/Scholastic, 1999.

Heck, C. J. *Barking Spiders and Other Such Stuff: Poetry for Children.* Pittsburg, Pa.: Sterling House, 2000.

Heide, Florence Parry and Judith Heide Gilliland. *A Day of Ahmad's Secret.* Bedford, N. S., Canada: Mulberry Books, 1995.

Henkes, Kevin. *Words of Stone.* New York Puffin. 1993.

Huynh, Quang Nhuong. *The Land I Lost.* New York: Harper, 1982.

————. *Water Buffalo Days: Growing Up in Vietnam.* New York: Harper, 1997.

Howard, Elizabeth Fitzgerald. *Virgie Goes to School with Us Boys.* New York: Simon & Schuster, 2000.

Hoyt-Goldsmith, Diane. *Day of the Dead: A Mexican American Celebration.* New York: Holiday House, 1994.

————. *Buffalo Days.* New York: Holiday House, 1997.

————. *Celebrating the Chinese New Year.* New York: Holiday House, 1998.

Hughes, Meredith and Tom. *Buried Treasure: Roots and Tubers.* Minneapolis: Lerner, 1998.

Jaffe, Nina. *The Golden Flower: A Taino Myth from Puerto Rico.* New York: Simon & Schuster, 1996.

Janulewicz, Mike. *Yikes! Your Body, Up Close.* New York: Simon & Schuster, 1997.

Jenkins, Steven. *Biggest, Strongest, Fastest.* New York: Ticknor & Fields, 1995.

Johnson, Joy. *Remember Rafferty: A Book about the Death of a Pet for Children of All Ages.* Omaha, Nebr.: Centering Corp., 1991.

Jordan, Delores and Roslyn. *Salt in His Shoes: Michael Jordan in Pursuit of a Dream.* New York: Simon & Schuster, 2000.

Kandel, Bethany. *Trevor's Story.* Minneapolis : Lerner, 1997.

Khan, Rukhsana. *Muslim Child: Understanding Islam through Stories and Poems.* Morton Grove, Ill.:Whitman, 2002.

Kimmel, Eric. *Hershel and the Hanukkah Goblins.* New York: Scholastic, 1990.

Knight, Khadijah. *Islamic Festivals.* Cyrstal Lake, Ill.: Heinemann, 1997.

Kohl, Mary Ann F. *Good Earth Art: Environmental Art for Kids.* Bellingham, Wash.: Bright Ring Publisher, 1991.

Kohlenberg, Sherry. *Sammy's Mommy Has Cancer.* New York: Magination Press, 1993.

Krull, Kathleen. *Wilma Unlimited.* San Diego: Harcourt, 1996.

Kuklin, Susan. *How My Family Lives in America.* New York: Aladdin, 1998.

Kurtz, Jane. *River Friendly, River Wild.* New York: Simon & Schuster, 2000.

LaMarche, Jim. *The Raft.* New York: HarperCollins, 2000.

Laminack, Lester. *The Sunsets of Miss Olivia Wiggins.* Atlanta: Peachtree, 1998.

Lansky, Bruce and Steve Carpenter. *A Bad Case of the Giggles: Kids Pick the Funniest Poems, Book Two.* Minnetonka, Minn.: Meadowbrook Press, 1994.

Lansky, Bruce, Steve Carpenter, and Stephen Carpenter, *Kids Pick the Funniest Poems.* New York: Simon & Schuster, 1991.

Lawson, Robert. *Rabbit Hill.* New York: Viking, 1944.

Leigh, Nila. *Learning to Swim in Swaziland: A Child's-Eye View of a Southern Aftican Country.* New York: Scholastic, 1993.

Levy, Janice. *Totally Uncool.* Minneapolis, Minn.: Carolrhoda, 1999.

Lewis, J. Patrick. *Arithme-Tickle: An Even Number of Odd Riddle Rhymes.* San Diego: Silver Whistle/Harcourt, 2002.

Lobel, Arnold. *Pigericks*. New York: HarperCollins, 1983.

Locker, Thomas. *Water Dance*. San Diego: Harcourt, 1997.

———. *Mountain Dance*. San Diego: Silver Whistle/Harcourt, 2001.

Lowry, Lois. *All About Sam*. Wilmington, Mass.: Houghton Mifflin, 1988.

MacLachlan, Patricia. *Sarah, Plain and Tall*. New York: Harper 1985.

———. *Caleb's Story*. New York: Joanna Cotler/HarperCollins, 2001.

Magill-Callahan, Sheila. *And Still the Turtle Watched*. New York: Dial, 1991.

Markle, Sandra. *Outside and Inside Alligators*. New York: Atheneum, 1998.

———. *Outside and Inside Dinosaurs*. New York: Atheneum, 2000.

McDermott, Gerald. *Zomo the Rabbit: A Trickster Tale from West Africa*. San Diego: Harcourt, 1992.

———. *Anansi the Spider: A Tale from The Ashanti*. New York: Scholastic, 1993.

———. *Coyote: A Trickster Tale from the American Southwest*. San Diego: Harcourt, 1994.

McKissack, Patricia. *Goin' Someplace Special*. New York: Atheneum, 2000.

Miller, William. *Richard Wright and the Library Card*. New York: Lee & Low, 1997.

Milne, A. A. *Winnie-the-Pooh*. New York: Dutton, 1926.

Montes, Marisa. *Juan Bobo Goes to Work*. New York: Morrow J, 2000.

Murphy, Stuart. *Safari Park*. New York: HarperCollins, 2002.

Naylor, Phyllis. *Shiloh*. New York: Dell, 1992.

Norton, Mary. *The Borrowers*. San Diego: Harcourt, 1998.

Numeroff, Laura Joffe. *The Hope Tree: Kids Talk about Breast Cancer*. New York: Simon & Schuster, 2001.

Nye, Naomi Shihab. *Come with Me: Poems for a Journey*. New York: Greenwillow, 2000.

Osceola, May and Alan Govenar. *Osceola: Memories of a Sharecropper's Daughter*. New York: Hyperion, 2000.

Park, Barbara. *Junie B. Jones and the Stupid Smelly Bus*. New York: Random House, 1993.

———. *The Graduation of Jake Moon*. New York: Atheneum, 2000.

Peet, Bill. *The Wump World*. Boston: Houghton Mifflin, 1970.

Pinkney, Andrea Davis. *Duke Ellington: The Piano Prince and His Orchestra*. New York: Hyperion, 1998.

———. *Let It Shine: Stories of Black Women Freedom Fighters*. San Diego: Harcourt, 2000.

Pinkwater, Daniel. *Mush, A Dog from Space.* New York: Atheneum, 1995.

———.*Fat Men from Space.* New York: Dell, 1997.

Polacco, Patrica. *The Bee Tree.* New York: Philomel, 1993.

———. *Pink and Say.* New York: Philomel, 1994.

Prelutsky, Jack. *It's Raining Pigs and Noodles.* New York: Greenwillow, 2000.

Rappaport, Doreen. *Martin's Big Words.* New York: Hyperion, 2001.

Ray, Mary Lyn. *Basket Moon.* Boston: Little, Brown, 1999.

Redfern, Martin. *The Kingfisher Young People's Book of Space.* New York: Kingfisher, 1998.

Reeder, Carolyn. *Shades of Gray.* New York: Avon Camelot, 1991.

———. *Across the Lines.* New York: Atheneum, 1997.

Ride, Sally. *To Space and Back.* New York: Beech Tree, 1991.

Rinaldi, Ann. *The Journal of Jasper Jonathan Pierce: A Pilgrim Boy.* New York: Scholastic, 2000.

Robbins, Ken. *Autumn Leaves.* New York: Scholastic, 1998.

Rockwell, Anne F. *Only Passing Through: The Story of Sojourner Truth.* New York: Knopf, 2000.

Rotner, Shelley. *Close, Closer, Closest.* New York: Atheneum, 1997.

Ruurs, Margriet. *Virtual Maniac: Silly and Serious Poems for Kids.* Gainesville, Fla.: Maupin House, 2001.

Rylant, Cynthia. *Missing May.* New York: Orchard, 1992.

Say, Allen. *Grandfather's Journey.* Boston: Houghton Mifflin, 1993.

———. *Tea with Milk.* Boston: Houghton Mifflin, 1999.

Schwartz, Betty Ann, ed. *My Kingdom for a Horse: An Anthology of Poems about Horses.* New York: Holt, 2001.

Service, Pamela. *Stinker in Space.* New York: Scribner's's, 1988.

Silverstein, Shel. *Where the Sidewalk Ends.* New York: Harper, 1974.

———. *Light in the Attic.* New York: Harper, 1981.

———. *Falling Up.* New York: HarperCollins, 1996.

Simon, Seymour. *Bones: Our Skeletal System.* New York: Morrow, 1998.

———. *The Brain: Our Nervous System.* New York: Scholastic, 1998.

———. *The Universe.* New York: Morrow, 1998.

Soto, Gary. *Chato's Kitchen.* New York: Putnam, 1997.

———. *Chato and the Party Animals.* New York: Putnam, 2000.

Spinelli, Jerry. *The Library Card.* New York: Scholastic, 1997.

Stanley, Diane. *Leonardo da Vinci.* New York: Morrow, 1996.

———.*Joan of Arc.* New York: Morrow Junior, 1998.

Stockdale, Susan. *Nature's Paintbrush: The Patterns and Colors around You.* New York: Simon & Schuster, 1999.

Takabayashi, Mari. *I Live in Tokyo*. Boston: Houghton Mifflin, 2001.

Temple, Frances. *Tonight By Sea*. New York: Orchard, 1995.

Thoreau, Henry David. *Henry David's House*. Watertown, Mass.: Charlesbridge, 2002.

Thornhill, Jan. *Before and After: A Book of Nature Timescapes*. Washington, D.C.: National Geographic Society, 1997.

Towle, Wendy. *The Real McCoy*. New York: Scholastic, 1993.

Uchida, Yoshiko. *Journey to Topaz*. Berkeley, Calif.: Creative Arts Book Company, 1985.

Van Allsburg, Chris. *The Garden of Abdul Gasazi*. Boston: Houghton Mifflin 1979.

———. *Jumanji*. Boston: Houghton Mifflin, 1981.

———. *Wreck of the Zephyr*. Boston: Houghton Mifflin, 1983.

———. *Mysteries of Harris Burdick*. Boston: Houghton Mifflin, 1984.

———. *Polar Express*. Boston: Houghton Mifflin, 1985.

———. *Just a Dream*. Boston: Houghton Mifflin, 1990.

Viorst, Judith. "Mother Doesn't Want A Dog." In *This Way to Books* by Caroline Feller Bauer. New York: H. W. Wilson, 1983.

Walker, Alice. *Langston Hughes, American Poet*. New York: Harper-Collins, 1998.

Warren, Andrea. *Surviving Hitler: A Boy in the Nazi Death Camps*. New York: HarperCollins, 2001.

Wick, Walter. *A Drop of Water: A Book of Science and Wonder*. New York: Scholastic, 1997.

Wild, Margaret. *Let the Celebrations Begin!* New York: Orchard, 1991.

Wilder, Laura Ingalls. *The First Four Years*. New York: Harper, 1971.

———. *Little House on the Prairie*. New York: Harper, 1973.

Wisniewski, David. *Golem*. New York: Clarion, 1996.

Yolen, Jane. *Letting Swift River Go*. Boston: Little, Brown, 1991.

Upper Elementary Level

Alcott, Louisa. *Little Women*. New York: Price, Stern, Sloan, 1983.

Alexander, Lloyd. *The Book of Three*. New York: Dell, 1964.

Anno, Mitsumasa. *Topsy Turvies: More Pictures to Stretch the Imagination*. New York: Philomel, 1968.

Arnold, Caroline. *Hawk Highway in the Sky: Watching Raptor Migration*. San Diego: Harcourt, 1997.

Arnosky, Jim. *Secrets of a Wildlife Watcher*. New York: Morrow, 1991.

———. *Wild and Swampy*. New York: HarperCollins, 2000.

Avi. *Poppy.* New York: Orchard, 1995.

Babbitt, Natalie. *The Devil's Arithmetic.* New York: Trumpet, 1991.

Banks, Lynn Reid. *The Indian in the Cupboard.* New York: Doubleday, 1981.

Bartoletti, Susan Campbell. *A Coal Miner's Bride: The Diary of Anetka Kaminska, Littimer, Pennsylvania, 1896.* New York: Scholastic, 2000.

Bauer, Marion Dane. *On My Honor.* New York: Clarion, 1986.

Baum, Frank L. *The Wonderful Wizard of Oz.* New York: Harper-Collins, 2000.

Black, Claudia. *It Will Never Happen to Me!* Denver, Colo.: M. A. C. Printing and Publications, 1982.

Blume, Judy. *Are You There, God? It's Me, Margaret.* New York: Bradbury, 1970.

———. *Then Again, Maybe I Won't.* New York: Bradbury, 1971.

———. *Deenie.* New York: Bradbury, 1973.

———. *Blubber.* New York: Bradbury, 1974.

———. *Superfudge.* New York: Dell, 1980.

———. *Fudge-a-Mania.* New York: Dutton, 1990.

Borden, Louise. *Good Luck, Mrs. K.!* New York: McElderry Books, 1999.

Brooks, Bruce. *Making Sense: Animal Perception and Communication.* New York: Farrar, Straus & Giroux, 1993.

Bruchac, Joseph. *Eagle Song.* New York: Puffin, 1997.

Bryan, Jenny. *Genetic Engineering.* New York: Thomson Learning, 1995.

Byars, Betsy. *Pinballs.* New York: HarperCollins, 1970.

———. *Summer of the Swans.* New York: Viking, 1970.

Carlson, Richard W. *The Feelings and Imaginations of a Barefoot Boy Still Inside My Head! Poems and Short Stories for Boys and Girls, Ages 9 to 12.* Campbell, Calif.: Authors Choice Press, 2001.

Carmi, Daniella. *Samir and Yonatan.* New York: Arthur A. Levine, 2000.

Carroll, Lewis. *Alice in Wonderland; and Through the Looking Glass.* New York: Knopf, 1992.

Christopher, John. *The White Mountains.* New York: Simon & Schuster, 1967.

Cobb, Vicki. *How to Really Fool Yourself: Illusions for All Your Senses.* New York: Wiley, 1999.

Coffer, Judith Ortiz. *An Island Like You: Stories of the Barrio.* New York: Puffin, 1996.

Cooper, Susan. *The Dark is Rising.* New York: Doubleday, 1996.

Coville, Bruce. *The Skull of Truth*. San Diego: Harcourt, 1997.

Creech, Sharon. *Walk Two Moons*. New York: HarperCollins, 1994.

———. *The Wanderer*. New York: Joanna Cotler/HarperCollins, 2000.

Degens, T. *Freya on the Wall*. San Diego: Browndeer, 1997.

———. *Tears of A Tiger*. New York: Atheneum, 1994.

Draper, Sharon. *Forged by Fire*. New York: Simon & Schuster, 1997.

Erdrich, Louise. *Birchbark House*. Thorndike, Maine: Thorndike Press, 2000.

Flor Ada, Alma. *Where The Flame Trees Bloom*. New York: Atheneum, 1994.

Forbes, Esther. *Johnny Tremain*. Boston: Houghton Mifflin, 1943.

Ford, Michael. *The Voices of AIDS*. New York: Morrow, 1995.

Frank, Anne. *The Diary of Anne Frank*. New York: Pocket Books, 1952.

Freedman, Russell. *Lincoln: A Photobiography*. New York: Clarion, 1987.

———. *Eleanor Roosevelt, A Life of Discovery*. New York: Clarion, 1993.

———. *The Life and Death of Crazy Horse*. New York: Holiday House, 1996.

———. *Babe Didrikson Zaharias: The Making of A Champion*. New York: Clarion, 1999.

Fritz, Jean. *Homesick, My Own Story*. New York: Dell, 1984.

Grahame, Kenneth. *Wind in the Willows*. New York: Aladdin Classics, 1999.

Gutman, Dan. *Shoeless Joe & Me*. New York: HarperCollins, 2002.

Hahn, Mary Downing. *Wait Till Helen Comes*. Boston: Houghton Mifflin, 1986.

Hamilton, Virginia. *In the Beginning: Creation Stories from Around the World*. San Diego: Harcourt, 1988.

———. *The People Could Fly*. New York: Knopf 1994.

Hansen, Joyce. *I Thought My Soul Would Rise and Fly: The Diary of Patsy, a Freed Girl*. New York: Scholastic, 1997.

Hearne, Betsy. *Listening for Leroy*. New York: McElderry, 1998.

Hertensten, Jane. *Home Is Where We Live: Life at a Shelter Through a Young Girl's Eyes*. Chicago: Cornerstone, 1995.

Hesse, Karen. *Letters from Rifka*. New York: Holt, 1992.

Highwater, Jamake. *Anpao: An American Indian Odyssey*. New York: HarperTrophy, 1992.

Jacques, Brian. *The Redwall*. New York: Philomel, 1986.

Jimenez, Francisco. *The Circuit: Stories from the Life of a Migrant Child*. Albuquerque: University of New Mexico Press, 1997.

Jukes, Mavis. *Like Jake and Me.* New York: Knopf, 1984.

Kehret, Peg. *Small Steps: The Year I Got Polio.* Morton Grove, Ill.: Whitman, 1996.

Krementz, Jill. *How It Feels to Fight For Your Life.* Boston: Joy Street Books, 1989.

Krull, Kathleen. *Lives of the Artists: Masterpieces, Messes and What the Neighbors Thought.* San Diego: Harcourt, 1995.

L'Engle, Madeleine. *A Wrinkle in Time.* New York: Farrar, Straus & Giroux, 1962.

———. *A Wind in the Door.* New York: Farrar Straus & Giroux, 1973.

———. *A Swiftly Tilting Planet.* New York: Farrar, Straus & Giroux, 1978.

———. *Many Waters.* New York: Farrar, Straus, & Giroux, 1986.

Lasky, Kathryn. *The Most Beautiful Roof in the World: Exploring the Rainforest Canopy.* San Diego: Harcourt, 1997.

Lauber, Patricia. *Summer of Fire: Yellowstone 1988.* New York: Orchard, 1991.

Littlechild, George. *This Land is My Land.* Emeryville, Calif.: Children's Book Press, 1993.

Lowry, Lois. *Anastasia Krupnik.* Boston: Mass.: Houghton Mifflin, 1979.

———. *Number the Stars.* New York: Dell, 1990.

Martinez, Floyd. *Spirits of the High Mesa.* Houston, Tex.: Arte Publico Press, 1997.

McCaughrean Geraldine. *The Golden Hoard.* New York: McElderry, 1996.

———. *The Silver Treasure.* New York: McElderry, 1997.

———. *The Bronze Cauldron.* New York: McElderry, 1998.

Murphy, Jim. *Across America on an Emigrant Train.* New York: Clarion, 1993.

O'Brien, Robert. *Mrs. Frisby and the Rats of NIMH.* New York: Atheneum, 1971.

Park, Barbara. *Mick Harte Was Here.* New York: Knopf, 1995.

Park, Linda Sue. *A Single Shard.* New York: Clarion, 2001.

Parks, Rosa and James Haskins. *Rosa Parks: My Story.* New York: Scholastic, 1994.

Paterson, Katherine. *Bridge to Terabithia.* New York: Harper, 1977.

———. *The Great Gilly Hopkins.* New York: Crowell, 1978.

———. *Parzival: The Quest of the Grail Knight.* New York: Lodestar, 1998.

Paulsen, Gary. *Hatchet.* New York: Viking, 1987.

———. *Nightjohn.* New York: Delacorte, 1993.

———. *Winterdance: The Fine Madness of Running the Iditarod.* San Diego: Harcourt, 1994.

———. *Brian's Return.* New York: Viking, 1996.

———. *Sarny: A Life Remembered.* New York: Bantam, 1997.

———. *Tucket's Ride.* New York: Delacorte 1997.

———. *My Life in Dog Year.* New York: Bantam, Doubleday Dell, 1998.

Peck, Richard. *Long Way From Chicago.* New York: Dial, 1998.

Polacco, Patricia. *Thank You, Mr. Falker.* New York: Philomel, 1998.

Pringle, Laurence. *Dolphin Man: Exploring the World of Dolphins.* New York: Atheneum, 1995.

———. *Fire in the Forest: A Cycle of Growth and Renewal.* New York: Atheneum, 1995.

Reiss, Johanna. *The Upstairs Room.* New York: Harper, 1972.

Riet, Seymour. *Behind Rebel Lines, The Incredible Story of Emma Edmonds, Civil War Spy.* San Diego: Harcourt, 1988.

Roberts, Willo Davis. *View from the Cherry Tree.* New York: Atheneum, 1998.

Rowling, J. K. *Harry Potter and the Sorcerer's Stone.* New York: Scholastic, 1997.

Ryan, Pam Munoz. *Esperanza Rising.* New York: Scholastic, 2000.

Rylant, Cynthia. *A Blue-Eyed Daisy.* New York: Bradbury, 1985.

Sachar, Louis. *Holes.* New York: Farrar, Straus & Giroux, 1998.

Schaeffer, Edith. *Mei Fuh: Memories from China.* Boston: Houghton Mifflin, 1998.

Simon, Seymour. *They Walk the Earth.* San Diego: Harcourt, 2000.

Sis, Peter. *Starry Messenger: A Book Depicting the Life of a Famous Scientist, Mathematician, Astronomer, Philosopher, Physicist: Galileo Galilei.* New York: Farrar, Straus &Giroux, 1996.

Soto, Gary. *Baseball in April and Other Stories.* San Diego: Harcourt, 1990.

———. *Crazy Weekend.* New York: Scholastic, 1994.

Spinelli, Jerry. *Maniac Magee.* New York: Little, Brown, 1990.

———.*Crash.* New York: Knopf, 1996.

———. *Wringer.* New York: Scholastic, 1998.

St. Exupery, Antoine de. *The Little Prince.* San Diego: Harcourt, 2000.

Stanley, Diane. *Michelangelo.* New York: HarperCollins, 2000.

Stanley, Jerry. *Children of the Dustbowl: The True Story of the School at Weedpatch Camp.* New York: Crown, 1993.

Staples, Suzanne Fisher. *Shabanu.* New York: Knopf, 1989.

———. *Haveli.* New York: Knopf, 1993.

———. *Dangerous Skies.* New York: Farrar, Straus, & Giroux, 1996.

————. *Shiva's Fire.* New York: Farrar, Strauss, & Giroux, 2000.

Taylor, Mildred. *Roll of Thunder, Hear My Cry.* New York: Bantam, 1976.

————. *Mississippi Bridge.* New York: Dial, 1990.

————. *The Land.* New York: Phyllis Fogelman Books, 2001.

Vos, Ida. *Key is Lost.* New York: HarperCollins, 2000.

Walter, Mildred Pitts. *Ray and the Best Family Reunion Ever.* New York: HarperCollins, 2002.

Whelan, Gloria. *Goodbye, Vietnam.* New York: Bull's Eye, 1993.

Wright-Frierson, Virginia. *An Island Scrapbook: Dawn to Dusk on a Barrier Island.* New York: Simon & Schuster, 1998.

Yep, Laurence. *Child of the Owl.* New York: Harper, 1977.

————. *Dragon's Gate.* New York: HarperCollins, 1993

Middle School Level

Flake, Sharon. *Money Hungry.* New York: Jump at the Sun, 2001.

Freedman, Russell. *Martha Graham: A Dancer's Life.* New York: Clarion, 1998.

Haddix, Margaret Peterson. *Don't You Dare Read This, Mrs. Dunphrey.* New York: Simon & Schuster, 1996.

Hesse, Karen. *Out of the Dust.* New York: Scholastic, 1997.

————. *Witness.* New York: Scholastic, 2001.

Jimenez, Francisco. *The Circuit Stories from the Life of a Migrant Child.* Boston: Houghton Mifflin, 1999.

Lowry, Lois. *The Giver.* Boston: Houghton Mifflin, 1993.

————. *Looking Back: A Book of Memories.* Boston: Houghton Mifflin, 1998.

Myers, Walter Dean. *Slam.* New York: Scholastic, 1996.

Peck, Richard. *A Year Down Yonder.* New York: Dial, 2000.

Relf, Pat. *A Dinosaur Named Sue.* New York: Scholastic, 2000.

Sleator, William. *The Duplicate.* New York: Bantam, Doubleday, Dell, 1990.

Thoreau, Henry David. *Walden.* Garden City, N.Y.: Anchor Press, 1973.

Twain, Mark. *The Adventures of Huckleberry Finn.* Los Angeles: Price, Stern, Sloan, 1983.

————. *The Adventures of Tom Sawyer.* New York: Random House, 1999.

Wilde, Oscar. *Complete Fairy Tales of Oscar Wilde.* East Rutherford, N.J.: Penguin Putnam, 1996.

Woodson, Jacqueline. *I Hadn't Meant to Tell You This*. New York: Delacorte, 1994.

Professional Level

Anderson, Richard C. et al. *Becoming a Nation Of Readers*. Washington, D.C.: National Institute of Education, 1985.

Bennett, Christine. "Genres of Research in Multicultural Education." *Review of Educational Research* 71, no. 2 (2001): 171–217.

Bettelheim, Bruno. *Uses of Enchantment*. New York: Knopf, 1976.

Bosma, Betty. *Fairy Tales, Fables, Legends, and Myths*. New York: Teachers College, Columbia, 1987.

Brinkley, Ellen Henson. *Caught Off Guard: Teachers Rethinking Censorship and Controversy*. Needham Heights, Mass.: Allyn & Bacon, 1999.

Bruner, Jerome. "Early Social Interaction and Language Development." In *Studies in Mother-Child Interaction*, ed. H. R. Schaffer (London: Academic Press, 1977).

Clay, Marie. *An Observation Survey of Early Literacy Achievement*. Portsmouth, N.H.: Heinemann, 1992.

———.*Change over Time in Children's Literacy Development*. Portsmouth, N.H.: Heinemann, 2001.

Cole, Elizabeth S. "An Experience in Froebel's Garden." *Childhood Education* 67 (1990): 18–20.

Cole, M. and S. Cole. *The Development of Children*. New York: Freeman, 1996

Comenius, Amos. *Orbis Pictus*. Kila, Mont.: Kessinger Publisher, 1999.

Cooper, Susan. *Dreams and Wishes: Essays on Writing for Children*. New York: Simon & Schuster 1996.

Cowper, William and Randolph Caldecott. *The History of John Gilpin*. London: Frederick Warne, 1925.

Daniels, Harvey. *Literature Circles: Voice and Choice in Book Clubs and Reading Groups*. York, Maine: Stenhouse, 1994.

Fletcher, Ralph. *Poetry Matters*. New York: HarperCollins, 2002.

Fox, Mem. *Reading Magic*. San Diego: Harcourt, 1977.

Giblin, James Cross. "Biography for the 21st Century." *School Library Journal* (February 2002): 45.

Glazer, Joan. *Literature for Young Children*. Upper Saddle River, N.J.: Prentice-Hall, 1999.

Goforth, Frances and Carolyn Spillman. *Using Folk Literature in the Classroom.* Phoenix, Ariz.: Oryx Press, 1994.

Goforth, Frances F. *Literature and the Learner.* Belmont, Calif.: Wadsworth, 1998.

Harvey, Stephanie. *Nonfiction Matters: Reading, Writing, Research in Grades 3–8.* York, Maine: Stenhouse, 1998.

Hawley, Suzanne. "Alma Flor Ada," In *The Eighth Book of Junior Authors and Illustrators,* ed. Connie Rockman. New York: H. W. Wilson, 2000.

Hickman, Janet and Bernice Cullinan, eds. *Children's Literature in the Classroom: Weaving Charlotte's Web.* Needham Heights, Mass.: Christopher Gordon, 1989.

Homa, Linda, ed. *Elementary School Library Collection.* Williamsport, Pa.: Brodart, 2000.

Horning, Kathleen T. *From Cover to Cover: Evaluating and Reviewing Children's Books.* New York: HarperCollins, 1997.

Huck, Charlette S. et al. *Children's Literature in the Elementary School.* 7th ed. rev. by Barbara Z. Keifer. New York: McGraw-Hill, 2001.

Jefferson, Margo. "Harry Potter for Grown-Ups." *The New York Times Book Review* (January 20, 2002): 23.

Karr-Morse, R. and M. Wiley. *Ghosts from the Nursery: Tracing the Roots of Violence.* New York: The Atlantic Monthly Press, 1997.

Kobrin, Beverly. *Eyeopeners II: Children's Books to Answer Children's Questions about the World Around Them.* New York: Scholastic, 1995.

Kohlberg, Lawrence. "The Cognitive Developmental Approach to Moral Education." *Phi Delta Kappan* 57 (1975).

Kotulak, Ronald. Series: "Unlocking the Mind," April 11–15 and special section: "The Roots of Violence: Tracking Down Monsters within Us." *Chicago Tribune,* December 12–15, 1993.

Krashen, Steven. "Phonemic Awareness Training for Prelinguistic Children: Do We Need Prenatal Phonemic Awareness?" *Reading Improvement* 35 no. 4 (1998).

Langer, Judith. *The Process of Understanding Literature.* Albany, N.Y.: Center for the Learning and Teaching of Literature, State University of New York at Albany, 1989.

Lewis, Valerie et al. *Valerie and Walter's Best Books for Children: A Lively, Opinionated Guide.* New York: Avon, 1998.

Lukens, Rebecca. *A Critical Handbook of Children's Literature.* 5th ed. New York: HarperCollins, 1995.

McDevitt, Teresa M. and Jeanne Ellis Ormrod, *Child Development and Education*. Upper Saddle River, N.J.: Merrill Prentice Hall, 2002.

Mikkelsen, Nina. *Words and Pictures: Lessons in Children's Literature and Literacies*. Boston: McGraw-Hill Higher Education, 2000.

Mitton, Jacqueline. *Zoo in the Sky: A Book of Animal Constellations*. Washington, D.C.: National Geographic, 1998.

Moe, Jerry. *Discovery: Finding the Buried Treasure*. Tuscon, Ariz.: Sierra Tuscon Educational Materials, 1993.

Newbery, John. *A Little Pretty Pocket-Book*. San Diego: Harcourt, 1967.

Nodelman, Perry. *The Pleasures of Children's Literature*. 2d ed. New York: Longmans, 1996.

Norton, Donna W. *Through the Eyes of a Child: An Introduction to Children's Literature*. 2d ed. Columbus, Ohio: Merrill, 1987.

Polito, Theodora. "Frederick Froebel's Illuminations on Kindergarten Children's Relatedness to Nature." *Education* 116 (1995): 223–229.

Price, Ann and Juliette Yaakov, eds. *Children's Catalog*. 18th edition. New York: H. W. Wilson, 2001.

Rosenblatt, Louise. *Literature as Exploration*. New York: Appleton, Century, Croftsman, 1938.

Routman, Regie. *Transitions*. Portsmouth, N.H.: Heinemann, 1998.

Sanders, B. *A is for Ox: The Collapse of Literacy and the Rise of Violence in an Electronic Age*. New York: Vintage Books, 1994.

Sanera, Michael and Jane S. Shaw. *Facts, Not Fear: Teaching Children about the Environment*. Washington, D.C.: Regnery, 1999.

Spillman, Carolyn. *The Integration of Language Arts through Literature*. Phoenix, Ariz.: Oryx, 1996.

Van Kleeck, Anne and Ronald B. Gillam. "The Relationship between Middle-Class Parents' Book Sharing Discussion and Their Preschoolers' Language Development." *Journal of Speech, Language, and Hearing Research* 40 (1997): 1261–1272, 1996.

Vygotsky, L. *Thought and Language*. Cambridge, Mass: MIT Press, 1962.

Waters, Elizabeth. *Painting*. New York: Dorling Kindersley, 1993.

Subject Index

Author and Illustrator Index

Title Index

About the Authors

Suzanne Hawley has taught children's literature at Florida Gulf Coast University and the University of South Florida and was an elementary school media specialist for over twenty years. She served as a member of the selection committee for the twenty-first and twenty-second editions of the *Elementary School Library Collection* as well as the Advisory Committee for the seventeenth and eighteenth editions of *Children's Catalog.* Hawley was also a contributing editor to the *Eighth Book of Junior Authors* and is currently working on biographies for the *Ninth Book of Junior Authors.*

As an active member of the American Library Association, Hawley has served on several committees, including the Newbery Award Committee, the School Library Media Program of the Year Award, and the May Hill Arbuthnot Committee.

Carolyn V. Spillman is a professor of education in the college of education at Florida Gulf Coast University in Fort Myers, Florida. Her master of education degree and Ph.D are both from the University of North Carolina at Greensboro. Her research and teaching in teacher education have been in the fields of child development and literacy.

Spillman has written two other books in the areas of reading, writing, and literature. She coauthored *Folk Literature in Elementary Classrooms: Encouraging Children to Read and Write* with Frances Goforth. She also wrote *Integrating Language Arts through Literature in Elementary Classrooms.*